THE
MURDOCH
MISSION

THE MURDOCH MISSION

The digital transformation of a media empire

Wendy Goldman Rohm

John Wiley & Sons, Inc.

Published by John Wiley & Sons, Inc., New York.
Published simultaneously in Canada.

Library of Congress Cataloging-in-Publication Data:
Rohm, Wendy Goldman.
    The Murdoch mission : the digital transformation of a media empire / Wendy Goldman Rohm.
        p. cm.
    ISBN 0-471-38360-0 (alk. paper)
    1. Murdoch, Rupert, 1931–   2. Mass media—Australia—Biography.   I. Title.
P92.5.M87 R64 2001
070'.092—dc21
[B]
                                                                          2001045612

Printed in the United States of America.

10 9 8 7 6 5 4 3 2 1

*For Jeffrey, who was
certain he would never
have enough potatoes.*

Contents

Preface

On February 20, 2001, in a News Corporation boardroom in Los Angeles, top executives leading all of Keith Rupert Murdoch's Sky Global companies gave a presentation to Mike Smith, the head of General Motors' Hughes Electronics— owner of pay-TV giant DirecTV—in the midst of a mammoth $70 billion merger attempt.

During the meeting, Murdoch's group presented strategic views of the most critical properties leading News Corp.'s expansion efforts around the globe. Murdoch's youngest son, James, leader of his Pan-Asian broadcaster Star, detailed the company's business model in the world's most rapidly expanding media markets: India and China. NDS, News Corp.'s technology arm, had its president, Abe Peled, reveal his company's role in providing the technological glue enabling new interactive applications and broadcast services across all of News Corp.'s properties around the globe. British Sky Broadcasting chief Tony Ball documented the U.K. pay-TV company's huge growth and innovation in the area of interactive television. And Gemstar TV Guide chairman Henry Yuen discussed Gemstar's worldwide plans for the ultimate consumer portal via the television screen.

All of these endeavors, and many more around the globe, were all feeding into Murdoch's new holding company, Sky Global, the embodiment of his grand plan to combine all of News Corp.'s satellite and technology businesses. Murdoch had lined up the building blocks for a new media platform that would support all of his properties around the globe. Sky Global, he hoped, would become an integrated platform for "interactive multimedia content distribution."

ix

Indeed, the Sky Global/DirecTV combination represented Murdoch's bid to create the largest global media platform of all time. Moreover, the result would be a strategic watershed for Murdoch's News Corp., positioning the company as the only truly global, vertically integrated media enterprise.

Not surprisingly, the Big Six, Murdoch's inner sanctum of top executives, from late 1998 till the present time have focused on the Sky Global promise as a top priority. Habitual Monday morning Office of the Chairman meetings have often been entirely consumed by plans for the growing entity. Rupert Murdoch, along with his oldest son, Lachlan Murdoch, deputy COO; CFO David Devoe; president Peter Chernin; chief counsel Arthur Siskind; and Sky Global CEO Chase Carey, were particularly keen on the building of Sky Global, given that, by the year 2000, they were staring down the likes of newly created mammoths AOL Time Warner and Vivendi Universal, the result of the megamerger of France's Vivendi and the Seagram Co.

While puzzling over the changes such monoliths would bring to the media world, Murdoch was the only one fully integrating his company's assets globally. His competitors were, for the time being, primarily focused on distributing existing programming and channels to platforms controlled by others around the world. Murdoch, on the other hand, is in the process of effecting the equivalent of continental shifts: implementing technology throughout the world that pushes media into new arenas, all the while transforming cultures and infiltrating previously remote worlds with data, ideas, and images.

But the building of Sky Global, and Murdoch's play for Hughes' DirecTV, are just the latest chapters in Murdoch's worldwide adventure, transforming the corporation for the digital age.

Toward this goal, in the past five years he has embarked on numerous high-risk ventures involving numerous business partners spanning a panoply of world markets and cultures.

This is a story of Murdoch's difficulties, successes, and single-mindedness in the course of shaping his corporation for the new millennium—both through technology and global platforms—and tutoring his two sons, Lachlan and James, to become leaders in the process.

Murdoch is viewed to be the most entrepreneurial of all the media titans—infamous for his high-risk approach. He has often pumped fortunes into new, money-losing ventures substantiated only by his belief that his investments would eventually reward him with a foothold in a new media world. And despite the skeptics, many of his most risky forays have paid off beyond anyone's wildest dreams.

While spending more than a billion through investments in Asia with Star over the past decade, for example, he also built the company into the number one media brand in the area. Murdoch is finally eyeing a 76 percent increase in revenue for Star, headed by his son James, for fiscal year 2001. As part of Star's efforts, Murdoch and his son were intent on transforming India's cable industry, rolling out the country's first premium digital service via a partnership with Hathway, a top Indian cable provider. What's more, between April 2000 and April 2001, Star managed to take over the number one spot in Indian programming—stunning rivals Zee TV and Sony—from having no presence in Hindi programming at all.

(Around the world, he is repeating the unlikely gambles he'd made years earlier in the United States when he was laughed at for attempting to launch the fourth television network, Fox.)

But Murdoch's boldness and success have also made him the object of much venom, paranoia, and envy. His power and success have also created enemies. Foreign officials have issued warrants for his arrest, and his own executives have sought to blackmail him over the years. Such is the level of fear and greed directed at him in the course of his bold inroads into new markets.

Not surprisingly, hurdles needed to be overcome in each country's market and would sometimes require dealing with situations outside the normal bounds of propriety. Murdoch has become adept over the years at changing the rules even in the most difficult environments. While launching a ground-breaking pay TV business using digital "smart cards," his executives had suffered police raids in Israel when they unknowingly got tied up with an international fugitive. In China, with Star, he learned to change his business drastically, tailoring his practices to comply with local mores. In India, he went from being vilified as a supposed pornographer and destroyer of culture to being regarded as royalty, becoming the number one Hindi television broadcaster. Much loathed in Britain for outshining competitors whom he considered to be uppity, he nonetheless almost single-handedly invented the market for interactive and pay television there. In the United States, after a failed takeover of Gemstar, he managed in the end to control a big chunk of the company, gaining an important stake in the most powerful emerging interactive consumer interface in existence: the television screen.

Mythology about Murdoch, the man and his practices, runs rampant, but up close he is a surprising and complex figure who often defies being pigeonholed. More than anything, he is independent; ironically, an iconoclast who traffics in icons.

He addresses his competitive foes almost with glee, and has been known to guffaw and giggle when reading criticism of himself by the most respected of his media rivals.

At the same time, he adores his victories. During a private

interview with me, he leapt to his feet and bounded gleefully to his phone to call his chief counsel Arthur Siskind on the phone (he was just down the hall), curious about whatever happened to an old business partner who had tried to blackmail him, and against whom he'd won a $25 million judgment. (He grinned wildly, speculating that the guy was still hiding out in Cuba.)

Murdoch is also surprisingly reflective about the legacy he will be leaving and the impact he has made on the world. He acknowledges shaking up the status quo wherever he's left his corporate footprints, and prides himself on being a "catalyst."

More than anything, perhaps, for better or worse, Murdoch's News Corp. is catalyzing new markets in areas of the world where none had existed.

While the media world at large is in the midst of a sea change, driven by new electronic methods of distribution and entirely new forms of media, it remains to be seen whether Murdoch, and News Corp., will succeed in fashioning an enterprise at the forefront of digital media and the Internet generation's next wave.

Aided by his sons, Murdoch is honing a long-term vision— one that transcends the early Internet business models that have had disappointing results. He has always viewed the Internet not as a core business in itself, but as a distribution medium, crucial in the way that, earlier, advances in transportation were essential to the print business.

Moreover, the fruition of Murdoch's vision for Sky Global requires a transformation that affects every aspect of the company's business, as old media dovetails into emerging digital media platforms. For example, News Corp. content across many properties—from Fox Film to book giant Harper-Collins—may soon be available on demand to consumers worldwide through a revenue-based Napster-like subscription service and new electronic book devices enabled by Gemstar technology.

New opportunities are being mined around the globe, and Murdoch has his key executives strategically scattered all over the world exploring the next phase of the digital revolution. His eye is on the satellite ball and on new services delivered to television sets across all platforms. Murdoch's prediction is that over the next five years, the number of homes hooked up to interactive television will increase 15-fold. Via his Sky Global platforms, and services delivered direct to homes all over the world, he hopes to further cultivate and extend what all media companies covet: an intimate, direct connection to consumers.

By the summer of 2001, Murdoch was briefing market analysts worldwide on Sky Global's plans for "explosive growth." While silent on the fate of his DirecTV deal with Hughes, behind the scenes a new management structure was being put in place at the pay-TV giant, in preparation for a new corporate life driven by mogul Murdoch.

At age 70, there is no sign of Murdoch slowing down. Tracking his worldwide business adventure means mapping the collision of one man's ambitions and the power of a single corporation on the media landscape worldwide.

1

THE DREAM BEAM

In the spring of 2001, Rupert Murdoch thought he'd reached the culmination of a deal he'd been working on intensely for months—the acquisition of GM's Hughes Electronics and DirecTV—a key component to the grandest plan of his career: the creation of Sky Global Networks. To pull it off, his company and another formidable giant, Microsoft Corp., needed to become bedfellows while waiting for a pair of CEO brothers at GM to sort out their priorities.

midst the midtown bustle, down the gray avenues of Manhattan, stark in the morning sun, Rupert Murdoch approaches the News Corp. office tower at 1221 Avenue of the Americas. Through the revolving glass doors, up the elevators, and past the third-floor reception area, silver-haired Murdoch—removing his jacket—arrives at his desk slightly slumped and paws through some papers like an old lion who can no longer be startled by anything laid before him. It is March 16, 2001, and the 70-year-old media mogul has been waiting to hear the final word on one of the biggest deals of his career.

Rupert Murdoch looks up in an oddly shy way at his colleagues who enter the room. "They're back!!" Murdoch's voice rises to a gleeful roar, as he sits suddenly bolt upright and pounds the table grinning mischievously.

For weeks Murdoch has believed that his supposed partners were trying to double-cross him. Perhaps because of the competitive decades he's weathered, he is disarmingly good-natured about such machinations—as if it's all part of his own karmic rodeo. Would-be partner General Motors had been leading him down the garden path for weeks. And now his tricky friends have reinitiated contact.

The slow-moving auto giant controlled Hughes Electronics' DirecTV, the pay television giant, and owned 30 percent of its shares. DirecTV for some time had been the apple of Murdoch's eye. Murdoch and his right-hand man, CEO Peter Chernin, had waited on GM for months, together flying to Detroit for tête-à-têtes with company executives. DirecTV represented the missing piece in the grandest plan of Murdoch's career: the creation of Sky Global Networks, a worldwide digital television enterprise that would beam all manner of content—entertainment, news, information, and the ability to purchase a plethora of consumer goods and services—to every corner of the planet. Wall Street called the plan Murdoch's "Dream Beam." Merging his Sky Global enterprise with DirecTV, Murdoch was hoping to recreate his successes with his British Sky Broadcasting in the United Kingdom, which he viewed as an interactive laboratory for his entire empire. Since America Online and Time-Warner announced their plans to merge, his goals in this area were even more urgent.

DirecTV boasted 8.7 million subscribers—about two-thirds of the satellite market. By the end of the year, it expected nearly 10 million customers, up 20 percent from the previous year. That meant it was reaching more homes than anyone except AT&T and Time Warner, and was on target to soon pass the cable giants.

These days, the media world is being transformed in an unpredictable way and at a lightning-fast pace—a pace that means huge success could suddenly come in one part of the world, while in another your supposed business partners could be stabbing you in the back.

Despite the setbacks, Murdoch's risk-taking in several world markets his rivals dared not enter was showing signs of paying off. Ironically, the biggest dream of his career—the creation of Sky Global—lacked one thing: a U.S. component. DirecTV was key to building his coveted global satellite platform. He had no presence in the United States with satellite, though his British Sky Broadcasting—known as BSkyB—combined with Asian broadcaster Star and Sky Latin America, had most of the rest of the world covered.

A merger with Hughes would give Murdoch the important U.S. piece he needed. Murdoch could not acquire the company outright; that would present hefty tax penalties for the seller. To avoid this, in a merger scenario, Hughes would need to maintain control of 51 percent of the company—but the deal would be structured in a way that ensured Murdoch was in charge.

Murdoch is pensive. Thick lenses magnify deep-set eyes. His shirtsleeves are rolled up to the elbows, and he is almost willowy as he moves about his spacious office, having been on a fitness campaign inspired by his new young wife. At age 70, Murdoch cuts a delicate figure that might have walked out of a T.S. Eliot poem rather than the cutthroat turf that is the media world—a surprising specter for a man who over the years has been reviled worldwide for his alleged crassness and reputation for catering to the lowest common denominator in order to make a buck.

(Murdoch says criticism of his media ventures has largely come from competitors he beat in the ratings, who simply were not as good as he at predicting popular tastes. "We were a huge catalyst for change," he says.)

Rupert settles into a white couch, relaxed, with one leg extended, to contemplate the latest perils and adventures of his worldwide empire. He is refined and softspoken, and even his indignant roars are moderated with a subtle sense of irony, as if his empire's battles are all just part of the churn. Indeed, the media magnate dispassionately views his life as an interlocking series of wars.

Murdoch's latest bid is just one in a seemingly endless series of deals since the 1950s that had resulted in his increasing control over newspapers, magazines, television, book publishing, radio, cable, and pay-television properties worldwide. From a single Australian newspaper he'd taken over for his father at age 23, he'd built a media empire that now spans six continents.

He is the gatekeeper of gatekeepers—shaping, interpreting, and distributing information to almost every corner of the earth. While some cried cultural imperialism, others believed Murdoch's influence was for the best, resulting in the democratization of information. In recent years, Murdoch and his young sons—who, starting in remote outposts, had gradually joined his most trusted inner sanctum of executives—had learned the importance of tailoring their business to local mores and cultures in country markets worldwide.

Of all the media companies on the planet, News Corp. was the only one to truly span the globe. Unlike the others, the ever-expanding News Corp. was the brainchild of one man— Murdoch—and it remained in his hands. While rival AOL Time Warner had become the largest media company in history, with Sony, Bertelsmann, Disney, and News Corp. following, only News Corp. continued to be controlled by a single man and his family.

Through dozens of acquisitions over the years, scrutinizing another mogul's industry had always been a fascinating exercise for Murdoch. GM chairman Jack Smith and his number two man, vice chairman Harry Pearce, inhabited another world. Compared to the media business, the automotive industry moved at a snail's pace. While GM owned a hot high-tech company with huge potential, getting the board to respond was like throwing tiny pebbles at an armored tank. Murdoch and Chernin had grown impatient over the months, and finally in late January—largely through Murdoch's secret conversations with Smith and Pearce, and subsequent meetings with the company's CEO Rick Wagoner and his CFO—they thought they had a handshake deal.

Moreover, there were understandings between the men that perhaps gave Murdoch a sense of solidarity. Vice chairman Pearce and Murdoch had some personal common ground. Both men recently had confronted their own mortality, faced with life-threatening diseases. Pearce, 58, had survived leukemia; Murdoch had "successfully" been treated for prostate cancer that summer, and liked to boast that he was now convinced of his own immortality, having not missed a day of work throughout the ordeal. For his part, Pearce was somewhat of a folk hero at GM, having been declared cured in September after a stem cell transplant from one of his brothers and two years in remission. Like Murdoch, his hair was white and wispy, and he was fit and proud of his physical strength. A partnership between the two men seemed right.

Just a few weeks earlier, News Corp. and GM had agreed on the outline of a deal that would merge Hughes with News Corp.'s satellite interests, while allowing GM to receive $8 billion cash in part payment for its stake in the company.

Like many other companies, News Corp. had to up the ante. Murdoch was at a precipice, having reached a turning point in the history of the media. He was like Shakespeare's Lear at the edge of a cliff; his old empire could easily slip away. But his plans were for growth, and his young sons, Lachlan and James, were playing a key role in helping him steer the enterprise into the new century.

Murdoch recognized both the implications of the changes taking place, and the potential role of technology in shaping the future of the media. Beyond narrower visions of first-generation applications of the Internet, and the struggle to find business models for making money, it was now not only possible to deploy technology to reach all corners of the earth, but also to have a two-way medium that allowed the audience to talk back, state what they wanted, and almost instantly receive it.

The printing press had revolutionized literacy all over the planet; communications technology and the Internet were likewise breaking down boundaries, making it possible to bypass intermediate steps in the distribution process: trucks, roads, planes, and rail cars were no longer needed. Wireless technology—satellite—meant that not even a land line or cable was needed to reach people in their homes. Those in the most hard-to-reach places on the planet could receive all the content the world had to offer via a small dish.

Rupert Murdoch's grand vision, Sky Global, at the moment was a holding company for all of his satellite and technology companies around the world. He had planned to take the company public by the end of 2000, but poor market conditions caused him to stall those plans. A merger with Hughes would obviate the need for an initial public offering in the United States. At the same time, the development of the new business he envisioned would be enormously expensive.

Shortly after he thought he'd made a handshake deal with GM to acquire DirecTV, and having heard what was going on behind the scenes, Murdoch figured that Pearce was not the problem holding up a deal.

It was a set of brothers whose machinations were now stalling Murdoch's plans. (The dynamics of brothers vying within a single corporation was not an unfamiliar theme to him. Since his cancer diagnosis and the promotions of his young sons in recent months, rampant speculation filled the press about a battle for supremacy between the scions. But such rumors were of little concern to Murdoch.)

The brothers Smith, however, were another story. Mike Smith, the chairman of Hughes, was GM chairman Jack Smith's sibling. Apparently, a war going on between the brothers was preventing Murdoch from nailing his $70 billion deal.

It was perhaps the first time in corporate history that two brothers had been CEOs at the same company at the same time. Years earlier, the Smith brothers had vowed to recuse themselves from any direct business with each other. (The issue of nepotism had to be dealt with by the Smiths as it had to be by Murdoch, who was accustomed to putting his offspring and in-laws at top spots at the company. Too, he'd leveraged the knowledge and diplomacy skills of his Chinese wife, Wendi Deng, whom he involved in forging new business relationships in China.)

Jack and Mike Smith had been close since childhood when they hauled ice cream together as part of the family business, Smithfield Famous Ice Cream, in Worcester, Massachusetts.

Jack, 62, was five years older than Mike, and had been president of General Motors since 1992. In the fall of 1997, brother Mike had been named chairman and CEO of GM's Hughes Electronics Corp., based just outside of Los Angeles. Hughes' former chief, Michael Armstrong, had left to become chairman of AT&T. Mike would report to Harry Pearce, and avoid direct contact with his brother, who insisted he had nothing to do with his little brother's appointment as Hughes' CEO. Pearce was also quite close to Jack, and inevitably acted as go-between.

Both brothers had started their careers humbly, in accounting at a GM car plant in Framingham, Massachusetts, not far from their home. Former GM chairman Roger B. Smith—who had no relation to these Smith brothers—personally went to Framingham to convince Jack to take a job working with GM's CFO. Eventually, Mike also got transferred to Detroit, and both brothers worked for the comptroller's office for some time.

Mike, however, preferred not to work for his brother, and got a transfer to a GM office in New York. Their paths did not collide again till the mid-80s, when GM was eyeing an acquisition of Hughes, and the brothers were on the same committee studying the options.

After the fact, according to executives present, GM executives were apologizing to Murdoch, not only for Mike Smith's courting other buyers, but for big shareholders who had allegedly forced them to backpedal on their supposed deal with Murdoch.

The word was that Hughes shareholders were chagrined that Murdoch would not pay a premium for the company. The plan had been to merge News Corp.'s closely held Sky Global Networks satellite business into Hughes, creating an independent, publicly traded company. Hughes shareholders would own about 65 percent of the merged entity, with News Corp. owning the rest. The resulting company would have a combined market value of as much as $70 billion. Shareholders, however, were balking, and so was Mike Smith—though presumably for reasons of his own. Rupert did not want him with the company. Smith would probably be out of a job if the News Corp. deal went through.

Jeffrey Bronchick, chief investment officer for Reed Conner & Birdwell Inc., which controlled 900,000 Hughes shares, said that, from an investor's point of view, he would not take the News Corp. bid lying down. "They're running right over the Hughes shareholders," he said. Indeed, Hughes shareholders complained that under the merger scenario, they wouldn't receive any premium, and News Corp. executives would end up running the combined company.

But also at issue might have been Mike's wounded ego, News Corp. executives speculated. Murdoch and his top advisors saw him as a "corporate guy", used to bureaucracy versus action, and Murdoch did not like "corporate guys." (Murdoch has made no secret of his distaste for Mr. Smith's leadership, at one point calling Hughes "undermanaged.")

Murdoch surrounded himself with executives who were as aggressive and risk-taking as he, but at the same time did not challenge his authority. Even his children had the habit of calling him "the boss."

In the midst of his wrangling with GM he'd celebrated his 70th birthday with a small party at his New York abode given with his wife Wendi Deng, a former employee of his Asian broadcasting company Star, whom he'd married a little more than a year earlier.

All his children had shown up for the occasion to honor their father: 29-year-old Lachlan, who now resided in New York; 28-year-old James, who flew in from Hong Kong, his new residence since taking the top post at Star about a year earlier; 34-year-old Elisabeth, who was mulling a return to her father's empire after departing for an independent venture the previous spring; and 42-year-old Prudence, Rupert's daughter from his first marriage, whose husband Alasdair

MacLeod was one of his senior executives. Despite rumors of warring for supremacy in the family dynasty, the clan was surprisingly close.

Number one son Lachlan was a rising star at the company, having recently been promoted to deputy chief operating officer, the number three position at the global empire, under president Peter Chernin. Son James was just cutting his teeth, as CEO of Star, after a stint heading up new media ventures. Elisabeth, who also had been on the fast track to the top, working out of London for her father's British Sky Broadcasting, had resigned abruptly the previous spring, citing the birth of her third child and a desire to start her own company. Prudence had never worked for News Corp., but her husband was a key Murdoch executive in the United Kingdom. At family events, the most dramatic deals of the day were often discussed, at least in whispered asides between Murdoch and his sons. His birthday party was no exception, and the GM intrigue was too juicy to ignore.

At his office, Murdoch slumps back and sinks into the white couch in the center of the room (before a bank of television monitors beaming Fox News images seemingly in perpetuity) and shakes his head in dismay at the thought of Smith's machinations: "So Mike was calling on a few friends!" he exclaims. Even while telling Murdoch he had a deal, the Hughes chief was shopping around for more money from someone else.

But a better deal was not to be had, Murdoch said. "I believe they're not only with us, they're with us for a set amount of money on a set of terms and we have a 99 percent completed deal with Microsoft that's waiting for these lawyers to write it up," he said. Software giant Microsoft had agreed to invest billions in Sky Global to help Murdoch get Hughes. Indeed, the market was in the doldrums. GM's stock had taken a hit just in the past couple of weeks; in the previous week alone, Hughes share price fell 16 percent, closing at $19 by week's end on rumors that News Corp. was giving up on the merger. That, however, was not the case.

"A deal is a deal!" Murdoch exclaimed.

Murdoch had smelled a rat on Tuesday, February 20, just a few weeks after his "handshake" with GM was complete. During a meeting at the company boardroom in Los Angeles, Murdoch was tipped off and he believed that he was being manipulated.

Though he, News Corp. CFO Dave Devoe, and chief counsel Arthur Siskind thought they had worked out all the details of the merger with GM's management, Hughes chairman Mike Smith had asked for an additional "due diligence" meeting, bringing their bankers in to hear detailed presentations about the Sky Global businesses. News Corp. executives—who never brought bankers to such meetings and relied instead on their CFO—felt the meeting was redundant, but Murdoch agreed to fly in executives from all around the globe to satisfy Smith.

Both of Rupert's sons flew in for the meeting. Lachlan had come back from London, where he was doing business, and James from Hong Kong. Gemstar chief Henry Yuen was present, as were Sky Global chief Chase Carey, News Corp. president Peter Chernin, BSkyB head Tony Ball, and Abe Peled, head of NDS, News Corp.'s technology arm.

Young James, tall and confident from his recent successes guiding his father's empire in Asia, got on well with the older, more experienced executives. For years he'd been championing to his father the brilliance of Henry Yuen, the Shanghai-born mathematician who was in the process of turning the world of interactive television on its ear. (News Corp. now was a close business partner of Yuen's.) Chase Carey and Peter Chernin were mentoring both Lachlan and James. NDS chief Abe Peled, an Israeli citizen born in Romania, had long ago enabled Murdoch—with his company's encryption technology—to participate in the pay-TV market in the first place. Each of the executives present played a critical role in the formation of the new Sky Global entity, and all had polished their spiels on Sky Global, given many times before to Wall Street analysts and prospective investors. The presentations had been fine-tuned before "the boss" for months now. The meeting, however, seemed odd, according to News Corp. executives. The bankers asked no questions, and Smith himself was sullen and oddly critical.

All were stunned when, at about 2:00 in the afternoon, Mike Smith stood up in the middle of James Murdoch's presentation on Star and announced that he was leaving for another meeting. Smith then abruptly walked out.

Murdoch was amazed. "He just sat there sullenly all day and then walked out! He didn't even wait for Gemstar!" he marveled to his colleagues. Gemstar, in which News Corp. held a 34 percent stake, was seen as one of the most valuable assets in Murdoch's arsenal of ingredients for the creation of Sky Global. Gemstar chief Henry Yuen was in the process of developing a new interactive television portal for worldwide use by Sky Global, essentially the ultimate portal for the future of digital television.

Later that day, Murdoch made some calls. He was flabbergasted to find out that just the day before Mike Smith had made a secret trip to Denver to discuss a merger with his rival, Echostar chief Charlie Ergen, the fearless entrepreneur who years earlier had had a disastrous falling out with Murdoch in an attempt to start a U.S. satellite business with him.

Rupert Murdoch was livid.

Lachlan Murdoch was about to see his father in rare form. He stood beside him as the mogul prepared to make it clear that he would not play fool to any other king—be it the head of General Motors or any other.

Pere Rupert arranged for a conference call in which he planned to confront his sneaky friends at the automotive giant. GM CEO Rick Wagoner and his cohorts were ready. Murdoch informed them that he heard all about what was going on—and the fact that Mike Smith was still shopping the company around.

Wagoner had become CEO of GM the previous June, taking over the job from Jack Smith, who remained chairman. Both worked closely with vice chairman Harry Pearce, who was a big proponent of e-commerce and technology. Wagoner had earlier served as CFO and head of GM's worldwide purchasing, running the company's North American operation.

His father, Lachlan noted, was angry but polite. He was not known for yelling and screaming, though many feared his wrath. His utterances at those times were more like roars. "We shook hands on this, Rick," Rupert rumbled. "Usually when I shake hands on a deal I mean it. It's a bond." Murdoch was regal, launching forth on a treatise about bonds that was worthy of any sovereign.

Wagoner and a few other corporate officers were stuttering a bit. Wagoner agreed that "our word is our bond," and protested that he didn't like to break their word, but this was a special circumstance . . . there's nothing they could do.

Murdoch pounded away. "We spent six months on this—a year and a half really. Six months full time . . ."

"I know," Wagoner said. "We hate to do this. We don't want to make an enemy of you, Rupert. But our hands our tied. It's coming from above. No one has the right to commit for the foremost senior director of the company."

Murdoch fell silent. It's coming from above? The foremost senior directors of the company were Jack Smith and Harry Pearce. Unbeknownst to these fellows, Rupert had been talking with Pearce himself for weeks. He wasn't going to divulge his little secret, however.

"Bullshit!" Murdoch said, his voice booming now. "The CFO was the proxy. I assumed a deal was a deal, and I still do!"

Months later, Jack Smith would discover that Murdoch was far from kidding. He would find out exactly how tenacious the News Corp. mogul could be when he saw the future in a business he coveted.

With DirecTV, Murdoch hoped to revolutionize the world of pay-TV in the United States just as he had in the United Kingdom with BSkyB. BSkyB was, in fact, leading the world in interactive television. Sky Digital, the cutting-edge division that was bringing BSkyB into the digital television world, was opening eyes around the globe.

Tony Ball, a silver-haired, quick-witted Londoner who'd enjoyed a meteoric rise within the News Corp. hierarchy, was at the heart of Murdoch's digital television revolution. He'd been at the helm of BSkyB only for about a year, and in early 2001 he'd overseen a mammoth accomplishment: the completion of the company's digital conversion. Its recent results were impressive: It had made $500 million in profits with 3.5 million analog subscribers, and was eyeing 5.5 million digital subscribers.

Ball had replaced former BSkyB chief Mark Booth, whose departure was said to be partially due to his difficult relationship with Elisabeth Murdoch, who'd been put in charge of BSkyB programming by her father. (Booth would leave to head up Murdoch's startup e-partners, a venture formed to invest in new media businesses. He remained one of Murdoch's trusted employees; so much so that Murdoch had outbid Microsoft when it tried to hire Booth away for a reported $25 million.)

Booth's successor at BSkyB, Ball, was going like gang-busters. As a young man, Ball started out as a television engineer, and worked at Thames Television, an independent television enterprise that competed with the BBC. Early in his career he was a local union leader. He worked at News Corp.'s Foxtel in 1996, Murdoch's pay-TV joint venture in Australia, and then moved to the United States, where he ran Fox Liberty Networks and worked on Fox's sports network, a joint venture with John Malone's Liberty Media. Under his watch, subscribers grew to 62 million from 38 million.

Murdoch had enormous confidence in Ball, and chose him to run BSkyB when the opportunity came. He'd slowly but surely become part of Murdoch's inner sanctum—the chosen elite augmenting the leadership of the Big Six who had earned a place on Murdoch's telephone speed dial. (Ball was said to be "number 3" on the boss's phone pad. Chernin and Chase Carey were ahead of him.)

BSkyB was clearly Murdoch's most valuable asset outside the United States, and at the center of his Sky Global strategy. From the company offices in an industrial park near London's Heathrow Airport, it had leap-frogged the U.K. and the U.S. cable industries, even in the eyes of Wall Street pundits who were bullish on the U.S. cable market. Early on, before anyone thought it was possible, the British pay-TV company was essentially offering an advanced interactive television service using cobbled-together technology—with enormous success. Interactivity was a problem that cable and satellite providers alike had been wrestling with. Satellite had been viewed largely as a one-way medium. But BSkyB used a telephone return path that allowed viewers to interact with the broadcast content. Worldwide, would-be interactive TV providers were learning from the BSkyB example.

With BSkyB, as with other assets, Murdoch had seized the moment, racing ahead of the slow cable operators in Britain.

Sure, it had taken a short-term hit to earnings, but Murdoch had always taken a long-term point of view; as a result, he hoped to win the lion's share of the digital market. He was becoming the dominant interactive TV player in the United Kingdom, and he planned to repeat that performance around the world.

The market was pointing to BSkyB as an example of what might be done—with online gaming, interactive shopping, and gambling. The pay TV company, for example, had a surprise success with interactive horse racing, with individual households spending large sums of money to participate. Critics might say that this type of application doesn't exactly promote cultural enrichment in the world, but Murdoch was no elitist. He provided what sold, what ordinary people had a passion for.

Such services were turning on their ear all expectations for the type of revenues that could be generated from interactive television services to the home.

In fact, Wall Street analysts were predicting that Murdoch's cutting-edge forays in digital television would have an impact on the pay-TV market and the growth of digital television worldwide.

Just as the Continent was way ahead of the United States in mobile phone use, it was out front in digital and pay-television. Murdoch and Ball were well aware of the figures and the untapped potential that remained in the United States. By 2001, more than 16 million European viewers subscribed to interactive TV—more than double the previous year. About a quarter of British and French households were subscribers, and 90 percent of customers regularly used interactive services.

In the United States, under 5 million households could interact with their televisions. That was less than 5 percent of the population. Where it was a commercial reality in Europe, it was just a niche market in America. What's more, Murdoch was betting that eventually, on a worldwide basis, television— already the device of choice for news and entertainment— would be more inviting than a personal computer for consumers purchasing all sorts of services and goods.

In that arena, analysts were predicting that while revenue from interactive commerce via the television set came to only $84 million in Europe the previous year, sales via interactive TV would increase to $655 million by the end of 2001 and soar to $2.1 billion the following year.

European retailers such as Woolworth's and Domino's Pizza were selling more product via interactive TV than via Internet sites. Vivendi, the owner of Canal+, Murdoch's biggest rival in Europe, merged with Seagram in part to eventually move its interactive television businesses to the United States.

Murdoch's BSkyB was way out front, and Murdoch had plans to imitate its successes in similar television endeavors in Germany and Asia, via Pan-Asian satellite broadcaster Star, now headed up by his youngest son James. In the United States, DirecTV would be the answer to his ambitions.

Murdoch's approach with interactive TV was much more targeted than some of his competitors, like Microsoft. Rather than providing viewers with full access to the Internet, which he believed was annoying and overwhelming, particular Internet sites would be accessible that were closely tied to programming and advertisers. He recognized that most people used the Internet for e-mail and for access to a few select sites—despite all the hype. People had no desire to surf the Web via their televisions, he believed, though a narrower interactive service allowed BSkyB customers to interact with companies and information sites in a more select way.

What's more, interactive shopping via TV was amazingly powerful when linked directly to a television program. Viewers could watch a football game and place a bet; watch a cooking show, and buy the cookbook instantly. Indeed, companies selling their products via interactive television versus the Internet were reporting that their sales via interactive TV were twice as high as online sales.

Such interactive systems were enabled by delivering digitized video signals via satellite, cable, or simple rooftop antenna. A set-top box decoded the signals into hundreds of channels. To allow two-way communications, versus one-way broadcast of programming, interactive television systems included a remote control or keyboard with an infrared connection to send information back to the broadcaster via phone line or through the cable.

In Europe, television viewers were customizing weather reports, picking camera angles for sports events, ordering pay-per-view films, and sending e-mail.

Unlike the Web, companies selling products and services via interactive television had to construct individual web sites for each interactive television system on the market, seeing that each company customized its system. This was expensive; some broadcasters were charging as much as $1.5 million a year just to list a company's interactive service. Another million could be spent on building the site. The business models, though in early stages, still were proving to work far better than any model for making money on the Internet.

In addition, such services appeared to be hugely popular. Subscriptions to BSkyB soared when the company began offering interactive betting on horse races and sports events. Murdoch and Ball were seeing dollar signs like they'd never seen them before; BSkyB's digital subscribers were spending 10 percent more than they did for the previous analog service for pay-TV films or programs, or about $450 a year.

Initially, in Europe, the popularity of digital television was fueled by the desire for more variety in programming. Free television offerings were very limited, often government-controlled channels. But Canal+ offered 23 channels, and BSkyB more than 200.

For e-mail and the Internet, interactive TV also proved to be less expensive than the PC. The charges for Internet access via the phone were repulsive to consumers; in Europe, Internet users paid huge per-minute phone charges. The difference in the country markets was fascinating—43 percent of American homes connected to the Internet via their PC; in Europe, only about 25 percent of all households connected via the PC.

Ball was in agreement with Murdoch: The television remained the ultimate way to reach a mass audience. His spiel to Hughes executives was compelling. What's more, in excess of 1.5 million of its viewers were using BSkyB e-mail addresses.

In addition, BSkyB's subscriber base was rising faster than analysts expected. It had doubled from 2.5 million in 2000 to almost 5 million in 2001. Most impressive, its "churn" rate, the buzzword in the broadcast industry that meant the percentage of viewers who end up leaving the service, had dropped from 14 percent to less than 10 percent over the past year. BSkyB's stock had risen about 40 percent since a year earlier, and Murdoch was in rapid expansion mode. With Sky Global Networks, he had worldwide scale in mind. His initial plan had been to raise $40 billion in an IPO, the largest in media history.

Rival Vivendi, with Canal+, was also expanding rapidly. It owned 23 percent of BSkyB, but its merger with Seagram required that it sell that stake. The Seagram merger would allow the expansion of its digital television efforts, enabling viewers to download Seagram music and film properties, and distribute these throughout Europe.

Murdoch at times has seemed surprised at his own success. In Britain, he had broken into entrenched television as well as newspaper markets where he'd had no presence. "Ours is a company that has prospered by injecting competition into industries and countries that for a long time favored monopoly suppliers," he said. "Britain is a case in point. Ever since television first became available, the government has favored BBC, allowing it to use tax revenues to finance whatever programming the elite thought appropriate to put on air.

"When we launched Sky Television, we had to cut through a thicket of rules, regulations and customs that were designed to preserve the broadcast monopoly—or, by then, duopoly—that had existed for decades. Through perseverance, and at considerable expense, we have been able to do that," Murdoch said.

He fully expected that, if Hughes finally accepted his proposal, his plans would be completely scrutinized by market regulators on a worldwide basis, as was routine for such mergers.

Most of Hughes Electronics' business was centered on DirecTV. Based in Los Angeles, the satellite TV company was the third-largest pay-TV service in the country, after cable giants AT&T and AOL Time Warner. Technologically, it was way ahead of its cable counterparts; it went digital in 1994, while cable companies didn't start offering digital service until 1999.

Six-year-old Hughes was actually outshining its century-old parent GM. In February 2001, the automotive company had a market cap of $31 billion; Hughes was valued at $35 billion.

For almost a year now, GM CEO Rick Wagoner had been hinting to would-be buyers that DirecTV was on the block.

GM's board was looking for about $40 billion to $50 billion—about $31 to $38 per share of GMH, the Hughes tracking stock. But by the winter of 2001, the market was in turmoil and GMH had plummeted to $27 from a high of $47 the previous spring. GM directors were getting a little desperate; if they'd sold the company months earlier they would have made out like bandits.

The Hughes story, like Murdoch's own, was a legacy of sons. Murdoch had grown his $40 billion News Corp. empire from a single Australian newspaper he'd inherited from his father.

In 1923, Howard R. Hughes Jr. inherited Hughes Tool Co. of Houston from his father, whose fortune grew out of the oil industry—developing patented drill bits. Armed with his newfound fortune, young Howard moved to Hollywood and immersed himself in the nascent film industry. Over the next 15 years, he managed to produce legendary films such as *Hell's Angels* and *Scarface,* and began a career as a director in 1943.

He also loved flying, and broke speed records with his H-1 aircraft, called the Silver Bullet. Driven by his love of the skies, he launched Hughes Aircraft Co. as a division of Hughes Tool in 1932, and it was quickly a success. He then took control of TWA in 1939, and during World War II branched into commercial aircraft. During the Cold War, the company was a major military and aviation supplier. Among other things, it developed the first geostationary satellites. Hughes died in 1976, but his defense powerhouse continued to grow.

In 1985, GM bought Hughes for $5.2 billion, hoping to apply its technology to cars. GM chairman Roger Smith said at the time that getting Hughes was like getting Cal Tech and MIT combined.

In the 1980s, Hughes inadvertently got lucky when the FCC opened part of the radio spectrum to those who wanted to use satellites for television broadcasting. The company already owned satellites used by cable operators to send programs to their systems. It applied for and won a piece of the spectrum in 1984—which enabled it to be a player in the pay-TV market with what would become DirecTV.

The man without whom satellite TV and digital services, accessible to consumers all over the country, would not have been possible is Eddy Hartenstein. In 1989 the engineer, along with eight employees, saw the opportunity in high-powered satellites and digital compression. DirecTV was formed with the notion of creating an orbiting system to broadcast scores of video channels to small satellite dishes on rooftops across the United States. He kept plugging away with his team despite repeated setbacks.

While Murdoch still lacked a U.S. presence in the pay-TV market, by 1994 DirecTV was ready for business, targeting customers who lived in out-of-reach rural areas not served by cable. But it was an expensive proposition: A set-top box, satellite dish, and installation cost customers $800. People were buying nonetheless.

By 1998 DirecTV was offering more than 200 channels to 4.5 million viewers, 70 percent living in areas where they also had access to cable TV.

With Hartenstein's persistence, Hughes had gone from missiles to MTV to become primarily a media company, after selling its defense business to Raytheon and satellite manufacturing to Boeing. And Hartenstein was promoted to the number two position at the company.

Murdoch now wanted Hartenstein as his number one man leading the combined company he hoped to create through a merger; Mike Smith, who fit in well at a company like GM, just did not have the "Murdoch stuff."

GM's vice chairman Pearce was often fond of saying that "ideas are cheap." It was execution that really showed the power of any organization. Murdoch had learned that lesson years earlier, when he launched his first attempt to create a U.S. satellite broadcasting operation with Hughes, and had first encountered Hartenstein. The early deal turned out to be ill-fated.

A decade prior to his play for DirecTV, Murdoch had sat in the same office on a conference call with three other giants—Bob Wright, president of GE's NBC; Cablevision's chairman Chuck Dolan; and Hughes' CEO—talking about how the four companies "were going to start this great service—before it ever got off the ground," Murdoch recalled. It was to be called Sky Cable, and hoped to provide satellite TV to viewers around the world.

The joint venture was announced in February 1990, with plans to launch the service by late 1993. Each of the companies already had a major investment in cable, broadcasting, satellite, and the movie business, but envisioned Sky Cable serving households that didn't already have cable TV, nor the space or funds for traditional satellite dishes. Nevertheless, it had the potential to cannibalize the basic cable and network businesses of NBC and Cablevision.

At the time, NBC president Robert Wright had said, "With this service, every conceivable audience can be served. The appetite for narrowly programmed channels is real. NBC will continue to be a mass marketing network, but we wanted to be able to explore other options as well."

The enterprise would use a new Hughes satellite that promised to be the most powerful space transmitter ever launched for communications purposes, allowing consumers to receive signals via a tiny napkin-sized dish placed on a windowsill or rooftop.

The plan was to sell the dishes for about $300 through

consumer electronics stores, and viewers would be charged a monthly fee to receive up to 108 channels of programming, including most existing cable program networks and pay-per-view services.

Murdoch, at the time, estimated that the company would need three to four million subscribers to break even.

But by June 1991, after 16 months, the effort was dead. "We fell out of it because we fell short of money, and GE lost their nerve," said Murdoch. "They'll tell you it's the worst thing they've ever done."

Conflicting interests among the partners and financial problems at News Corp. all played a part. The partnership had fallen apart, Hartenstein told those who asked, because the partners all had different needs. NBC was focused on acquiring the Financial News Network, and News Corp. was in the midst of restructuring. The focus wasn't there, but Murdoch had not lost the vision. (Years later, he would regret having given up.)

In addition, the partners were squabbling over how to sell the service to consumers. Cablevision was said to be pushing for cable operators to be the local sales agent, but direct-broadcast satellite TV competed with the cable business.

The idea eventually turned into DirecTV. Hughes—with Hartenstein and his group—succeeded after much persistence. DirecTV has steadily forged partnerships with other companies to provide more interactive services to customers, and was visionary about the potential of linking online services and the Internet with entertainment through these alliances.

DirecTV had been courted by others, prior to Murdoch's offer.

Back in the spring of 1999, DirecTV had also been approached by AOL's CEO Steve Case. Case had contacted

Mike Smith to ask if he was interested in selling the company. The two met, though Smith was not interested in selling at the time. Nevertheless, AOL had very specific plans in the television arena. Hughes received a $1.5 billion investment from AOL three months later, and a pact to comarket AOL TV—an entity designed to provide DirecTV satellite customers with AOL's interactive content, Instant Messaging service, and e-mail services. AOL said it hoped to make this available to customers in late 2001.

Like Murdoch's BSkyB, DirecTV was looking for solutions to provide two-way communications to its customers. Satellite remained a one-way medium without partnerships that would provide technology for a more interactive platform.

A pact with Wink Communications forged in the fall of 2000 enabled DirecTV to offer 30 interactive channels as part of its service. Using an advanced set-top box, customers could access sports scores and weather information. An alliance with TiVo, the personal video recording and service provider, also enabled viewers to pause broadcasts midstream and record up to 35 hours of programming.

Hughes was also working with Microsoft to develop Ultimate TV; the plan was to let viewers record programs and surf the Internet via their TVs.

Hughes' film connection was also still alive. In the summer of 2000 Hughes, together with PanAmSat (it owned 81 percent of the company), IBM, Lucent, and Creative Artists Agency, formed a venture known as NeTune Communications. Among other things, it was developing a communications system that would allow film directors to digitally transmit daily footage on location via satellite to their production studios. Hughes had ambitions to once again become a presence in Hollywood.

Aside from the DirecTV business, a division known as Hughes Network Systems since 1996 had developed satellite technology for the Internet using a high-speed online service called DirecPC, which let customers download data from a small satellite dish at speeds similar to those of a cable modem. It was originally offered at $40 a month plus $650 for the equipment, and the satellite communication was still only one-way. A phone line was needed for sending data to the Internet. By December 2000, however, two-way satellite service was enabled, and the same dish could also deliver DirecTV broadcasts. Dubbed "satellite broadband," the service was not expected to overtake cable as the delivery mechanism for movies and data services.

For super-high-speed broadcasting, Hughes was eyeing the 2003 debut of a service known as Spaceway, using new "spot-beam" transmission that was ten times faster than a cable modem.

Behind the scenes, after the phone call from Murdoch in late February, Jack Smith, his brother, and vice chairman Pearce had many serious discussions. Mike had a matter of weeks to come up with a better deal, or GM was going to go ahead and sell its stake to Murdoch. By a better deal, he meant more cash for GM. GM would have come away from the News Corp. deal with about $8 billion in cash. Meanwhile, the press was reporting that the deal was dead.

"General Motors is motivated, as all big companies are, by the credit ratings they get. GMAC, Ford Credit, all these things depend on their credit ratings. They're borrowing hundreds of millions all the time. Daily. If their ratings go, it costs them a lot of money," said Murdoch, musing over the fact that it would be difficult for GM to walk away from that much cash at a time when the economy seemed to be heading south. With the cash the News Corp. deal would bring, GM will be "a lot stronger company," he said.

For weeks now, during their habitual Monday morning Office of the Chairman meeting, Murdoch and his top five executives had pondered the realities and the possible routes GM might consider. All of the company's most important strategies began and ended with the Big Six.

Son Lachlan, deputy COO; CFO Devoe; president Chernin; legal eagle Arthur Siskind; and Sky Global CEO Chase Carey, along with "the boss," all had high hopes that GM would soon come back, grateful for a deal.

"Wall Street has been putting pressure on GM for three years at least to spin this company off and to monetize its value. If they'd done it last year, they would have had a little bit more money than this year but because this has been allowed to drag on and on they don't get as much money and it's very very much more difficult operating in a low market," Murdoch said.

While Mike Smith could try a leveraged spin-off of the company, that did not seem practical. GM owned about 424 million of Hughes' 1.3 billion shares; the rest were owned by the public. It was possible Hughes could borrow the cash to buy out GM, and sell its 84 percent stake in satellite carrier PanAmSat for as much as $6 billion, but borrowing could be difficult in the current market, with banks losing lots of money on leveraged transactions. What's more, a spin-off would limit growth by using up cash to pay off interest.

While the Hughes deal was up for grabs, Murdoch and Chernin were making sure their other most important allegiances were intact. They made the rounds in Washington D.C. in early February, courting George W. Bush's new chairman at the FCC, Michael Powell.

The two also hobnobbed with House Energy and Commerce Committee ranking Democrat John Dingell of Michigan (home to GM) and Committee chairman Billy Tauzin, Republican from Louisiana. Telecommunications Subcommittee Chairman Fred Upton, Republican from Michigan, also discussed the industry with the News Corp. honchos.

The rules of the game were in the process of being changed on many fronts beyond technology, too.

Indeed, in the previous decade, Murdoch had transformed News Corp. from a print publishing operation with a presence primarily in Britain and Australia, with only 20 percent of its operations in the U.S., to a global enterprise 70 percent based in the U.S., with 50 percent of revenues coming from digital or electronic sources.

Opportunity never ceased to knock. With the advent of George W. Bush's new administration and the changing of the guard at the FCC, Murdoch was elated at the prospect of an environment similar to the one he had enjoyed in the mid-80s, when he became an American citizen and three of his children, Elisabeth, Lachlan, and James—at the time 17, 14, and 12, respectively—sat in the courtroom to witness the ceremony.

While the likes of Chicago journalist Mike Royko and others blasted the move, Murdoch was welcomed with open arms by the Reagan administration. At the time, Murdoch and FCC chairman Mark Fowler had been virtual soul mates, proponents of the free market and determined to do away with regulation at all cost. (Murdoch had described him as "one of the great pioneers of the communications revolution.") Fowler had welcomed Murdoch's plan to create a new television network, Fox, ownership of which required that Murdoch change his citizenship.

Fowler was said to keep a Mao cap adorned with a red star in his office, which he placed on the head of his commissioners anytime they came up with an idea he felt was "collectivist." Indeed, public interest groups dubbed him the "mad monk of deregulation." Fowler's easing up on ownership rules at the time, indeed, had enabled Murdoch's purchase of Metromedia, which was his stepping stone to the creation of Fox.

Murdoch and Chernin were now having a déjà vu of sorts. Bush's Powell was all for changing the rules and allowing greater freedoms to pioneers in new markets. Antitrust departments at the FTC, DOJ, and FCC were being put back to sleep by Bush, as they had been in the Reagan days. (George W.'s own father had been more enforcement-minded than his son, reversing some of Reagan's antiregulatory efforts during his own presidency.)

But Murdoch was heartened. The signs were clear.

Back in Fowler's day, no one could have envisioned that the media and communications industry a decade later would be almost unrecognizable in terms of the technologies and competitive dynamics at work.

Was this a brave new world, a world where only the might of a giant could succeed?

F or his part, Murdoch viewed himself as a catalyst for competition, whereas regulators were inadvertently maintaining existing monopolies, he believed. He hoped to be remembered for "creating competition and choice in the media.

"But the battle is on-going: regulators yield power every bit as reluctantly as private monopolies," Murdoch said. "So we have to do more than accept passively the rules as given: We have to work to change those rules when they interfere with our ability to provide consumers with choice, and our ability to compete with established and often government-sponsored media companies."

Checking himself, Murdoch noted, "But, at the same time, we cannot be cultural imperialists, imposing Western notions of decency and openness on countries that have different histories, different values, and different cultures."

As a global media company, he had to consider the vastly different mores of the countries in which he operated. "In America, for example, the laws include a constitutional guarantee of the right to print and show almost anything we think consumers want to read or view," he said. "But in Britain, the government has the power to restrict what may be shown on television before 9 P.M., and to suggest just how far newspapers may go in reporting purely private matters."

Said Murdoch, "It is in balancing these three interests—those of our shareholders, our customers and our host governments—that our most important master comes into play: our consciences.

"We have special powers: We can help to set the agenda of political discussion. We can uncover government misdeeds and bring them to light. We can decide what television fare to offer children on a rainy Saturday morning. We can affect the culture by glorifying or demonizing certain behavior, such as the use of drugs." Indeed, he'd gotten in a fight with son Lachlan about his disapproval of a film his studio had produced, *The Fight Club*. Lachlan had enjoyed the film, but respected that his father just did not "get" that "in your face" culture.

But Murdoch is a man of shifting tastes and loyalties; he is an iconoclast who traffics in icons.

With the shape-shifting talents of a Proteus, Murdoch was also poised to adjust his allegiances in the face of Mike Smith's attempted coup with DirecTV. He was not going to sit by idly while the man did his shopping.

Said Lachlan Murdoch, "When we heard they were talking

to Charlie, we said, 'well, we're not going to sit here and get screwed, we'll talk to Charlie as well.' "

Rupert, in fact, considered Echostar's Charlie Ergen an old friend, despite the fact that the two men had a disastrous time with a failed merger years earlier. He admired the man whose high-risk, gambling spirit was much like his own. No matter the problems of the past, the man unquestionably had the "Murdoch stuff."

Charlie Ergen had put himself through college playing darts; like Murdoch, he had the fearlessness of a gambler. For years, he sold tiny satellite dishes out of the back of his car, targeting backwater America, entertainment-hungry citizens living in remote, rural areas of the country. Now he was a billionaire.

With Ergen having 90 percent voting control within Echostar, any attempted merger with News Corp.'s Sky Global would be impossible without his backing. Echostar now had more than 5 million subscribers and a market value of $12.4 billion.

It was unlikely that this independent spirit would ever be open to being controlled by another fiercely independent mogul: Rupert Murdoch.

In fact, he'd been through that exercise once, and had failed miserably. In 1997, Murdoch had announced plans for another attempt to combine a U.S. satellite system—American Sky Broadcasting—with tiny Echostar. The new service would simply be called Sky, and had ambitions to cover 75 percent of the country by the end of 1998. It would transmit local stations as well as cable networks, and hoped to beam up to 500 channels over an 18-inch dish.

With such a system, Murdoch could rebroadcast Fox News, and other Fox programming, clear across the country, without relying on partnerships with cable operators. Murdoch had his eye on all of North America—and two-thirds of the world's television screens.

But cable competitors went ballistic and lobbied Congress to block Murdoch's plan. "The cable people made a lot of threats to us," Murdoch said.

Lobbyists argued too much control of the U.S. media would be in a single mogul's hands. He already owned 22 television stations nationwide. One critic even accused Murdoch of practicing "egonomics." He was willing to sustain big losses in return for what he predicted would be a huge payoff in the future.

There were other problems. Charlie Ergen was having trouble conforming to the desires of News Corp. executives over him. "He wanted 100 percent of votes," Murdoch said. "And there were a lot of people who invested a year of their lives and were very passionate about ASkyB. In the end we broke it up." And Ergen sued Murdoch for breach of contract, to the tune of $5 billion.

Nonetheless, Murdoch considered his relationship with Ergen still strong, despite press reports that there was much bad blood between the two men because of their earlier failed deal.

Now, in 2001, Murdoch believed that if Echostar was to be a possible alternative solution for a U.S. stake in the satellite market, it would have to be in the form of an equity swap between the two companies—and Ergen would have to maintain control of U.S. operations.

He described his relationship with Ergen as "very good." Said Murdoch, "People said it's bad, it's *always* been very good with Charlie personally as far as he and I go, and as far as most of his company goes."

As for the past problems, Murdoch said, "It was basically just Charlie's sheer determination to be a loner, to do it on his own, do it cheap, and you've got to admire him. So far, he's pulled it off.

"I like him, I respect him, and he remains some sort of alternative," Murdoch said. If such a deal occurred, Murdoch said, Ergen would "still want to run the show in this country."

Despite press reports at the time, Murdoch added, "We never ended up talking in great detail about it, you know, how it would really work out."

Indeed, Murdoch more than anyone knew that it was folly to believe everything you read. The press had seized upon the idea that Echostar had approached Hughes with a merger offer, and that Murdoch had been courting Echostar. In fact, it had been an apparently desperate Mike Smith who had started the free-for-all with his February 19 sojourn to Denver. Now most everyone was waiting for GM to make up its mind about the only real and viable offer on the table: Murdoch's.

While Hughes' talks with Echostar concerned him, Murdoch highly doubted whether federal regulators— another big consideration—would approve such a combination anyway.

"It's a ridiculous idea to say that you're going to put these two together in order to be competitive because they're both growing pretty fast. Much faster than anybody in cable. Even if it may be a possible battle to win in Washington today it would be a long one. GM would have had this hanging over their head for years," he said.

Still more damage control was needed. Next, Murdoch was told that Mike Smith's shopping expeditions included a trip to Seattle to court software giant Microsoft. News Corp. CEO Peter Chernin immediately got on the phone with Microsoft president Steve Ballmer;

Murdoch had won Gates's approval for a $5 billion investment in Sky Global, and the Hughes merger was part of the deal. While Murdoch had his eye on the DirecTV prize, Gates coveted a place on the "World Box," the secret plan Murdoch had for a set-top box that would be customized for markets all over the world. The Microsoft pact was "99 percent" final, and had been set up in two parts—in case Hughes bailed out.

Chernin told Ballmer, "We're very close to being done with this Hughes deal. But Mike Smith is trying to get a better deal. We want you to know that we are still committed to doing this deal with Microsoft, and we want DirecTV."

The intention was to give Ballmer complete confidence that News Corp. was still in the game as originally envisioned, so that Ballmer could definitively say one thing to Mike Smith: "No."

2

WALLED GARDEN

Months earlier, in the summer of 2000, at the time of his younger son's wedding, Murdoch had been courting Microsoft, initially at a retreat in Sun Valley, Idaho, and working on his sometimes friend John Malone, the cable billionaire, to take an interest in Sky Global as well. As was his wont, business and family life were often indistinguishable, and these days both sons, who were quickly climbing the corporate ladder honed by their father, were often by his side for key deals and strategy meetings. Ironically, Murdoch discovered in crafting his plans for World Box that the need to protect his properties was greater than ever before in the world of the Internet and interactive television; forging electronic "walled gardens" would accomplish this, much as the hedges of Dame Elisabeth's Cruden Farm had enclosed and protected him as a boy.

Ties, knots, liaisons, mergers, marriages, links, pacts. Murdoch knows all about them; his familial bonds say much about not just the future of his empire but also hint at the seriousness with which he approaches issues of loyalty, trust, and forming unions.

Talks regarding a possible partnership with Microsoft Corp. had been intensive since the summer of 2000, and had dovetailed with Murdoch's initial idea to take Sky Global public by the end of the year. He still had no U.S. satellite component to the business; although informal talks had been going on with Hughes and GM throughout the previous year, they did not become serious until December. Even without a DirecTV component, Wall Street had estimated Murdoch's proposed float of Sky Global to be worth some $40 billion.

Back on June 18, Murdoch was still pondering his options as he stood in a tuxedo on the grounds of a small ferry house framed by a vast expanse of sea and sky. It was the occasion of his son James's wedding.

At the same spot a hundred years earlier, wooden ferry boats had traversed the Connecticut River. Family and business were one; life was work and work was life. Rupert Murdoch himself had fallen in love during a business trip to Hong Kong a few years earlier. James, who'd just taken his wedding vows, was now running the same Hong Kong headquarters of Star TV where pere Rupert had met his wife.

Now wedding guests were steadily arriving at James's recently purchased getaway just outside of Old Saybrook, Connecticut, driving in a downpour from the wedding ceremony at a tiny church nearby.

Meanwhile, behind the scenes, father Rupert was lining up some of the most interesting marriages of all. John Malone was about to fork over $500 million for Sky Global. Murdoch was also eyeing a meeting with titan Bill Gates the following month, hoping for a multibillion-dollar partnership with the software giant.

All through the party, hugs and squeezes were interspersed with quiet asides regarding the latest buzz in the industry, and how Rupert's sons and in-laws and spouses—new and old—were faring in their lives. He rarely got to see them face-to-face all at once.

Rupert had first been introduced by James to his new bride, Kathryn Hufschmid, years earlier aboard his yacht *Morning Glory,* when the Murdoch clan took a 10-day cruise together around Australia's Great Barrier Reef.

James initially had met his wife-to-be at a party aboard a yacht in Australia given by a friend of Lachlan's. She was working as a model at the time, but relocated to New York for a marketing job, and to be with her true love. (Hufschmid hated the modeling profession, but had decided to do it long enough to travel the world for a few years. For the Oregon-born young woman whose mother had passed away the previous year, the Murdoch clan was now all the family she had in the world.)

James and Kathryn had planned the wedding and reception to be small—about 80 close friends and family members. During the ceremony, James had read Kathryn a poem by Pablo Neruda, and Kathryn read to him from James Joyce. Father Rupert shed a few bittersweet tears. He was facing his own mortality, having been diagnosed with prostate cancer the previous spring. Wendi Deng, whom he'd married in the summer of 1999, had seen him through the tough times. He'd separated from his wife of 32 years, Anna Murdoch, in April 1998, the year son Lachlan wed supermodel Sarah O'Hare. Wendi had been at his side all through the summer for his treatments, which he pronounced to be "a success" to all who inquired about his health. "I'm now convinced of my own immortality!" he said.

Rupert's 92-year-old mother, Dame Elisabeth Murdoch, had traveled from her abode, Cruden Farm, in Australia for her grandson's wedding. All the children worshipped her. Cruden Farm was 30 miles south of Melbourne, and was the boyhood home of Rupert and his three sisters. Dame Elisabeth's was a large country house, American colonial in style, with Georgian porticoes and large open fireplaces. It was a lush place, with her lavish gardens, tennis court, and stables.

The clan now congregating represented the past and future control of News Corp. Eventually, financial control of Rupert's empire would be divided between James and Lachlan, and daughters Elisabeth and Prudence. The Murdoch family held a 31 percent stake in News Corp., the largest controlling share in a single family's hands of any media company on the planet. That stake was held by an Australian trust, Cruden Investments.

Over the previous five years, News Corp.'s revenues had grown steadily, but net income was erratic. That was largely because of Rupert Murdoch's tendency to take a long-term approach to his investments. It was "Very Rupert," as one Wall Street analyst liked to call it, for News Corp. to pay an outlandish sum for some asset, based on the mogul's visions of the potential to reinvent a whole business sector in some way.

Murdoch was proud to pronounce he would not "play the quarterly-earnings game so beloved of Wall Street and other financial analysts." News Corp.'s focus was on the long term, and his goal was to reap the benefits of his company's investment in that future. Said Murdoch, "We see ourselves as a growth company, but one with the patience and courage to invest now to develop higher earnings in the future, rather than attempt to capitalize on whatever fad happens to be this week's darling of Wall Street."

Dinner was served under a tent in the yard. Rupert and Wendi were charming and witty together, many guests noted. It was hard to believe that Murdoch had been undergoing cancer treatments; he was his usual ebullient and irreverent self.

Ex-wife Anna Murdoch Mann and her new husband,

American financier William Mann, were present, as was daughter Elisabeth with her new beau, Matthew Freud, the grandson of Sigmund Freud. Daughter Prudence, 42, Rupert's first child from his first marriage, was in from London, with the tall and refined Alasdair MacLeod, her husband. Lachlan with his wife Sarah toasted the newlyweds.

News Corp. president Peter Chernin was one of the few outside-the-clan executives present. But Chernin was like family, almost a second father to the Murdoch sons, who were being closely tutored by him in all aspects of the business.

James and Lachlan were both fascinated by the machinations that were in the works surrounding the launch of what could be the largest IPO in the history of the media industry. All through the wedding reception, an old college chum of James's noted Rupert pulling his sons aside to talk business.

That same month, following briefings with Murdoch and sons, Merrill Lynch's Jessica Reif Cohen—whose firm planned to underwrite the float—targeted the price of $33 a share on the future Sky Global stock. She told the media this was "ridiculously cheap," because of the value of News' unlisted satellite TV assets.

Given all the competing media technologies, only two delivery platforms mattered as far as interactive pay TV was concerned. "In most parts of the world, it's either cable or satellite. And there is just no other company that is better positioned than News Corp. If we are even remotely right, they are paying you right now to take the stock," Cohen had said.

In frequent meetings over the months, Cohen noted that the Murdoch sons were equally impressive: bright, intellectual adventurers, not the spoiled kids that sometimes came out of New York's wealthy families. Cohen had just seen James Murdoch recently, during a secret meeting about the float of Sky Global.

New digital media, for all diversified media and entertainment companies, meant being able to repurpose existing assets—programs and all types of published content—and extending existing platforms to reach new audiences and create new brands and businesses. It was all upside, in the eyes of the Street. News Corp. was reaching deeper to consumers using its brands, and creating new businesses as well. On the other hand, everyone was struggling with the Internet. How do you make money at it? What's the successful business model to follow? News Corp. was no exception.

Cohen, in fact, had given Murdoch a virtual gold star, "for not having spent too much money and really having thought it through, whereas a year ago there was a demerit against them for not being active enough."

Numerous companies had invested much time, management attention, money, and promotion, trying to drive Internet-based businesses, but did not have a lot to show for it.

Nevertheless, it was inevitable that traditional media would have to move in a big way into new media. Two decades earlier, none of the traditional media companies started cable networks, but eventually moved into cable. Now cable was concentrated in five or six hands. Wall Street was expecting the same type of consolidation in new media, though none could yet predict what it would mean to the bottom line.

Cohen viewed News Corp. as the most entrepreneurial of all the traditional media companies. It was the freest-thinking organization. Time Warner had been viewed similarly 15 years prior, but no longer.

Rupert saw things that others didn't. When he bought the Metromedia television stations, nobody believed he would be able to successfully start a network. Now all the Street's top seers snickered when they thought of Larry Tisch's famous statement that he wouldn't pay a nickel for the Fox network. Until recently, Fox was worth more than CBS.

Rupert built the Fox network, a fourth network which everyone thought was impossible, but he also built the largest and the most profitable TV station group rivaled only by Viacom. He'd taken second-rate production assets and made them first-class, and News Corp. was by far the dominant producer of prime-time entertainment programming, providing some 25 percent of programs to six networks by the end of 2000.

News Corp. was in good shape to be the content provider for all kinds of new enterprises in need of compelling content. Merrill Lynch's Cohen saw it poised to be the dominant TV syndicator over the next several years, with the huge amount of programming coming off the networks into syndication. Rupert had turned laggard assets into powerful platforms, created the Fox network, and made the Fox brand, which in the fall of 2000 was the strongest it had ever been.

What's more, Wall Street was abuzz about the most incredible platform of them all—the massive interactive satellite network that would be enabled with the float of Sky Global Networks. Indeed, Rupert Murdoch believed that, with Sky Global, he would be able to export the company's best businesses on a global basis, migrating them to worldwide media platforms.

Courting John Malone came naturally to Murdoch, though Malone was sometimes his partner and sometimes his rival. Malone, 59, was the son of a GE executive and one of the world's wealthiest media moguls, personally worth some $2.4 billion. He was a cable pioneer who spent decades growing TCI as the largest U.S. cable operator. He was now pretty much out of the cable business and a dealmaker extraordinaire.

Malone sold off TCI, which he'd joined in 1973, with company founder Bob Magness, to AT&T for about $54 billion, while retaining programming assets via Liberty Media, a holding company for a range of his interests. His Liberty had a stake in all kinds of media endeavors, including 22 of the top 50 cable channels, and pieces of Time Warner, News Corp., and Sprint PCS. While Murdoch had been forced to sell his yacht *Morning Glory* as part of his divorce settlement, Malone still loved piloting his *Liberty,* an 80-foot-long vessel. He could also be spotted along the highways of America, driving between his homes in Colorado and Maine in a custom-built luxury camper. He was fond of telling gapers at truck stops that the $750,000 extravaganza was owned by country superstar Garth Brooks.

Malone had not always been an ally of Murdoch's, though Murdoch professed great admiration for the man, as did both the Murdoch sons. In 1996, Malone—whose TCI cable network boasted 14 million subscribers—partnered with Murdoch for the launch of Fox News. Murdoch had at first tried to woo Ted Turner and acquire CNN, but Turner sold the all-news channel to Time Warner. Murdoch even considered buying Time Warner for a whopping $40 billion, but decided to launch his own news channel instead. He vowed that it would be "much better than CNN." Meanwhile, Turner, who loathed Murdoch, described his rival as "the schlockmeister." Murdoch accepted the description, he said, if one defined "schlock" as such hit properties as *X-Files,* the *Times of London,* NFL football, *The Simpsons,* and films such as *Waiting to Exhale.* Murdoch dismissed his detractors as being green with envy.

For the Fox launch, Murdoch was paying big incentives to cable networks that agreed to carry his channel. Murdoch, as was his habit, turned customary practices on their ear, and the Fox debut was no different. While cable operators usually paid a small fee per subscriber to channels they featured, Murdoch promised to pay cable operators large sums for every sub-scriber they brought to Fox News. In their first pact together, Malone provided Murdoch with ten million subscribers, at the cost of $20 each. In return, Malone also received an option to buy a 20 percent equity interest in the channel. Murdoch also paid $10 a subscriber to other large cable operators, for a total of about eight million more subscribers.

At the same time, Time Warner, in which Malone held a substantial stake, had banned Murdoch's Fox News, largely because of their new executive, Ted Turner, whose hatred of Murdoch was legendary.

Malone's Liberty Media Group held an 18 percent non-voting stake in News Corp., second only to the Murdoch family's 31 percent controlling interest. Malone over time had been instrumental in helping News Corp. grow its overall cable programming business from zero to more than 350 million subscribers in just a few years.

Now, while trying to woo investors for his Sky Global plans, Murdoch was also considering giving Malone a board seat.

While Murdoch had been talking up Sky Global to Malone for months, in about a month his merger deal with Gemstar's Henry Yuen would be complete. Murdoch had talked with Malone about Liberty Media giving up its 21 percent stake in Gemstar in exchange for a stake in the larger Sky Global, of which Gemstar would be a part. Murdoch was in aggressive talks with other would-be investors. In July, he and son Lach-lan were set to go to the Allen & Co. conference in Sun Valley, Idaho, for a private meeting targeted at winning over Bill Gates.

The Microsoft courtship, shepherded by Rupert, began a few weeks later.

It was one of those blazing July days in Sun Valley,

Idaho, and the Sun Valley Lodge was filled with billionaires and tycoons of all shapes and sizes, bedecked in tennis shoes and shorts for the occasion of Herb Allen's yearly conference.

Film director Francis Ford Coppola had stationed himself at the bar. Most likely he was eyeing what was indeed a darn clever bunch as they passed through.

Murdoch's competitors were swarming all over the place. In one room, America Online chairman Steve Case and Time Warner's Gerald Levin had been holding forth about their new octopus AOL Time Warner.

The power structures in the media business had been realigned in recent months as though a colossal earthquake had hit—the aftermath of all the megamergers that had gone down. Warner Brothers' chairman Edgar Bronfman Jr. was at the bar wagging his tongue about the mind-boggling collision that was the Vivendi/Canal+/Seagram merger. His movie studio crony at Vivendi Universal, Pierre Lescure, sat in a bar outside the conference rooms cavorting with 45-year-old tycoon Jean-Marie Messier, the chairman of Vivendi, whom Murdoch had recently e-mailed to say "you've got guts!" when he heard of the Vivendi-Seagram megamerger.

In the midst of this incestuous world, where everyone had a stake in everyone else's business, it was hard to keep up with who owned whom anymore. Barry Diller, head of USA Networks, who ironically had introduced Peter Chernin years ago to his former boss Murdoch, was scrambling to take advantage of the new media giant. Vivendi held a 43 percent stake in his company, and he had high hopes that USA's Home Shopping Network, Ticketmaster, and Sci-Fi Channel would be distributed to Canal+'s 13 million European pay-TV subscribers.

Diller had also come to butt heads with Sony chief Howard Stringer and Intel's Andy Grove on a panel discussing "The Impact of the Internet on Corporate Culture." As moderator, it was the job of NBC's Tom Brokaw to keep them in line.

The world had permanently been changed by technology and by the financial and business transactions that defined the times. And surely as they had throughout history, such monumental industry shifts would breed more transformation. The biggest changes were yet to come.

The $98.6 billion marriage of America Online Inc., the world's largest Internet provider, and Time Warner Inc., the number two cable provider in the United States, was just the beginning.

There would be a wave of activity on the part of media companies doing deals with Internet and digital broadcasting companies to combine content with new methods of digital distribution.

"In the television business, we used to worry about what other networks were doing. Now we worry about what hundreds of specialist channels are doing to woo audiences, and what is going on in the video game industry and on the Internet, both of which now compete for people's time and advertisers' money," Murdoch said.

In the newspaper business, where he used to worry whether other papers had scooped him, now News Corp. had to "worry about where newspapers fit in a world in which television, radio and the Internet transmit news as it is happening, and hundreds of specialist magazines provide expert commentary and analysis."

Nevertheless, "We are confident that when the time comes that these new systems begin to affect the bottom line in a positive way, we will be in a position to share in that flow of profits," Murdoch said. "Not that life is as easy as it once was. We have to work harder, take more risks, and manage smarter."

Traditional media companies were increasingly willing to cannibalize their own traditional revenues by establishing new digital forms of media—delivered via the Internet, digital cable, and wireless devices such as cell phones and e-books.

While online-only media ventures had been experiencing disappointing declines in online advertising revenues, compelling content was being viewed as the ingredient that would save the day—attracting viewers regardless of distribution method. Exploring new uses of interactivity was another ingredient that held promise.

Internet portals that were advertising-based were recognizing that distribution via the Internet was not as powerful an asset on its own; traditional media could boost their appeal.

While the original AOL Time Warner pact lost 40 percent of its value as AOL's share price plunged (it was originally valued at about $164 billion when it was announced), the industry, still reeling from its implications, was eyeing similar pacts.

For his part, Murdoch was shunning Internet plays and keeping his eye on the satellite dish.

N ow, in July 2000, tucked away in a room in Sun Valley, Bill Gates sat opposite Rupert Murdoch, who had his older son Lachlan beside him. Gates was accompanied by a few of his deputies, but his right-hand man Steve Ballmer (Gates's counterpart to Murdoch's top man Peter Chernin) was noticeably missing.

Although James was honeymooning in Tanzania and the Seychelles, both sons had been involved for almost a year now in the secretive talks held at the top levels of the company concerning Sky Global's creation. By the time James took over at the helm of Star TV in the spring of 2000, he had become even more intensely involved, participating in regular meetings with bankers and corporate officers. Star was an important asset in the array of the Sky Global companies.

Now "the boss" was doing all the talking.

Rupert was holding forth eloquently about the biggest

dream of his career. Chernin and News Corp. CFO Dave Devoe sat by patiently to answer any questions.

With Sky Global, in addition to a distribution platform that would reach all over the globe, Murdoch had a treasure trove of content to offer, unlike most other cable and satellite companies. By 2001, indeed, News Corp., with Fox, had become the dominant content supplier to broadcast and cable networks—producing nearly one-quarter of all broadcast network prime-time programs—which eventually translates into enormous syndication profits. The company could boast that it had produced Disney's number one comedy *Dharma and Greg*, the drama *The Practice, Ally McBeal, X-Files*, and many others.

Sky Global would also enable economies of scale that would make it possible to develop inexpensive set-top boxes customized for every country market in existence. It had plans to launch new interactive digital services on the latest generation of set-top boxes in select world markets. The initial rollout would be slow, Murdoch expected, but the eventual market would be huge.

For Microsoft's part, it coveted a presence in interactive TV, an area viewed as having more growth than the personal computer market over the next five years. News Corp. insiders talked about the fact that the software giant "has hopes that it can dominate digital television sets of the future just as it did the personal computer with Windows."

James had explained to his father, "They definitely want to get Windows into the operating system of some of these set-top boxes. I think they're realizing on the PC now, they're being attacked on different fronts, both from servers and Internet appliances, and at the same time the TV is becoming more intelligent."

Indeed, Murdoch and Chernin envisioned that soon no

company in the world could afford *not* to be carried on Sky Global's digital platforms.

The presentation lasted about an hour, and Murdoch senior discussed all the worldwide assets he hoped to join together in the new venture—BSkyB, Star, the powerful technology and patents Gemstar would bring to the table, and NDS, the Murdoch technology company that Gates knew well. NDS had helped him out of his own interactive TV disaster.

With the economies of scale that would be made possible through the creation of a global satellite business, Murdoch's vision was for a worldwide project code-named World Box—developing set-top boxes customized for markets in every corner of the world.

Providing set-top boxes to customers had been an expensive proposition. In Europe, France, and elsewhere, broadcasters subsidized the hardware by giving a $400 set-top box away for free to subscribers. On average, Murdoch's BSkyB spent $250 in marketing costs for each new subscriber, but BSkyB's payback for each subscriber's set-top box was less than a year. With the economies of scale enabled by Sky Global's World Box, Murdoch could subsidize infant markets in remote parts of the world with profits pouring in from more sophisticated television viewers.

Gates expressed eagerness for a version of Windows to be at the heart of these interactive television devices, which represented a much larger market than personal computers as the entertainment and information devices of the future.

Murdoch detailed the plan. "We'll operate three World Boxes. We'll have a very basic introductory box, cheap, it can take unlimited television channels. It will be for unsophisticated viewers, those in underdeveloped markets like China, where people can't afford to spend much. Then you'd have your general World Box where you can do at least what you can do in Britain [with BSkyB] but probably also have a hard disk so you can be recording programs while you're watching something else.

"And then you'd have a super box, which could sing and dance, so to speak," he laughs. "It will run your security system in the house, turn on your microwave, read the gas meter, all those things."

By the end of the meeting, Gates expressed his interest in being a partner and investing billions. Murdoch promised that another meeting would be arranged soon; he and his CFO were just in the process of defining the structure of the company.

L ater in the summer of 2000, another round of talks began, this time headed by Peter Chernin and Microsoft's Ballmer. Microsoft got more specific about wanting a version of its Windows software to be at the heart of the World Box. In exchange for a large investment, News Corp. agreed, as a quid pro quo, that it was open to putting a version of Windows and other Microsoft technologies in the box, under the condition that the software "worked well and was available on time for the product rollout, and the quality is as good as software from other set-top box software providers," Ballmer was told.

For its part, Microsoft explained its plans with its Ultimate TV box, its own interactive TV endeavor for which it also had a partnership with Murdoch's archrival AOL Time Warner. It made sense for Microsoft to merge its lackluster Ultimate TV plans with Murdoch's Sky Global World Box, if a partnership was to go forward.

News Corp.'s top technology executive was up on all the issues, and unintimidated by being confronted by the world's top computer nerds sitting before him. His forte was satellite broadcast technology, and he plunged deep into the issues.

Chase Carey, the president of Sky Global, also held forth on News Corp.'s concerns about Microsoft and customer control.

All along, Murdoch had been instructing his lieutenants, who were paranoid about Microsoft's ability to gain control of News Corp. customers, to make sure that "it's *our* walled garden."

That is, a relationship with Microsoft would require a partition, or walled garden, within the television set-top box for interactivity and shopping and access to the Internet. It was important to understand how Microsoft saw its Microsoft Network online service, MSN—its answer to AOL—fitting in. No cable operators, News Corp.'s customers, wanted to give direct access to their customers to Microsoft and have the software giant, for example, gaining access to pay-per-view revenues.

Peter Chernin was Murdoch's most trusted executive. All through the fall and winter of 2000, he continued the negotiations with Microsoft.

Over the months, continued wrangling over how to separate each company's services offered via the set-top box began to bog the deal down. James Murdoch observed that the problem with partnering with Microsoft was, "for service operators like us, or for a cable company, how does the Microsoft .Net project fit into their system software and services?" Microsoft's much promoted .Net strategy meant transferring essential parts of its software businesses to an Internet-based foundation. News Corp. executives were uncertain about how Microsoft's strategic plans might overlap with News Corp.'s—Murdoch was cautious about inviting the aggressive software giant too much onto his own turf.

Indeed, there is "a fine line," James noted, between a partnership where you pay a license fee to a component supplier—hardware or software—to get what you need for the inside of a set-top box, and allowing the partner to control and have access to your customers.

Rupert and sons agreed that, in reality, Microsoft needed News Corp. more than News Corp. needed Microsoft; Murdoch had relationships with dozens of technology suppliers. Licensing what he needed for the guts of the set-top box was not a hurdle. But the market presence and clout of Microsoft, along with the huge financial investment it could make, kept interest high as News Corp. executives wrestled with the question: How should Sky Global control interactive TV applications, and how much control is it willing to give up?

"In the area of e-mail, for example, and other customer applications, no service operator or cable operator is going to want its customers doing e-mail over the network at MSN.com," James pointed out.

"Application provision gets into really sensitive issues about whose customer it is," he said. "For a set-top box business it's just simply about cost—wrap plastic around chips in a reliable cost-effective way and those things are going to win the contracts. We can get what we need from other companies besides Microsoft."

James said, "But if you can have 'em on board, it's better than having them against you. The devil is in the details."

Indeed, said one senior executive, "Everyone loves Microsoft when they come in with a check, but then you never want to see them again because that's the last you'd see of your company."

Tech-savvy James, whom Rupert had been relying on for some time for advice on his digital investments, actually viewed AOL as more predatory than Microsoft, having spent years testifying against the online service provider during litigation News Corp. was involved in with the company years earlier. (That contract dispute was eventually settled.) James had served as a key witness in that case, and was hence savvy about how perilous "partnerships" with potential competitors could be.

In the end, the companies worked out a plan for making sure the walled garden protected News Corp.'s core businesses, guarding its pay-TV revenues and customers from mingling with those from Microsoft's online and interactive endeavors via the set-top box.

By December, however, it was clear from Murdoch that not only had he "lined up a great deal of money to go the development of this [Sky Global] business," his new plan was to use the funds to "take out GM."

3

BIG GUNS

News Corp. president Peter Chernin had over the years risen to become Murdoch's most trusted executive, which went a long way when the big boss had to announce to shareholders in the spring of 2000 that he'd been diagnosed with prostate cancer. By the time Sky Global plans were in full swing, the Murdoch sons had taken on more and more responsibility, fueling speculation about which one would inherit their father's throne. Rumors ran rampant about a war for supremacy between the brothers, but they in fact remained close—which boded well for the future of the family-controlled empire. By the end of 2000, the Big Six were closely monitoring the market, poised for a possible IPO with Sky Global. But a glitch in the market one October day was a harbinger of things to come; the market was headed for the doldrums, and suddenly the talks with GM became red-hot. While dealing with the pressing issues of the moment, Murdoch also had Chernin looking out for the future, lobbying Washington to protect content in the Internet age.

hile the young scions, Lachlan and James, were learning the ropes, Rupert Murdoch had slowly but surely put COO Peter Chernin in a position of increasing power. The investment community had been skittish, perceiving News Corp. as a one-man show. Starting back in the summer of 1999, that perception began to change. Murdoch said that his sons would have to prove themselves first, before they would be in any position to take over the top spot at the company. Peter Chernin, on the other hand, was viewed as his immediate successor, should Murdoch become incapable of performing his job. He at times mused that Lachlan could possibly serve as chairman, in such a scenario, with Chernin still running the day-to-day operations of the empire.

But Murdoch on many occasions remarked that he did not intend to die or leave anytime soon, noting that his heirs would have to "carry me out or push me out." Still, at the end of the 90s, he was increasingly aware of the need to have a contingency plan in the case of his unanticipated demise. "We have had to assemble a world-class international management team. A one-man band cannot play the tunes that will be the hits of the next century," he said.

Chernin started to make his mark back in July 1999. London's Royal Lancaster hotel was overflowing with investment bankers attending a conference hosted by Merrill Lynch. Peter Chernin held court, pointing out to investors that revenues from just a few of the programs in syndication from Fox would result in a whopping $1.5 billion in profits over the next few years.

It was one of the first times that investors felt comfortable that News Corp. wasn't being guided just by Rupert Murdoch. Not surprisingly, Chernin's ambitions were just as grand as Murdoch's. During one CNN broadcast, he stated that News Corp.'s overall strategy was to "try and build the world's preeminent, vertically integrated global communications company, create the most amount of content in television and movies and sports, and have the most number of outlets to display them whether those are satellite outlets around the world, newspapers, television stations, [or] cable channels."

During an executive retreat in 1998, Chernin gave a keynote speech in which he made it clear how much the top brass emulated "the boss."

Chernin said, "You know those 'Be Like Mike' commercials?" alluding to the Nike advertisements featuring the basketball star Michael Jordan. "We have to be like Rupert. We have to institutionalize the imagination, nerve and vision he represents." Those who know him attribute Chernin's success as one of the most powerful people in the media business to just that—emulating "KRM," as insiders refer to Murdoch.

Chernin had come into Murdoch's fold via Barry Diller, Murdoch's former Fox chief, who had hired him to run the Fox network programming division.

Chernin's background was in publishing, having graduated from Berkeley University to a short career in book editing. He joined the cable television station Showtime in 1983, and was recruited by the Fox Network to become president of entertainment. He went on to run the network and, later, Fox Studios.

Murdoch, who had never met Chernin before, noticed him during a company management retreat in Santa Barbara, California. He asked Chernin to give him a ride back to Los Angeles, and the two immediately hit it off. Their friendship continued to grow over the years as Chernin climbed the corporate ladder, heading up the Fox network and then the film studio.

Chernin also was viewed to be unthreatening to Murdoch; unlike Diller and others, he did not question Murdoch's vision.

In 1996, Rupert made him his right-hand man, his closest

strategic confidant outside the family. Chernin played a key role in News Corp.'s expansion—its move into German TV, the purchase of the LA Dodgers baseball team, and continued expansion of Fox in the United States.

Then, in 1999, Murdoch was on a big push in Europe, and Chernin accompanied him on many trips around the continent, including France and Germany. The previous December, Chernin had overseen News Corp.'s $40 billion takeover of TM3, the women's cable channel in Germany with a small subscriber base and $25 million in annual losses.

Astoundingly, he then had TM3 spend in excess of $400 million for the viewing rights to soccer's popular European Champions League. Germany was a soccer-crazed place, and the move mirrored the rationale behind Fox's purchase of NFL viewing rights for $1.6 billion in 1993, which was credited with solidifying Fox as the "fourth network." Although Chernin projected losses of about $100 million for three years running because of the soccer purchase, he and Murdoch believed the gamble would pay off.

Rupert and Peter were very close. They talked many times a day, more often than not, and Chernin was the only News Corp. executive to be invited to attend the boss's wedding to Wendi, as well as the weddings of Lachlan and James.

Chernin, like Murdoch, was seen to possess a rare knack for both the creative and the corporate sides of the business. His presence was unassuming, his mixture of right- and left-brained-ness seeming to stem from being a Berkeley-educated literature major from a long line of accountants.

He was admired for his managerial discipline, which the company was sorely lacking back in 1990 when it was on the verge of bankruptcy because of global debts. Chernin brought the film and TV businesses to greater profits, and approved the creation of *Titanic,* which turned out to be the biggest-grossing film of all time.

In the mid-90s, he proved himself by convincing Murdoch to spend some $70 million to hire away Hollywood's top writers and producers. These included David Kelley, the man behind *Ally McBeal* and *The Practice* (a Fox creation that was sold to Disney's ABC), and Chris Carter, who developed *X-Files.* Needless to say Chernin steered the company in the right direction.

Wall Street really got its first big jolt in regard to News Corp. in Manhattan on April 16, 2000, and key management like Chernin would necessarily be called upon. Green buds were just beginning to appear on the drab avenues, and Rupert Murdoch held forth before a group of Wall Street pundits, disclosing that he was about to begin treatment for prostate cancer—two months of radiation.

Rupert had been adamant that his condition, diagnosed a week earlier during a checkup with his doctor in Los Angeles, not interfere with his job. Indeed, prostate cancer was a fairly common thing among older men, and rarely fatal. Fellow tycoon Andy Grove, the chairman of Intel, had become an activist promoting education about the disease, following his own diagnosis and apparent cure.

Among his audience, Murdoch follower/analyst Jessica Reif Cohen was stunned. "The man is unbelievable. So full of energy and so full of life," she said, indulging in a bit of Rupert worship. "You can ask him anything about anything and he'll know."

But there were lots of things he couldn't know.

Despite Murdoch's optimism about his health, News Corp. shares all over the world plunged that day on news of his illness, losing some $10.9 billion in value on the Australian market. It was the largest one-day plummet in a company's value in the history of the Australian Stock Exchange. (The company's stock is listed on numerous exchanges worldwide.) After all, Murdoch's intimate involvement in managing his empire was legendary on Wall Street. If the man was gone, what would happen to the company he founded 40 years ago?

The news also launched a barrage of speculation about his successor, which annoyed Murdoch to no end.

By October, partly in response to concerns about leadership at the company, Murdoch had promoted son Lachlan to deputy chief operating officer, the number three position at the company, under Chernin. James, who had made the leap to Hong Kong as the head of Star TV, also was soon given a board position on his birthday on December 13, 2000.

Their promotions fueled rampant speculation about a bitter war between them to become their father's chosen heir. But James just laughed that notion off. So did Lachlan. The brothers are closer to each other than any of the Murdoch siblings, and aggressively dismiss tales of their supposed power grab.

If Pop was King Lear whose empire was slipping away, they were portrayed as the greedy scions trying to prove their love and worth to win the riches. (Both Lachlan and James bow out of any scenario that smacks of rivalry between them. Except, of course, when shooting skeets at their father's Carmel ranch, one of their favorite pastimes.)

The rivalry myth is "frustrating," James said. "It usually

doesn't come up because it's not, it's just simply not what we think about. So it's not even on the radar screen really. And we work together on things, we get on really well, we're very comfortable with each other professionally as well and there's no tension there. . . . People forget that the company is a public company, it's not Dynasty or something, ya know what I mean?" he said, with notable youth and informality.

Rupert Murdoch, too, dismisses myths about the brothers' feuding: "They talk to each other a lot, and they're very good friends," he said.

Lachlan likewise shrugs off the notion that he and his brother are competing for the top spot. "The truth is good stories are good stories, and you don't blame anyone for trying to find a story in something when it has a different element— whether it's a family element or a feud, or whatever it is. But at the end of the day, if there's no story there, you'd like to think they'd move on," he said.

When sister Elisabeth was still working for the company, the notion was that the three siblings were duking it out for their father's attention, Lachlan said. "But people would see my brother and sister and I working together, and after so many years of being reported on, when they can find no evidence of that sort of feuding, you'd like to think that people say, well, it's obviously a normal family."

Rupert acknowledged the "story" to be irresistible for the media, which seemingly had made it up out of thin air. It made great headlines, though. The grains of truth were: Yes, he had two brilliant sons, both an important part of his empire, close in age, and close to their father. They were completely different people, and got on splendidly. There was no insecurity regarding their father's affections. And neither wished the demise of their father, nor coveted stepping into his shoes.

Since their promotions, the mud had been flying at the two in press reports skeptical that their qualifications went any further than their surname. James, however, who was not quite as far up the corporate ladder as his brother, was being intensely scrutinized for the first time—having, until now, been in relatively low-profile jobs since joining his father's company in 1977.

"I was kicking around in pretty small stuff for a while," he said, compared to his brother and older sister Elisabeth who, prior to leaving the company in the spring of 2000, was running the show at News Corp.'s U.K. pay-TV operation British Sky Broadcasting.

But when you're a Murdoch, you've been brought up to take the heat. Like his father, James shrugged off the noise of the media, and instead dug further into work. "I adore my job," he said.

Perhaps wisely, early on Rupert sent both sons to remote parts of the world to cut their teeth as chief executives. Lachlan, who ran the company's Australian newspaper operations for three years, valued the chance to try out a CEO job in a remote part of the world, which gave him the freedom he needed to learn the ropes. "It's so important to be away from New York and L.A. and the other executives, and to be 100 percent in charge of your own business—because it really gives you the room and the space to grow and learn lessons," he said. Lachlan was now back in the states, working out of News Corp.'s New York and Los Angeles offices, as deputy COO and a member of the Big Six—the office of the chairman.

Meanwhile, James was in the position Lachlan had been in, sent off to prove his management skills running Star out of Hong Kong. "He's loving it and loving that freedom," Lachlan said. "You're able to make decisions without being second-guessed. And it's entirely your own to succeed at or fail at, and it's a very important experience, and he's doing a great job.

"You're still dealing with the head office in New York or L.A., still doing budgets, reporting in, but it's a totally different thing when you're thousands of miles away responsible for all the management issues that come up, and strategies and everything else," Lachlan said.

Neither son at the moment could fill his father's shoes, a rather obvious observation, seeing that Rupert himself stresses that, as "men in their twenties," both sons are executives in training.

If Rupert died tomorrow, Peter Chernin would take his spot and could remain there indefinitely.

The closeness of the Murdoch brothers may in the long run turn out to be a boon for the News Corp. empire—though market watchers by the spring of 2001 were still uncertain as to their qualifications. Both were clearly now running key parts of the company and having a strategic impact. Their performance was being closely monitored by the market, and by their father, needless to say.

Yet not much was widely known about these brothers who were now running a very public company. Mostly mythological stories had been published about James and Lachlan, and their relationship with each other, as the family is quite private. But the various strengths of the Murdoch brothers, and their apparent preference to remain close and in constant communication, bodes well for a Rupert-like "information stream" governing all of the company's moves.

Their upbringing within the Murdoch clan bears scrutiny.

Nature at least intended the brothers to be close. They were born only 15 months apart in London's Wimbledon Hospital: James on December 13, 1972, Lachlan on September 8, 1971. Anna and Rupert had moved from Australia to England in the late 60s when Murdoch bought *News of the World* and

The Times, and launched *The Sun* a couple of years later. Older sister Elisabeth, three years older than Lachlan, was born in Australia. Lachlan remembers she fulfilled her duties as big sister by "ordering her two brothers what to do."

(As for half-sister Prudence, Rupert's daughter with his first wife Patricia Booker, a former model he married in Adelaide in 1956 and divorced in 1966, she joined Rupert and his wife Anna when she was nine, around the time Elisabeth was born. Prudence, while visiting them at age 8, begged her father to allow her to stay. First in London and then in New York, Prudence lived for a decade with her siblings Elisabeth, Lachlan, and James, who lovingly call her "Prue.")

The brothers clearly were brought up with the sense that family and loyalty were cherished things to be protected and nurtured at all costs, especially given the demands of an always-distracted, globe-trotting father who was often in the company of the world's power brokers and heads of state.

The family moved back to New York in 1973 when the boys were small, settling on the East Side of Manhattan near the United Nations. They stayed a year or two in their apartment there, but both sons have only vague memories of the place. The next move was to Fifth Avenue and 64th Street, where the family lived for five or six years. This is where the memories of both brothers really start.

Compared to their New York boyhood friends, the Murdochs were considered to be pretty formal. "We would have a sit-down dinner every night. My dad would get home from work, he'd make an effort to be home from work on time so we could have half an hour with him before dinner, and he'd usually have guests over for dinner," Lachlan said.

Those guests represented a Who's Who of the world. The brothers grew up breaking bread with muckety-mucks ranging from heads of state to publishers and film stars. At the sit-down dinners, from the time James and Lachlan were six or seven years old, both recall that an intellectual debate was always going on.

"Political debates," Lachlan said. "There were people from in the company but also pretty interesting people from media—from a creative side, authors and journalists, and also people who were in the news. Back then Mayor Koch would come to dinner, and other interesting people. And then generally speaking we'd be sent off to bed before it got too late."

At the same time, the Murdoch children grew up feeling that company executives were also part of the family. "And it's not actually even just merged with your true family, but it's merged with other people you work with in the company. There's great loyalty. James and I have grown up with people in the company—whether it's journalists, to advertising execs to TV execs, from the time we were babies.

"When you grow up with that upbringing, family and work become completely merged. Your home life and work, you never sort of shut off, because when you're in the office you never think, 'Oh, I'm in the office, I'll talk to my brother and my dad differently,' " Lachlan said.

In that Fifth Avenue house, the brothers shared a room for a while, until age 10 or 11. There was a connecting room where a nanny had stayed; when Lachlan got older, the nanny was dismissed and he moved into his own space. Their rooms were always connected; the brothers were not only emotionally, but physically, close throughout their childhood and into adulthood.

When the boys were adolescents, the family moved to an apartment on 88th Street, between Madison and Fifth Avenue, overlooking the Guggenheim Museum. At ages 12 and 13, the brothers often would "climb around the roof and pretend we were Ninjas."

"Lachlan was into karate, martial arts and stuff like that," muses James. "I wanted to do that and wasn't very good at it. Because he was older than I was, it was kind of, 'look up to your big brother doing karate.' "

The family had a country house in upstate New York, a getaway about three hours north of the city, a small house that Lachlan says he remembers as being much bigger, on 100 acres of forested land, with a lake and a dirt road. It was the place where all the children learned to ride bicycles, and were free to roam by themselves for miles in an expansive natural world that was quite different from the confines of New York. "It was really out of the way. We both had little motorcycles, and used to go through the trails in the woods," Lachlan recalled.

By the time the boys were 14, however, James and Elisabeth were into the city life in Manhattan, and Lachlan was heading for Colorado to boarding school. "And I think my parents were tired of driving us all up there for the weekend. They sold the place," he said.

As teenagers they began to have a different circle of friends, and attended different schools. In tenth grade, while Lachlan attended boarding school in Colorado, which he loved, James stayed behind in New York, going to the Horace Mann day school.

When James was 17, he crashed his brother's motorcycle. "And I hadn't told him that I had taken it out," he confesses, noting that his father helped him break the news to Lachlan. "Lachlan called and wanted to know how I was. He didn't want to know what happened to his motorcycle. He wanted to know that later. It wasn't pretty," James said. "He was a good brother. He *is* a good brother."

James then went off to Harvard after a year on an archaeological dig in Rome, and Lachlan went to Princeton to become a philosophy major.

Lachlan's thesis was on Kant and Hegel. "I did then, and I don't now, understand a word of what I wrote."

In the past couple of years, the brothers seem to have done some role-swapping. Conventional wisdom has it that while James has an innovative flair that the more conservative Lachlan perhaps lacks, the younger son's impetuosity also makes him a less stable candidate for the job. But, these days, Lachlan is more outspoken in his expressions and improvisational in his thinking—about everything from reality TV to sheep breeding in the Australian outback. He loves adventure and danger, regularly throwing himself into the often spine-chilling Sydney-to-Hobart sailboat race, and motorcycling whenever he has the chance. James speaks more conservatively of all of his endeavors, and describes his brother's motorcycle habit as "dangerous," having learned firsthand from his escapade on his brother's bike at age 17.

James now is an interesting mixture of spontaneity and caution, while his brother has become more fun-loving and gregarious. Oddly, while calling his brother's motorcycling "dangerous," he hurled himself into a helicopter-skiing adventure in the Himalayas the previous winter—having trained for months in anticipation of the grueling jaunt. He dismisses the danger of that. "It's run by pros," he said.

The switch is noticeable, according to those closest to the brothers. James is pulling in and settling down to a more conservative life and job, while Lachlan is discovering wider social circles and interests.

In boarding school in Colorado during his high school years, Lachlan led a quiet, "natural" life, and loved to be in the mountains climbing and hiking. As for James, "you couldn't have dragged him out of New York," said a friend.

In high school, Lachlan was very "straight" and didn't go out much, say his long-time friends. James had a much wider circle of friends from "all walks of life," and would always be out—uptown, downtown, exploring every nook and cranny of New York.

Both brothers were also tight with their sisters, and James was particularly close with Elisabeth, who also loved art and music. When she left News Corp. in the spring of 2000, she called James to confide in him before announcing her decision. "She had thought about it a lot, and she wanted to have this other baby and focus on that for a while," said James. "She called me about it, it was actually late at night. I was in Singapore. And I thought it sounded like the right thing for her to do. She was eager to do something on her own in the sort of creative community there . . . and also get some more flexibility what with a third baby on the way. I think it was probably the right thing to do."

(James objects to the tales the press weaves around his family's activities. "Everybody said, Ohhh look, it's this succession stuff and all that jazz, but it's just like anybody dealing with a lifestyle choice and a change in their life like having a child. And everyone makes those kinds of choices all the time.")

Lachlan only later became an art and music enthusiast, say friends of both. Lachlan now goes out much more than he used to in New York. And—like James—hangs out with people not necessarily in his immediate world. James, however, with marriage and increasing work demands, has "gotten that out of his system," says a longtime friend. He's tightened his circle of friends, and "doesn't have the need for the partying anymore, he's done it before."

Lachlan's restraint in the area of drinking was catalyzed by a bad experience while overindulging. After a bad experience in high school getting "smashed" with one of his friends, Lachlan vowed he'd never drink again. And for about ten years he didn't—until he moved to Australia for his News Corp. job. According to his friends, his decisiveness was a dominant personality trait; he was not known to waffle on important issues, business or personal. "That's the kind of person he is," said a longtime friend who speaks with both James and Lachlan on a regular basis. "He is intense and disciplined," the friend continued, noting that Lachlan is a professional-level rock climber, and spent years when he lived in Colorado devoting himself to that demanding physical endeavor, shunning socializing and partying.

During high school, James's wild side was kept in check by a Portuguese couple known as George and Isabella, who had cared for the Murdoch clan since the children were small. At the time, his parents were often on worldwide travels, and he would stay alone in his parents' large Manhattan house, brother Lachlan having gone off to boarding school, and sister Elisabeth attending college. George and Isabella still look after Rupert's home in Los Angeles.

Father and sons these days have turned the world into their playground; skimobiles and minibikes have given way to red-eye flights and due-diligence meetings all over the planet.

Rupert enjoyed his younger son's persona, which was much different from that of the more pragmatic Lachlan, who had graduated Princeton in philosophy. James, the Harvard dropout, was considered by his friends to be a "warrior poet"—creative, powerful, incredibly erudite and well read, and with an agile mind that could carry him from Roman history to business mergers in one breath.

Rupert himself did not participate very often in that imaginative world. He preferred the real world. His mother would always say that her son "didn't like pretendy games."

Yet Rupert respected James's artistic nature, and fiercely defended both sons from any detractors. If someone described

James as being intellectually superior and more entrepreneurial than Lachlan, Murdoch would disagree, pointing out that Lachlan merely had a "quiet side." If James was called too rebellious, a renegade who spoke in profanities during public speeches, his father would say that was "a pose more than anything."

Guests of the Murdochs' would marvel at how "normal" the family was, given their fame and fortune. Both Rupert and Anna were enormously proud of their children and were open and affectionate about it. One News Corp. executive would get all choked up recalling what he observed in the Murdoch home. "It was always 'I love you' all the time, with Rupert. I tell my own father I love him, but it's rare for men to express themselves that way, and I used to see it in business meetings on occasion. This may sound corny, but it was touching."

They also knew how to horse around together.

Rupert Murdoch spent much time talking to his sons about Sky Global over the months, during James's bachelor party, back at his midtown Manhattan office, and any- and everywhere he happened to see them.

Father and sons together blew off steam during James's bachelor party just before his wedding. Two weeks before the big event, the brothers Murdoch, together with their father and their closest family members and friends, had reveled in an all-male rite of passage.

At a shooting range in Las Vegas, Rupert Murdoch had held a machine gun in his hands. Lachlan stood beside him and James manned a large 44-magnum revolver. The occasion was James's weekend-long bachelor party at the Bellaggio Hotel, formerly owned by Rupert's friend Steve Wynn.

A group of about ten, including James's brother-in-law Alasdair MacLeod; Robert Carlock, a *Saturday Night Live* writer who was an old friend of James's since his Harvard days; and

Jesse Angelo, a young deputy editor at the New York *Post* who was a boyhood friend of James's, horsed around at an indoor gun club, shooting at paper targets just for laughs.

"It was fun. It was irresponsible, you know what I mean," James said. "We played cards, hung around. It was nice. We had big dinners and drank too much. We went to a firing range, which was entirely adolescent. We were all a little uncomfortable. Then we left."

The entourage, with Rupert as their leader, was intent on having as much "fun" as possible—playing cards, hanging out, eating steak dinners, and "drinking too much," according to James.

During the gun club escapade, the Murdoch men got a bit spooked and left when it suddenly dawned on them that they were standing in an open room with total strangers, wielding lethal weapons.

While Lachlan and James aren't hunters, Las Vegas was not their first experience with firearms. At their father's ranch in Carmel, California, they kept a couple of rifles and had a ritual of sitting at the end of the hill and shooting skeets while getting drunk.

"We put some targets up and shoot, you know, clay pigeons with shotguns. James will have a Scotch and I'll have a Vodka and tonic, and we'll get drunk shooting skeets," Lachlan laughs boisterously, his normal sophistication melting into boyishness. "Probably not the smartest thing to do," he adds, like the self-correcting executive that he has become.

The brothers actually bought the skeet trap for their Dad years ago. "And he rarely uses it, so when we go there we use it," James acknowledged, noting that he and Lachlan are "not into guns."

"It's just kind of a fun thing to do in the afternoon. And everyone gets annoyed," James said. "It's noisy."

Like his sons, Rupert Murdoch was fiercely loyal to those closest to him, and to those who returned his trust and loyalty. At the Las Vegas bachelor party, and elsewhere, Alasdair MacLeod was like a second son. Murdoch's loyalty and concern for his now-deceased first wife, Patricia, also was impressive.

In the case of MacLeod, Rupert's daughter Prudence had met him in Australia in the late 1980s. Rupert instantly adored the man, who was tall and refined—a newspaper-loving Scotsman. MacLeod at the time was in banking, but not enjoying it. Murdoch eventually offered him a job, and he soon rose to general manager of the *Times of London*.

Prudence, like her half brothers, believed her father to be a good and even sensitive man. But, she told *The Sun* in 1999, "I do see the other side sometimes, and I walk away because I don't have to deal with it. I'm sure he can be ruthless, I am sure he can be unpleasant, but Dad is not evil."

Indeed, Rupert Murdoch's generosity at times was unequaled. Years earlier, Prudence's mother, Patricia, fell on hard times healthwise and financially, and suffered after a bad investment in a disastrous orange juice venture in Spain. She'd had a gorgeous house on Tynte Street in North Adelaide, where she'd originally lived with Rupert. It was gone, along with art, paintings, personal treasures, and jewelry that she had received from Dame Elisabeth, Rupert's mother, for her wedding. All Patricia had left was a string of pearls Rupert had given her.

Prudence said in 1999, "There are people who ripped her off until very very recently—she was very ill for a long time—it is just appalling."

Without laying blame, after the Spain venture collapsed, Rupert and Prudence brought Patricia to Adelaide to receive medical care. Rupert's marriage to her had been over for more than a decade. Well aware that her house and possessions had been squandered, he nevertheless set her up again, and bought her a flat in North Adelaide where she lived until her death. Murdoch visited her whenever he was in Adelaide.

James was infamous for engaging in heated political arguments with his libertarian father. These days, however, he evaluates his politics as being "pretty close" to his father's. Rupert's political beliefs, he believes, were vastly misunderstood. Father and son both defended China's human rights record, no matter how grisly the facts.

James, more than Lachlan, is a futurist. Brainstorming about the future of the Internet is one of his favorite pastimes. He is fascinated by the claim that, while half the current Internet users are American, that figure was expected to drop to one-third by 2004.

Investment banker Goldman Sachs was forecasting that there would be 96.6 million Internet users in China by 2002. Internet growth in China was outstripping forecasts by 25 percent.

When doing business on a global scale, the issue of language was fascinating to James. Worldwide, Mandarin was the most commonly spoken language, with 835 million people speaking it; this was followed by English, with 470 million speakers, Spanish at 330 million, and Hindi with 300 million.

While his father had been criticized by some as being a destroyer of culture, James believed that, more than any other media company, News Corp. was studying local markets and developing programming in native languages, and using local talent to do so.

On the other hand, in the United States and Britain, cultural imperialism was marching onward, he believed. Media in those countries, he thought, were unaware of "surging non-English markets, or worse, quite aware of them but still believing that the lingua franca of the modern age is and will continue to be English."

English would not be the default language of the default world, he concluded, though it had been the predominant language of the Internet to date.

These days, both sons look up to mentor Peter Chernin. While Rupert had numerous times stated that Lachlan would most likely one day serve in his shoes, that would not be for some time.

"If I went under a bus today, I'm sure Peter would be appointed chief," he said. He figured that in five to eight years, perhaps one of his sons would be up to doing the job, as co–chief executive officer with Chernin.

No one close to him had their minds much on Murdoch's demise—he was going strong. He'd spent the summer of 2000 undergoing cancer treatments in Los Angeles, but kept working at the same pace as always, courting Sky Global investors, attending James's wedding, and goofing around with the young lads during the bachelor party. By the fall, talks with GM regarding Hughes had intensified, and the Big Six were monitoring the market like bees hovering over a pot of honey.

Glip, glip, glip. The second-by-second pulse of News Corp. shares flickered across the computer screens of fourth-floor executive offices at Rupert Murdoch's midtown office tower.

In October 2000, the Big Six were still eyeing a possible IPO with Sky Global. Chernin and Murdoch were hoping it could happen by year-end. Both were also closely monitoring the performance of U.S. satellite TV leaders Echostar and

DirecTV, whose value could also impact the perceived value of Sky Global.

News Corp.'s bid for DirecTV was in the works. A slump in the market could result in it being called off or rescheduled. A tumble in value for the corporation could completely change the dynamics of the upcoming deal.

On October 5, 2000, an overcast fall day in Manhattan, Rupert Murdoch issued a worldwide news release announcing the promotion of Lachlan as chief operating officer, the most senior position next to that of Chernin.

At around 3 P.M., the phone calls were flying between Murdoch and his top advisors. He was alarmed. News Corp.'s shares had taken a dive in the past hour, and the adrenaline rush seemed almost palpable. A handful of executives were suddenly on their feet. Phones were ringing.

A corporate officer put in a call to his closest ally on Wall Street. "What's going on with our stock?" he asked. "There's a rumor that someone downgraded News . . . it's been in the last hour, a free fall, it's totally down, like $4. Fox is up."

Some information is being offered. The executive is attentive, then, "Is Dave alright with this? He's not freaking out?" he asks, referring to Devoe, Murdoch's chief financial officer.

Hang up. The phone rings again. It's Rupert, his boss. Murdoch's voice can be heard across the room, coming through the handset clenched in the executive's right fist. The man attempts an explanation, ". . . It's a function of Belotti taking the numbers down yesterday," he says, speaking of Wall Street's influential analyst Rich Belotti. He goes on, ". . . Jessica helped us yesterday . . . Fox came back at the end of the day. . . ." Jessica Reif Cohen, a top analyst at Merrill Lynch, had been a News Corp. watcher for years. The words between Murdoch and his advisor, who is actually speaking just a few feet away from Murdoch in another fourth-floor office, are still flying. ". . . It looks like a big seller . . . an East German sold a million shares . . . ," the executive says. Murdoch shoots back something. His man is still excited, ". . . I've never seen it go down like this."

The News Corp. chief's syllables are coming across haltingly, unintelligible to a listener across the room. "Lachlan's news just crossed," the executive offers, looking up nervously at the guest waiting in his office. Coincidentally, the stock dive seemed timed to the announcement.

The phone is hung up, and another number is dialed. "Jessica?" the executive is attentive, and does not even have to ask the question. The Merrill Lynch analyst is offering her ideas. The News Corp. executive is appreciative. "Let us know how we can help you do that," he says. "Rupert is home in California next week."

Indeed, one of Murdoch's most relaxing places to be was his ranch in Carmel, California. Despite his cancer treatments, the News Corp. chief hadn't missed a single day of work, and made sure everyone knew it. The current glitch in the stock price was just one dip in a white-water rafting adventure that seemingly had no end.

Cohen said goodbye to Murdoch's advisor, who was instantly on another call. "Is Rupert there?" The executive was on his feet, standing over the computer monitor sitting on the counter behind his desk. Momentarily, the voice of Rupert Murdoch is again heard across the room through the telephone handset. Murdoch is speaking loudly, in apparent agitation over the real-time stock readings now pulsing over the monitor on a wall in his office.

"The thing to take into account . . . ," the information stream is delivered in rapid fire, as the executive calms his boss. "DirecTV and DISH [Echostar] are also getting trashed . . . ," he says, "there may be some residual . . ."

Murdoch is lobbing his own syllables between the phrases, which do not stop. "Cable is going up as a result . . ."

Murdoch is saying something, and the man pauses.

"Is that right?" he said. "They're not in touch with their customers enough?" Murdoch was on a tirade about Echostar's management problems. He was certain he could do much better with the company.

Just as Lachlan Murdoch had been promoted to COO, News Corp.'s share price started on a tumble that would continue through the winter months. But the market downtrend was not just Murdoch's problem; the entire media industry was going through the same thing.

By December, the Sky Global strategy had been revamped. An IPO was not the only way to get the resources Murdoch needed to accomplish his vision. Talks with Jack Smith at General Motors were suddenly red-hot; it didn't hurt that GM was also suffering from the low stock market.

While Murdoch was courting GM, and Lachlan was broadening his scope as deputy COO, James was touring India, eyeing another $500 million investment through Star in new broadcast businesses, and Peter Chernin was looking out for News Corp.'s digital rights in the future.

Chernin was Murdoch's best lobbyist in Washington. In the winter of 2001, he was in the capitol making sure that politics would not get in the way of interactive media in the near future.

He was encouraging book publishers to join Hollywood in

lobbying Congress to provide greater ways of protecting all types of content flowing over the Internet—and to continue to clarify the law. Without guarantees that movies and other content would be protected from Internet pirates, Hollywood movie studios could not afford to open their libraries. Companies like News Corp. feared a Napster-like scenario occurring in the future with movies, for example, being pirated over the Internet.

Copyright law and the Web were still murky areas, even though in 1998 Congress passed the Digital Millennium Copyright Act, which made it illegal to circumvent electronic safeguards on copyrighted works. But, by 2001, the law was being disputed in the courts.

At a meeting before the Association of American Publishers, Chernin said, "The single most important issue, I believe, for all entertainment companies and certainly for every publishing house, is that of copyright protection, a fundamental right that has become endangered in the digital age."

The same day, he met with legislators on Capitol Hill to discuss copyright protection. It was one of his new regular visits to Washington, along with lobbyist Jack Valenti, head of the Motion Picture Association.

"It is time to consider copyright infringement a profound and immediate threat to publishers as well as record producers, to editors and their authors as well as movie executives, and to the right of everyone here to make books for a living," Chernin said. "Together we must put pressure on the new president and Congress to update previous copyright laws in the face of new broadband technologies."

Back in 1989, Murdoch had anticipated that the theft of News Corp. content in the digital age would be rampant, if he did not find a way to encrypt his treasure trove.

4

THE CODE

Murdoch's satellite broadcasting business had been enabled by the foresight he had had back in the late 1980s, and the hard lessons he learned when he searched the world to find technology that would protect content beamed to audiences all over the world. He found it in Israel, but inadvertently found himself in the middle of a thriller when he discovered one of his business partners had orchestrated an international fraud scheme that would take years to solve.

ecurity. And glue, to keep the world together. That was what Rupert Murdoch needed.

His success in the pay-television arena was largely because of his early recognition of these things in the late 1980s. It was then that he found the missing ingredient he needed—near Jerusalem.

A lot had changed since the days of Greek historian Herodotus, who recorded that, to protect valuable information, a messenger's head was sometimes shaved to create a slate for a written text. The messenger would not travel to the recipient with the precious scrawl until his hair had grown back. He would then journey to his destination, where his head would be shaved and the message revealed. Or wooden writing tablets were covered with wax to hide messages under a seemingly blank surface.

Finding ways to deliver precious words to a select and rapt audience through ciphers and cryptography has sometimes been driven by intense human passions. Even in Victorian England lovers would post forbidden romantic messages encrypted in the personal advertisements of newspapers, which became known as "agony columns."

As early as 1987, Murdoch had a flash of insight into the future importance of cryptography to all kinds of electronic commerce. His holdings in a bank, a securities company, and in Reuters, the news wire service, gave him insight into the role of information delivered electronically. He saw that the ability to encrypt information would leave the specialized realm of government and business, and would eventually enable secure transactions via such phenomena as e-mail, satellite uplinks, cell phones, online shopping, and delivery of content directly to consumers via computer, television, and a range of new electronic devices.

Murdoch embarked on a worldwide search for an appropriate venture to satisfy this need, and an expert to head up such an endeavor. Murdoch's technology director at the time, Peter Smith, was dispatched on a trip around the world to find the best encryption expert on the planet. Cryptography, then and now, was not a crowded arena; worldwide, there were only a handful of renowned cryptographers in existence.

His quest was made even more urgent by the fact that, in 1988, when Murdoch was setting up British Sky Broadcasting, his satellite pay-TV operation in the U.K., Hollywood movie studios told him if he couldn't protect access to pay-TV programming, he couldn't show their movies.

Smith found what he was looking for in Israel that year.

Adi Shamir wandered around the Weizmann Institute of

Science in Rehovot, Israel, in blue jeans and sandals. That was typical attire for the mathematician who revolutionized cryptography. In 1978, when at the Massachusetts Institute of Technology, he developed a groundbreaking "public key" algorithm known as RSA with his fellow professors Ronald Rivest and Leonard Adelman. Shamir was the "S" in RSA. (In 1982, they went on to found RSA Data Security Inc., and the three eventually became millionaires.)

Shamir, some would say, was also the "S" in secretive. Perhaps not surprisingly, as one of the world's few genius cryptographers, Shamir was not very accessible—it was virtually impossible to get him to talk.

On a fall morning in 1987, Shamir received a phone call at his Weizmann office. "Rupert Murdoch would like to talk to you," said the voice on the phone.

Murdoch consultant Bruce Hundertmark, a News International director and Australian engineer, had known another Israeli technologist Uzi Sharon, a larger-than-life character who served in the Israeli military as a teenager. Sharon was legendary, having reportedly helped to sink the *King Faroud,* an Egyptian cruiser, by ramming it with an explosives-filled speedboat. Sharon was also a world-renowned laser technologist at Weizmann, and had turned Hundertmark on to encryption guru Shamir. Sharon had also introduced Hundertmark to a British/Israeli businessman, Michael Clinger, whose trustee company International Developments Group NV later became a partner with him in a surprising Murdoch company that was about to be formed.

A few weeks later, two of Murdoch's "scouts" showed up in Rehovot, and spent a few days with Shamir. They returned to Murdoch with a glowing report.

"This is fantastic. Shamir is your man, he's great," Murdoch was told, followed by an awkward silence.

"Well, what are we waiting for?" Murdoch asked.

"There's only one problem," the big boss was told. "He belongs to the Weizmann Institute of Science."

Pause, as Murdoch glanced at one man and then the other. "What's the big deal?" he demanded. "Let's just buy the Institute."

Of course, the Weizmann Institute was not exactly for sale.

It did have a commercial arm, known as Yeda, formed to set up ventures for capitalizing on inventions of its scientists. And Shamir and a number of other scientists had been given a mandate: take all your research and your theoretical mathematics, and bring it all into the real world as quickly as possible. In February 1988, News Datacom Research Ltd was set up in Israel. It was founded as a joint venture between News Corp. and Weizmann's Yeda; its parent was a Hong Kong company, News Data Security Products Ltd. NDSP was owned 60 percent by News Corp., 10 percent by Weizmann, 10 percent by Shamir, and 20 percent by Michael Clinger's trustee company, International Developments Group.

Banking was at first the key area for cryptography, for transaction-secure exchange of funds and so on. "But then television quickly overshadowed everything," said Dov Rubin, a company founder. Pay-TV would open up a massive area for "revenue protection" for cable and satellite television broadcasters around the world.

After three years, in July 1992, Murdoch exercised his buyout option, and bought 100 percent of NDSP. By 1999, Murdoch floated the company and renamed it NDS, retaining an 80 percent stake in the company. (Shamir today serves as an NDS consultant.)

From the beginning, NDS had a unique approach to television encryption. Instead of putting Shamir's algorithm in the set-top box, it was held on a microchip in a smart card, a plastic card that gives subscribers access to programming when inserted into the box. If the encryption was broken by hackers, NDS had only to issue a new smart card.

In May 1995, Murdoch recognized he needed a world-class executive to head up NDS if it was to realize its full potential.

Abe Peled, a Romanian by birth, had become an Israeli citizen when he immigrated with his parents at age 13. At a young age, he'd grown accustomed to being adaptable to vastly different cultures. He had worked for IBM some 20 years when Murdoch came after him.

Peled was startled when he got the call saying Rupert Murdoch wanted him to come to London to speak with him. He'd discussed the opportunity with his wife, was convinced that it would require him leaving his home in Israel, and decided beforehand that he didn't want the job. He also agreed to go meet with Murdoch; he'd heard so much about the man and was dying of curiosity.

Peled flew to London to meet with Murdoch. Standing before the media mogul, Peled confronted him, "Why would you bother interviewing somebody to run a company that's only around $45 million in sales—and a company that's not in your immediate business?"

Murdoch looked Peled up and down, and smiled. "You know, it is a little company, but with the right man and the right vision and the right leadership it can become a very valuable and important asset," Murdoch said, and then paused. "Furthermore, it's strategic to our future."

Peled pondered that a moment, and then asked, "Why in 1989 did you even decide to start this company, in Israel of all places?"

Murdoch replied, "I thought everything would become

digital. Without some sort of encryption technology, it will be easy to steal all our newspapers and television programs."

Peled was still concerned. "This company cannot be a captive technology supplier for News Corp. If you have a vision for it to become a real company, it has to be able to supply anybody in the world with the best technology—not just News Corp. Otherwise it becomes fat and lazy."

Murdoch responded without a blink. "That's fine," he said. "You can sell NDS technology to anyone you wish, even our competitors."

Peled returned home, informing his wife that he wanted to take the job, at great personal inconvenience.

By the fall of 2000, some 18 million pay-television viewers were being served by NDS technology. NDS was protecting about $4 billion in revenues annually for its broadcasting clients, including Murdoch's own companies.

But this success came only after a wild and preposterous turn of events.

Unbeknownst to Baroness Niva Von Weisl, she was at the center of a love triangle that unleashed a surreptitious campaign of fraud, extortion, death threats, phone tapping and eventually an international hunt by the FBI.

Niva Von Weisl had been a *Vogue* model, a former beauty queen, and a ballet dancer who held a math degree from Cornell University. She was also a genuine Austrian baroness.

Her husband was Michael Clinger, who, unbeknownst to News Corp., had fled the United States after the SEC accused him of fraud in 1997. In November 1990, he was indicted by a New York grand jury, and has been an international fugitive since.

Clinger and his accountant Leo Krieger had been running News Datacom in Israel since 1990, when partner Hundertmark left in bad health to live in his native Australia. For a time, he lived at Dame Elisabeth Murdoch's house in Melbourne, seeing that Murdoch had known him for years and had a trusted relationship with him.

In 1994, Clinger left Niva Von Weisl, who was pregnant with their third child, for another model by the name of Daphna Kapeliuk. Daphna was an attorney, a highly respectable woman, and the daughter of a very influential journalist in Israel.

Two weeks later, Clinger's long-time accountant and confidant, Leo Krieger, who was a very orthodox man with a wife and six children, moved in with the irresistible Baroness. This was too fast for Clinger, and a war began between the two men.

Clinger went to Israeli tax authorities and accused Krieger of not declaring taxes. (Kreiger was later vindicated.)

In retaliation, Krieger went to News Corp. and offered to give the company some very alarming information about Clinger.

Having formally started his job on July 1, 1995, after a few months Abe Peled was invited to one of Murdoch's executive retreats. He headed for a "boondoggle," as he likes to describe such trips, in Australia.

Upon his return, News Corp. chief counsel Arthur Siskind called him into his office. He began talking of general business pleasantries, and then said, "By the way, Abe, I want to fill you in on something: We suspect that a former partner has set up some kind of deal and is in cahoots with a senior executive of NDS in Israel. He's forcing the company to buy smart cards from a single source. He, in turn, gets a cutback, overcharges the company, and pockets millions."

Peled almost fell over. A criminal investigation was under way, he was told. "You'll be briefed further," Siskind said.

Michael Clinger, unbeknownst to News executives, had Indian-born smart card supplier Bharat Kumar Marya providing the cards to NDS at an inflated price, and was pocketing a big percentage of the profit. What's more, he was in cahoots with an NDS executive, whom he'd convinced to agree with the scheme. Marya's 60 percent silent partner was Clinger himself.

One thing that had amazed Peled, in his few months on the job, was that the company had only one supplier. He pointed out the company needed to diversify its suppliers, and pay less. "But the [executive] manipulated things such that no supplier could be qualified," Peled said.

To put it mildly, knowing that an employee close to you is a crook was an unusual experience for him. At the same time, NDS was under pressure to keep the card supply coming. "We were at a critical phase of supplying new cards to Sky and we could not face a disruption in the supply," said Peled.

By 1995, News Datacomm supplied 19.1 million smart cards to BSkyB and Hughes' DirecTV.

It was a touchy situation. A secret investigation was under way and, at the same time, News Corp. senior executives could not afford to do anything that would disrupt its business.

Siskind became a bulldog, hiring British private investigative firm Argen to begin an international fraud investigation. The investigation continued for six months, and Peled began asking questions, pretending not to know any better, seeing that he was new on the job. "I don't understand what's going on. Why do we have only one supplier? Let's qualify others," he said to the executive at NDS's Israel headquarters. Unlike the previous CEO, Peled had a technical background, indeed had been a research scientist at IBM, and couldn't be sold a bill of goods. Additional suppliers were put in place, and by the time a new system was set up, the investigators had all they needed to clearly prove that the NDS executive was a crook.

Meanwhile, Arthur Siskind was going after the big brains behind the scheme: Michael Clinger.

Throughout the investigation, Peled had to maintain a working relationship with his executive, without letting on that he suspected anything.

"There was all sorts of speculation going through my mind," Peled said. "What does a man say when you tell him this? It was hard to believe he was really a crook. He was such a nice man, everyone in Israel liked him, he was their defender and protector from the previous CEO—very much loved by the people," said Peled. "I thought somehow he would come up with an explanation, I must say. Because I never dealt with a real crook. It's not something you get to deal with usually."

Finally, after six months, with a lawyer at his side, Peled looked his executive in the eye, told him he was fired, and that the smart card scheme had been found out. He informed him that a suit had simultaneously been filed against him and Clinger and his other partners. He half expected the man would offer some kind of reasonable explanation, that Clinger perhaps was blackmailing him. Instead, the man demanded the three-months' separation payment stipulated in his employment contract.

"That was the most unexpected thing," Peled said, disappointed that he had completely misread the man's character. The executive has since been convicted.

Filed in February 1996, the News International and NDS suit went after Clinger and his partners in British High Court for $38.3 million, accusing them of a conspiracy to overcharge the company for smart cards. Clinger countersued News for allegedly defrauding him by undervaluing the company when it bought out his stake in 1992. Clinger had multiple residences in England, Israel, and Switzerland at the time.

Those close to him say that Clinger had a particular way of

operating to get others to do his bidding. "His modus operandi was to find a weak spot and blackmail people. He'd corrupt them a little bit and then blackmail them. He would try to get you a little bit dirty and then say if you don't cooperate, I'll reveal that, and gradually pull you in," Peled said.

Once News Corp. filed suit, Clinger's representatives came a few months later with a hardball attempt to blackmail News Corp. They showed up in Arthur Siskind's New York office threatening that if Siskind did not get off Clinger's case and pay them a large sum of money, Murdoch and company would have "tax problems."

Siskind threw them out of his office.

T he big payback came months later, on October 20, 1996.

As Rupert Murdoch was having a laid-back Sunday afternoon in Australia, he received an outrageous phone call.

Israeli police had just raided the Jerusalem offices of NDS.

Back in New York, CFO David Devoe was receiving the same news.

In Jerusalem, Israeli security offices cordoned off the building and television camera crews were swarming all over the place. Michael Clinger had fed a tale to Israeli tax authorities that Murdoch's company had been under-reporting some $150 million in revenue.

While the Jerusalem offices were being raided, Abe Peled's apartment in Haifa was also being raided. "At 7 A.M., they woke us up," Peled said.

The news was leaked to the press and labeled as the biggest tax fraud in the history of Israel. Clinger was a state witness. "My wife was quite alarmed," Peled said.

By afternoon, News Corp. issued statements that the

charges were "groundless" and a result of an extortion campaign by Clinger.

It took a while for News Corp. and NDS executives and lawyers to convince the Israeli government and tax authority that it was all a sham.

Peled was next the focus of Clinger's blackmail attempts. "They went to our lawyers and said unless we settled, since I'm so important to Murdoch, they'll cause me major damage and accuse me of wiretapping—a big offense in Israel," he said.

NDS lawyers immediately went to the police with a transcript of the conversation. Amazingly enough, two days later a cassette with recorded phone conversations between Clinger and his lawyers in London was found, allegedly taken from a safe in Peled's office in Jerusalem.

Clinger had provided this to Israeli officials, apparently trying to make it look like Peled himself had wiretapped the conversations.

Peled was hauled in for questioning. He rarely used his Jerusalem office, and the last executive to use it was the man he had just fired, who was in cahoots with Clinger. The man, and perhaps a secretary, was the only one to know the combination, according to Peled.

The punishment for wiretapping in Israel was ten years in jail. A special unit devoted to investigating wiretapping, known as Major Crimes, called Peled in for an interview.

Peled was grilled for 16 hours, and had the absurd sense he'd somehow landed in the midst of a James Bond movie.

According to Peled, Clinger also tried to frame Niva Von Weisl, his former wife, by planting the same wiretap cassettes in her house. At first glance, the police thought Peled was in cahoots with the baroness.

During his grilling, a sergeant confronted Peled. "You know Niva Von Weisl?"

Peled responded, "No, I don't know her. I know her name, and I know about her, I've never met her."

The sergeant continued, "Well, you know she's a very beautiful woman."

To which Peled answered, "Yes, I've heard she's a former beauty queen."

"Weren't you curious to meet her?" the sergeant asked.

"No, not really," said Peled.

"What's the matter, you're not interested in women?" the sergeant shot back.

The attempts to get him to confess to their notion that he'd been dating the woman seemed comical to Peled, seeing that he was innocent.

He said other "tricks" were used to try and get a confession out of him. "They have this poor secretary who used to help me out. They kept her in the room next to me and were screaming at her. Then they said to me, do you want the secretary to take the blame? Are you going to let this poor woman be the fall woman? Don't you have pity for her?" Peled said.

Peled responded to his interrogators, "Listen, you should treat her nicely, I don't think she had anything to do with it."

One of Clinger's tales was that NDS was manufacturing smart cards in some secret apartment in Israel, according to Peled. Eventually, the whole concocted story fell apart. "He was very good, a misplaced genius, a con man," Peled said.

Throughout, Rupert Murdoch never questioned Peled's innocence.

"Rupert is very savvy. The guy kept saying he's going to screw Rupert. To Rupert, Clinger was like a fly," Peled said.

But "the fly" succeeded in getting the press to print stories that Israel had issued an arrest warrant for Rupert Murdoch.

Eventually, "because we had evidence it became clear what was going on," Peled said. The police questioned Clinger's accomplices and accused them of blackmail, and the whole scheme started unraveling.

All of this chaos was throwing a monkey wrench in NDS's plans to go public. "The tax authorities in Israel can keep you in check forever, they don't have to push charges nor do they have to say you are cleared. Because we wanted to go public, we needed a clear bill of health, so we eventually settled with them in the interest of getting it off the table," Peled said.

In late 1988, in News International v. Michael Clinger et al., a British judge ruled against Clinger, and ordered him to pay about $50 million—$34.5 million in damages and the rest in interest from smart card suppliers who overcharged for cards needed to view BSkyB's satellite channels. The court found that Clinger, among other things, had defrauded News by selling cards from various offshore companies he'd set up. Meanwhile, prosecutors in Israel proceeded with a blackmail case, and the tax authorities finally understood who he was and that he'd spun a humongous web of lies that they had fallen for. Clinger was forced to flee Israel.

There was also a case against Clinger in Switzerland—and he was still wanted as a fugitive in the United States.

His Indian partner in the smart card business, Bharat Kumar Marya, eventually settled with NDS, provided information, turned witness against Clinger, and paid damages.

By 1998, Clinger was a wanted man in Israel, England, Switzerland, and the United States. "That's when he disappeared," said Peled.

"Every once in a while people say why don't we join forces and look for him," Peled said. "A lot of people were cheated."

Investigators believe Clinger may be hiding in Cuba.

But Siskind went after Clinger's assets with a vengeance. The man had an art collection he bought with some of the money he stole from News Corp., that turned out to be "very bad art," said Peled. "He paid like $500 million and it was worth $600,000."

"Clinger corrupted a lot of people, including some early management in Australia," said Peled.

News Corp. eventually got its hands on $25 million worth of Clinger's assets.

"It was a complex management challenge—dealing with this while building the company," the understated Peled mused.

Murdoch, in retrospect, laughs at the whole affair. "He was a crook. We don't know where he is, but we have suspicions of where some of his money is. We don't know for sure," he laughed, musing over the characters who have tried to "get" him over the years. Every now and then Murdoch picks up the phone to call Arthur Siskind, who is just down the hall from him, to ask if anyone has found Clinger yet.

"It has become a personal mission of Arthur's," Rupert laughed. "He has to get that money. But we got half of it."

Peled years later was still flabbergasted by Murdoch's vision more than anything else, committing to a business in a remote part of the world that was out of his control, in recognition that there was no better technology to be had. "Here is a man who in 1989 was thinking he should be in this area because it's going to be important," he said.

5

THE PATENT LORD

The media industry was changing dramatically, largely through the impact of technology. A Chinese mathematician took everyone by surprise with his algorithms that promised to change the way audiences viewed television forever. James Murdoch had urged his father to go after this tiny company, Gemstar, before anyone really realized what Henry Yuen was up to, but Murdoch ignored his son. By the time he realized Gemstar represented the future, Murdoch was pushed to make a hostile play for the company—which was rebuffed. In the end, however, with his usual persistence, he got a large piece of the company and a partnership that was strategic to his Sky Global plans.

While NDS was growing and becoming more successful, its technology enabling a new industry, a Shanghai-born mathematician was pushing the envelope in a different area of broadcast technology, catalyzed by his own frustration in trying to record a Red Sox game on his VCR.

By the year 2000, Henry Yuen and his company, Gemstar, had outsmarted Rupert Murdoch and John Malone, and had the entire cable industry so angry that companies were banding together to fight him. Even giants Microsoft and AOL had to bow and pay license fees to the visionary Yuen.

The walls of Gemstar's Pasadena offices were covered with framed patents. To some, Yuen was a "patent terrorist." He had managed to lock up some 90 patents on the way information is displayed and manipulated on a television screen—the ingredients for most interactive television and "t-commerce" transactions now and in the future.

"He was just out there quietly doing all these patents," said Murdoch. "From a little back room in Pasadena. He's brilliant." Murdoch predicted that Gemstar would be the "key player" in the future of digital information services, with "enormous advantages as the broadband revolution takes hold."

Henry Yuen was raised in Hong Kong and schooled in the United States, earning a Ph.D. in applied math from Cal Tech. He served as a research scientist for 18 years at TRW, specializing in mathematical patterns of ocean waves that resulted in technology for global weather forecasting and defense applications.

Insatiable for knowledge, Yuen studied law at night and earned a law degree, and began a part-time practice representing Asian companies in the United States.

At age 40, he launched his own company, Gemstar, with some grad school friends. He had dwelled in a buttoned-down academic and scientific environment for most of his life, and considered business "a free for all."

Yuen's first product, VCR Plus, was invented to cure his frustration in trying to program his VCR to record a baseball game. VCR Plus enabled TV viewers to record a show with their remote controls by entering a mathematical code printed in the TV listings.

His first challenge was to convince publishers to print the codes in their TV listings, electronics stores to carry the new remote-control devices, and viewers to buy them for about $60 apiece.

Newspapers not only printed the codes but also paid for

them. Yuen also asked *TV Guide* to print his codes. At the time, Murdoch agreed to buy 20 percent of Gemstar, but backed out due to a credit crunch—something he greatly regrets.

Gemstar sold millions of VCR Plus remotes. Yuen then licensed the technology to VCR makers, which built it right into their machines. Gemstar's profit margins rose to more than 40 percent. By 2001, the VCR Plus system was being used in about 80 million homes in 40 countries, and was built into 60 percent of all VCRs sold.

In 1995, when the company was worth about $250 million, Yuen took Gemstar public and went on a spending spree, buying early television guide companies VideoGuide and Starsight, which together had lost close to $100 million waiting for interactive TV to catch on.

The acquisition made Yuen a force to be reckoned with, going head-to-head with John Malone's United Video. Gemstar had the patents—the intellectual property—and Malone controlled cable relationships.

Meantime, Malone and Murdoch were competing to control the gateway to television viewing. Murdoch had *TV Guide*, the magazine, and Malone, with Liberty Media, had United Video, a cable channel with scrolled program information.

But Yuen was onto something no one could touch. Said Murdoch, "James was actually pushing for us to take over the company."

Indeed, even John Malone said he considered Gemstar to be "one of the most intelligently run intellectual-property companies in the world."

James Murdoch in 1997 had a keen interest in interactive television, according to his father. "We were talking, and he was developing a few Internet things for us and looking at stuff. It was his idea to go out there" and make a bid for Gemstar.

"But then we found out that Liberty was also bidding, and that pushed the price up. We were very close," Murdoch said.

To this day, says Rupert Murdoch, son James still regrets that his father did not take his advice and make an early bid for Gemstar. "He's still angry that we joined forces with Liberty instead of getting it then. Maybe we could have, it seems like a common sense thing to do."

Lachlan Murdoch too was impressed with his brother's early recognition of Gemstar's potential. "We were criticized for not being as aggressive on the Internet," said Lachlan. Yet, he said, James was one of the first people to focus on Gemstar as an important company.

Indeed, the Gemstar interface is seen as the ultimate interface for television sets in the digital broadcasting world.

"We started to realize with Sky Global Networks—with Gemstar—you really do have in this company a huge interactive platform that covers the world," Lachlan said.

But instead of making a play for the company on its own, News Corp. and Liberty in 1988—through United Video Satellite Group—decided to combine their assets and make a bid, to the tune of $2.8 billion, for tiny Gemstar.

But Yuen went ballistic, said Murdoch. "We were bidding together at that stage," he said, "and Yuen just went nuclear and had a board meeting in Tokyo at midnight or something, and issued [poison pill] shares and made it impossible. Now, [however,] we have 43 or 44 percent of Gemstar and an option to buy Henry's shares when he retires."

Yuen, unimpressed with the lavish sum the two moguls were offering—a 50 percent premium over the company's share price—resisted the takeover, despite shareholders' and bankers' urgings. He believed his company would soon be much more valuable.

Following the failed bid, Gemstar's share price went soaring, and the eccentric mathematician became a billionaire.

By October 1999, Yuen had turned the tables on Murdoch and Malone, persuading them to give him *TV Guide* in exchange for Gemstar stock valued at $9.2 billion at the time. (The talks regarding the sale of *TV Guide* to Yuen happened only because a judge urged them to resolve their differences after Yuen sued Murdoch for violating his patents.)

As part of their merger, Gemstar and TV Guide settled a six-year-old lawsuit over the patents for interactive guides; the court rulings were leaning in Gemstar's favor.

Rupert Murdoch had reason to unload *TV Guide* magazine: It had suffered from declining readership and profits for years. Its circulation plunged from 14 million to 11.8 million since the mid-1990s, and its operating income dropped from $203 million to $155 million.

The TV Guide cable channel, created with Malone, was being phased out. It made no sense, given the plans for Yuen's interactive guide.

Now, with Gemstar in control, Malone's Liberty Media and Murdoch's News Corp. each owned about 19 percent of the combined Gemstar-TV Guide International. CEO Yuen owned about 10 percent of the stock, and ran the show.

Adding more icing to the cake, and exciting Rupert Murdoch's competitive juices even further, in January 2000 Yuen bought the leading electronic book manufacturers, NuvoMedia and Softbook, along with their patents.

He hoped to drop the price of e-books and distribute 500,000 of them to consumers. Market analysts were predicting that 28 million people would spend $2.3 billion annually on e-books by 2005. It was no wonder that Gemstar was being valued at some $30 billion. Its prospects were viewed to be gargantuan, but it was being valued at 20 times its current revenues, and 75 times its cash flow. The future was everything. It remained to be seen if it would meet the same fate as so many overvalued Internet stocks that never managed to monetize their businesses. There was one big difference: Gemstar's business was not centered on e-commerce via the Internet, but on t-commerce transactions that took place via the television set, and interactive services of the future.

While the Justice Department reviewed the Gemstar-TV Guide merger, competitors were sending an avalanche of briefs to antitrust attorneys complaining that the combination would create disadvantages for others in the market. A Senate subcommittee warned that the pairing "may decrease competition" as TVs increasingly take on some of the functions of personal computers.

Of competitors' animosity toward Gemstar's patents, Murdoch said, "Well, people resent them. I did too before we owned them."

In July 2000, around the same time Rupert Murdoch was at Sun Valley giving his first Sky Global pitch to Bill Gates, federal regulators at the Department of Justice approved Gemstar's merger with TV Guide, paving the way for Henry Yuen to create the ultimate portal for interactive television. Despite bad blood that continued through Yuen's acquisition, by this time Rupert and sons spoke of Yuen as if he were a hero and a close friend.

With the merged Gemstar-TV Guide, Gemstar would contribute about 20 percent of the revenues and 35 percent of the operating income of the combined company, but its stockholders would own about 55 percent of the equity. Gemstar's part was viewed as the ingredient that would provide all of the company's growth.

Murdoch and Malone made sure the company structure protected their interests. CEO Yuen would run Gemstar from Pasadena, with copresident and CFO Elsie Leung. Joe Keiner, a former News Corp. executive, and Peter Boylan, a Liberty executive, would also serve as copresidents. Keiner would operate *TV Guide* magazine, the scrolling cable channel, and advertising sales from New York; Boylan would manage the cable-based interactive guide, a horse-racing channel, and other assets. Yuen could not fire Keiner without approval from News Corp., or Boylan without consent from Liberty.

By the fall, Murdoch upped his stake to 43 percent and announced that his friend John Malone would swap his 21 percent stake in the company for a stake in Sky Global.

But competitors were not happy with the powerhouse that had been created. While it was possible that someone smarter than John Malone, Rupert Murdoch, and Henry Yuen might come along, it remained to be seen if anyone could ever figure out how to get around Gemstar's patents.

Henry Yuen had turned the tables on Murdoch and his partner John Malone, but their continued alliance with him was now dovetailing in unexpected ways, providing the ingredients for a global platform that might in the digital television world rival Bill Gates's control over personal computers.

Seeing that TV is more pervasive than the Internet, the Gemstar interface, with the potential of appearing on most of the world's television sets, dwarfs the exposure of any current Internet portal. Yuen and Murdoch envision shepherding millions of viewers all over the world to television program destinations and Internet sites alike.

By the summer of 2000, Gemstar's guides appeared on about 3 million television sets; TV Guide's interactive guides were distributed over cable and satellite, reaching about 3.5 million homes. Yuen hoped his electronic guide would eventually become as pervasive as the remote control.

Protecting Yuen are 90 broad patents he holds covering the electronic program guides and how information can be presented on a television screen. Every TV manufacturer, cable operator, satellite TV provider, or Internet company that installs a guide in a TV or set-top box must obtain a license, and pay a fee, for Yuen's technology. Microsoft and America Online pay him tens of millions of dollars, as do RCA, Sony, Philips, and scores of others.

Microsoft, for example, paid Gemstar $45 million in license fees for the program guide used in WebTV. It also pays an estimated 30 percent of the revenues generated by the guide as a royalty to Gemstar.

Electronic guides not only list upcoming television shows but allow consumers to order movies, buy products, and record television programs. Already, Hughes' DirecTV is offering some of these features—it is also a Gemstar licensee.

Murdoch believed that the ability for television viewers to instantly make purchases while they're watching TV by simply clicking on the screen—something enabled by Gemstar technology—would be the most profitable use of television advertising so far, greater than anything that could be generated through sales via the Internet. It was in its early stages of testing in the United Kingdom with BSkyB; when unleashed across his worldwide satellite platforms, and in use in World Box set-top boxes, the potential would be astronomical.

Research analysts were predicting that, by 2005, as many as 80 million U.S. homes would be using electronic program guides, generating $23 billion in advertising revenue and $13 billion in commerce.

Peter Boylan, who became copresident and COO of the new company, recognized that Gemstar's patents were exceptional and—after years of litigation—would bring "patent peace" to the cable and satellite businesses.

The joint venture that is expected to generate billions in

revenues, however, is @TV, Gemstar's alliance with NBC and Thomson, the French electronics company that makes RCA TV sets, popular in the United States.

The plan, which has ambitions to be the ultimate in t-commerce, involves Thomson equipping at least 30 million new TVs with two-way paging technology, enabling viewers to shop at home using their remote control.

Litigation is ongoing, however, with Gemstar being challenged—for allegedly abusing its patents and monopolizing the set-top box market—by set-top box makers General Instrument, Scientific Atlanta, and Pioneer Electronics. Gemstar itself sued TiVo for allegedly infringing on its patents with its program guide, and has threatened Echostar with a similar suit. So far, however, Yuen has won all his patent-related court challenges.

While Rupert Murdoch had designs on dramatically increasing his stake in Gemstar over time (he had the right to buy all of Yuen's shares when Yuen retired), John Malone had reason to be an uncomfortable bedfellow, seeing that Time Warner cable went to extraordinary lengths to stymie it as a competitor, rendering Gemstar's guides useless in some cities by technologically blocking its TV listings from traveling through its cable wires. Federal regulators were reviewing that dispute, and in the meantime cable operators were scrambling to build television portals of their own, determined to stay out of the control of Henry Yuen.

Analysts now were recognizing that News Corp. had more potential for growth in strategic new areas of business than any of its media rivals. Tied together with a global satellite platform it was hoping to forge through the creation of Sky Global Networks, it was mining fortunes in 5 key arenas: the ultimate portal for the digital television world, with the Gemstar-TV Guide electronic program guide; satellite platforms around the world; cable networks; syndicated television programming; and the Fox film studio and television network delivering content worldwide.

Lachlan Murdoch said it was his brother James's pushing their father that eventually ended in News Corp.'s pact with Gemstar and strategic use of the Gemstar interface across all of its future television platforms. "James was one of the first people to focus on Gemstar as an important company for us," Lachlan said. "And that was when it wasn't the huge company it is today. James is the first person at the company to realize that if we can do a deal with Gemstar where you effectively have access to that electronic program guide, it will be important. As time has gone on it has become even more interactive, and for a company like ours, that's critical."

6

RUPERT, JAMES,
AND THE DRAGON

After a money-losing decade in China, Murdoch was making progress break-
ing into what promised to be the largest media market on the planet. In the
winter of 2001, after less than a year on the job, James Murdoch was hosted,
with his father, by President Jiang Zemin at a private dinner in Beijing. Not
so long ago, Murdoch had been viewed by Chinese officials as a "Western
devil." Son James was also proving adept at forging business relationships in
difficult parts of the world.

Dozens of executives in suits traverse the grid of the city, on foot and by bicycle, down the wide, straight avenues or through the narrow hutongs of old Bei-jing. Skirting endless traffic jams on this hazy morning, they breeze past children playing in the square, and scores of noo-dle shops interspersed with Internet cafes.

Above the clatter of overflowing rickshaws and mahjong players squatting in the streets, the air is full of the music of Putonghua, the spoken version of Mandarin, and China's "official language."

It is early 2001, and skyscrapers seem to be overtaking the city's skyline, piercing the rectangles arranged symmetrically around The Forbidden City. Beijing had originally been designed in a grid that reflected the harmony of the cosmos. Now, within the limits of the grid, a remarkable change is taking place that promises to disrupt its boundaries as well as its proverbial harmony.

A private dining room is filling up not far from the site of the imperial palace and Mao Tse Dong's tomb; in it, the order of one of the oldest monopolies is being challenged. Since the time of the Qin dynasty, more than 2,000 years ago, the rulers of China have controlled all communications—what could be published or written or spoken. Is the breaking of the system a necessity, and key to the future of China? That is the view of leaders from multinational corporations scrambling to gain a foothold here, and the Chinese officials they are courting seem to be in cautious agreement.

A sturdy older man in a European-style suit sits at the center of a long dining table, and peers out from dark-framed glasses. He nods and smiles, half skeptically, half kindly, at the lanky young American sitting before him in the middle of a Beijing government compound within the Imperial Garden.

It is January 5, 2001, and Jiang Zemin begins to speak, the staccato of his syllables coming like little explosions from his mouth. James Murdoch, who has just been introduced to the Chinese president, and his father Rupert hang on every word coming slightly delayed through a translator.

Murdoch senior, who in recent years has become a surprisingly welcome and regular guest here, is beaming proudly, having anointed his youngest son as his full-time envoy in this difficult part of the world.

The stolid Jiang is studying 28-year-old James in his impeccable blue suit, light-brown, slightly tousled hair, and small, fashionable eyeglasses, and notes, "He is so very young. . . ."

Silence and glances all around.

"Working for my father, I am aging rapidly," pipes up James, the young artist-turned-executive known for his wit during his days at *The Harvard Lampoon*. As the translation flies, James glances at his Chinese-born stepmother Wendi Deng, who sits at Jiang's left side, then at his father, who sits just to the right of the president. The dinner guests break into waves of laughter that spread across the table, which is covered with plates of Western-style pepper steak.

Despite his jocularity, James is in the hot seat, having been elevated by his father to the helm of Asian satellite broadcaster Star—one of the most strategic, though money-losing, operations across his father's $40 billion News Corp. empire.

A couple of weeks earlier, Rupert had sat in while Lachlan—who was ahead of his brother on the corporate ladder—led a top-level executive strategy summit in the outback of Australia. James and Lachlan continue to be closely tutored by their father.

Now Australia-born Laurie Smith, a sinologist and former diplomat who serves as News Corp. China chief operating officer, is on hand as a backup translator, making sure that Murdoch's words hit their mark. Along with Rupert, Smith has been tutoring James in this area of the world for months now—accompanying him, his father, and stepmother on dozens of tête-à-têtes with local Chinese business owners and government officials alike.

Jiang's top three ministers are also at the table, and a gift box filled with items from Fox Film and HarperCollins, two of News Corp.'s many properties, has been presented to Jiang, bearing digital video disks of some of Hollywood's most popular movies and a book on the Sydney Olympics. (Zemin was proudly promoting Beijing as the site for the 2008 Olympics, and the city was plastered with banners and posters. Murdoch knew well Jiang's favorite topics of discussion with foreigners these days.)

As the dinner proceeds, Murdoch and his youngest son are cementing their plans for a media summit in Shanghai the following fall. They need Jiang Zemin's approval for the high-profile event, which they hope will take place during the upcoming Asia-Pacific Economic Cooperation summit and be attended by 5,000 journalists from around the world.

For the most part, however, the private party is of a very personal nature.

Toward the end of the dinner, Jiang—as he is known to do at large gatherings with guests and even at large receptions in the United States—encourages his guests to join him in a song. The Chinese leader has an impressive voice, and his preference is to sing one song in English and one in Chinese. He urges Wendi to accompany him on the piano, but she is too shy.

The guests depart, sans musical entertainment, for their quarters at The China Club, the elite and iconoclastic establishment owned by Hong Kong tycoon David Tang. It is itself emblematic of the worlds that are colliding. In elegant refurbished quarters that were once home to several Chinese emperors, guests are couched in ancient history and relax at The Long March, the club's irreverent bar. (The China Club reportedly commands membership fees of $20,000, about ten times the annual income of the average Chinese citizen.)

"It was private, strictly not a business dinner," said Rupert Murdoch. "We had a meeting beforehand for half an hour, and his broadcasting policy was just touched on. Then we went to dinner and had a terribly personal conversation. His only disappointment was we didn't get up and sing with him. He loves to sing. He has a very good voice. And people will go away completely charmed.

"Wendi was too shy to accompany him on the piano," Murdoch said, laughing.

"We talked about world events to family events," Murdoch said. "He was very curious about the new Bush administration. In fact, he knew more about it than I did. I think he assumed that I was very close to it or something. Whereas I have met President Bush once in my life, for one minute at a reception. So I couldn't enlighten him very much. Although I was sort of going on what my impressions were. But he had a pretty good relationship with Bush's father and mother. The Chinese are like that. They put huge store into the personal relationship," Murdoch said.

Murdoch, needless to say, was pleased to start the year with this chummy tableau, painstakingly forged by News Corp. after a money-losing decade in China, years of political blunders rife with government hostility.

Indeed, "These days it's like a meeting of old friends," said one high-level Star TV executive. "It used to be like war."

The going had been rough. Back in 1993, Beijing officials were so offended by Rupert Murdoch's public comments on the impact of technology that they banned satellite broadcasts to the mainland.

Murdoch had said that telecommunications "have proved an unambiguous threat to totalitarian regimes everywhere." Satellite TV, he went on, "makes it possible for information-hungry residents of many closed societies to bypass state-controlled channels."

(Murdoch, whether he knew it or not, was echoing his grandfather Patrick Murdoch, who had said that freedom of the press is "probably the strongest foe of tyranny," and "no autocrat can tolerate the widespread dissemination among his people of a free discussion of his conduct." Interestingly, Murdoch himself, unlike other moguls, never discouraged criticism of himself and his power.)

Murdoch subsequently pulled out all the stops to regain favor with Beijing decision makers. He removed BBC news from Star and sold one of his papers, Hong Kong–based *South China Morning Post,* to a Chinese tycoon who was pro-Beijing. He then cancelled a book contract his publishing company HarperCollins had with ex-governor of Hong Kong Chris Patten. Slowly, over the years Rupert and News Corp. had come back in favor.

Now, said James, "There's recognition that as long as independent media is going to be sensitive to issues and doesn't push too hard, largely things will be alright."

After years of losses in Asia, and a string of political and cultural blunders, James's mission was to change his father's fortunes in one of the most unpredictable regions on the planet—and the highest growth market for the company.

His preliminary task: Shore up News Corp.'s assets, and expand Star's broadcasting endeavors in two of the world's largest markets—China and India—which were on the cusp of explosive growth.

Since his appointment in May, James has been working on transforming the company from a free-to-air, money-losing television broadcaster to a multiplatform media company with varied assets—delivering original and licensed programming and direct-to-customer services via cable, satellite, and new broadband channels. It is a role his father views as not just crucial to the success of News Corp.'s expansion but critical to the future of global media.

While skeptics say that James inherited "a mess" from his father, others view Murdoch's positioning of his son, and his ongoing investments in the area, as being prescient. Despite the fact that the company's been bleeding cash for years—to the tune of tens of millions a year since Star was acquired in the mid-90s—Michael J. Wolf, senior partner and media and entertainment consultant at McKinsey & Co., says five years from now, "people will look at the company's involvement in China as an investment similar to the cheap land Disney bought in Orlando." India and China both promise to be "the biggest media markets in the world—bigger than the U.S.," he says.

Back in New York, in his fourth-floor office at News Corp.'s midtown office tower, Lachlan Murdoch is monitoring the movements of his father and his younger brother closely. During their travels on the mainland in early January, Lachlan spoke with both for a progress report. "They both sounded ready to collapse," Lachlan says. Sounding like an old veteran of worldwide business diplomacy, he notes, "Those are the kind of trips where you have breakfast meetings, lunch meetings, dinner meetings, plus all the meetings in between. Because of the language barrier, you're always having to concentrate—it becomes more tiring than if you were traveling anywhere else." Back in 1995, Lachlan had done a brief stint as deputy chairman of Star, though he'd never taken up residence in the area.

James's first experience in mainland China was at about age 12, on a family trip with father Rupert, mother Anna, brother Lachlan, and sister Elisabeth. That was some ten years before Rupert had acquired Star. The clan had stayed in a government guesthouse in Beijing, and then moved on to hotels in other cities. Rupert was conducting some of his first meetings with Chinese government officials at the time, and the children were also taken sightseeing to The Great Wall, The Forbidden City, and Mao's tomb.

Mainland China was much different then—no McDonald's or other Western companies that now litter the major cities. James remembers that the strong smell of a certain Asian liquor that seemed to be consumed by adults at restaurants everywhere had repulsed him.

"There were a few official things that my father was doing. We spent most of our time on the mainland. I remember having difficulty with the food. I was young and I wasn't used to international food. I also remember we would go to all these official dinners, everyone would go, and we were all guests. The kids had their own table. Mai tai, that's drunk often with dinners in China, and I remember that being pretty strong—not drinking it, just smelling it," James said.

The family moved on to Shanghai, then Xian in eastern China, and on to Guangzhou, the home of Rupert's future bride. They also stopped for a few days in Hong Kong before returning to their home in New York.

"He was fascinated—my father has always been fascinated by China. And he's always had a big international vision," says James. "I think a lot of media companies, particularly U.S.-based media companies, look at the U.S. and then international. And I think the history of our company, coming from Australia and then going to Europe and the States has been more . . . we look at it in a more reasonable way. My father has always been fascinated by international markets and wanting to grow the businesses in places like this, and India and Europe."

"**A**nd there were the lions and the crocodiles and everybody eating them."

James Murdoch is describing one of the sights he saw while on a safari in Tanzania during his honeymoon, but he may as well have been describing the competitive landscape for the media business.

Back in the United States, while James and his father were dining with Jiang Zemin, a major battle was being won. After a year of scrutiny, AOL and Time Warner won regulatory approval for their merger, creating a media octopus with enormous reach. In exchange for the green light, they'd agreed to some restrictions on their businesses. The new giant agreed to open up aspects of its instant messaging, cable TV, and interactive television systems to competitors.

That concession, many competitors felt, would have little impact on the giant for some time to come. "Now we're all minnows," Rupert Murdoch had said.

The deal had melded AOL with Time Warner's Time Inc. publishing holdings, cable networks CNN and TBS, and the music business of Warner Music Group. The combined AOL Time Warner company had 26 million online users, 148 million registered instant-messaging users, 12.8 million cable subscribers, and millions of magazine readers. It also had an expansive library of films and thousands of television properties and recording artists.

Murdoch was betting on a different strategy. News Corp. now spanned six continents. Across all of News Corp., its key strategic areas were viewed to have more growth potential than all those of its media rivals Viacom, AOL Time Warner, Bertelsmann, and Disney.

Wall Street and market analysts were watching Murdoch and his sons with a mixture of skepticism and eager anticipation. They'd been taken by surprise before when Murdoch succeeded in new businesses that had been deemed impossible for him to enter.

Now a free-for-all was unfolding in Asia, because of deregulation and the explosion of the Internet. Technology of all sorts was proliferating. In the previous three years, the number of mobile phone users in China had gone from zero to 33 million. Each day the number of Internet users was doubling, and under President Jiang Zemin, Beijing officials were pushing digital technology to promote economic growth and modernization.

While there are currently 95 million television homes in the United States, there are already 300 million in China, with a total of 900 million television viewers—and that number is growing fast. "No doubt having James there will ensure the business is aggressive and gets fully developed," McKinsey's Wolf said. "There's a big difference between remote control and having the owner there."

China's cable and satellite advertising market was worth more than $800 million a year and growing at 30 percent annually.

Da-kuai-guang. Great, rapid, and expansive. *The People's Daily,* the newspaper and official voice of the communist state, now used the words once used to describe China's "Great Leap Forward" of 1958 to 1960 to describe the Internet revolution. The leap China was about to make was nothing short of world-shattering, and Murdoch was determined to be there.

James considered the visit with Jiang "a courtesy call." He said, "It is important in an environment like that—and when we have a lot on the agenda—to try and maintain good relations as we go along, so when my father is here we try to make sure we do a lot of work in Beijing."

Jiang and his top government ministers "like to see my Dad, he's had long relationships with a lot of those guys," said James, who has a habit of peering over or around the small, metal-framed eyeglasses that are always slipping down his nose, giving him the air of a man much older who is scrutinizing the world skeptically. Not much skepticism can be found in the young man, though; he has an air of ease and fearlessness, and indeed is described as being easygoing and fearless by his cohorts and colleagues.

James is boyish and sophisticated by turns, moving from startlingly astute talk of business models to gleeful accounts of merriment with his older brother Lachlan. He is a curious mixture of the worldliness that comes from growing up a Murdoch, and the childlike, wide-eyed wonder of a young man on his first odyssey.

Like his father, he also has an alarming ability to look the other way when confronting ugly political realities in the course of forging ahead in business.

While the West criticizes China for human rights abuses, James Murdoch echoes China's Communist Party rhetoric, calling the Falun Gong spiritual movement a "dangerous" and "apocalyptic cult." (Falun Gong, also known as Falun Dafa, is a movement involving meditation and exercise that was banned by the Chinese government after 10,000 followers staged a protest in Tiananmen Square in 1999. The U.S. State Department estimated that hundreds of its followers had been detained and tortured by the Chinese government; many lost their lives in prison.)

But James scolds the Western press for its negative portrayal of China and its human rights record. "I think these destabilizing forces today are very, very dangerous for the Chinese government," he said.

At Harvard, James was known for his memorable *Lampoon* cartoon, "Albrecht the Atypical Hun," a satire of World War I propaganda posters. His "Hun" was a bookish, gentle spirit with poetry in his soul. Now, apparently for business favors in China, James was being outrageously gentle about China's human rights record. Having poetry in one's soul about such abuses was hardly palatable even to the most adamant of China supporters.

Clearly, the business "Hun" lurked behind those generous words; Murdoch and sons clearly knew how to say the right things to win China's favor. Surprising for the liberal bohemian who not so long ago had been wandering around Harvard campus in a beard and red shoes. James described himself as "apolitical," but clearly, like his father, his political views shifted as needed.

James was showing signs of following in his father's footsteps. Up until about 1970, Murdoch leaned toward the left, but then he began to move toward the center. He was malleable, actually; it seemed he always liked to be on the side of the governing party. This could be seen in his ability to be chameleon-like, as the environment in world markets dictated.

Indeed, historical letters show a left-wing young Rupert.

The young heir ironically had been a supporter of the Australian Labor Party. Between 1949 and 1951 Rupert's father, Sir Keith Murdoch, and Rupert himself sent letters to the ALP leader, Ben Chifley. In one letter, Sir Keith described his son as a "zealous Laborite," but added that "he will I think (probably) eventually travel the same course as his father."

He was right on the money. Rupert might have said the same thing about son James, who was showing signs of being a chip off the old block. In his own letters to Chifley, Rupert criticized "Tory quackery" and praised "the rightness of socialism."

At the time, Sir Keith confided that he was worried about his son's "alarming left-wing views." Indeed, in college in London, Rupert kept a bust of Lenin on his mantelpiece, perhaps to aggravate his father.

James's views in China now clearly echoed those of his father. Defending China, Rupert Murdoch said, "There are human rights abuses in this country too. The Chinese government is about keeping China together—they're nationalists in that sense. While they're doing this, I think they're very frightened of any organized dissent.

"If you go to a Chinese home today, you will hear criticism of Chinese policy, government, or open discussion, which you certainly didn't get seven, eight years ago. On the other hand, if you want to go up the street and find someone on a soapbox making a speech, you won't. They'll be very quickly moved on. But I'd say it's much freer. Much more open than it was for the average citizen. But because they think their job above all else is to keep China together—remember over the course of civilization they'd been broken up, conquered and messed around with many times, they['ve] got to keep it together. Therefore they're trying to keep very strict control over the media and what goes out over television channels. I think they're getting a little looser about that, but I couldn't say radically," Murdoch said.

A t the same time, Murdoch and son admired Chinese culture and history. When he was stationed in New York, James had two posters of Mao Tse Dong, a gift from his pal Matt Jacobson, a former News Corp. executive, on one wall of his New York office until an anonymous office mate removed them. That was in his younger days, and Mao was a stylish and camp icon, more than being a man James particularly admired.

James was a history buff, and loved mining the history of his new surroundings. Unlike in modern times, China had historically been a leader in technology. Medieval China had in fact led the world in technological innovation. It was the first with cast iron, the compass, gunpowder, paper, and printing. It was the world leader in navigation, control of the seas, and political power. China lost its technological lead to Europe in the mid-fifteenth century and again in modern times because of local political issues; shipyards were dismantled and fleets were grounded, for example, when one faction of the Chinese court gained power. It abolished mechanical clocks after being a world leader in clock construction, abandoned development of a water-powered spinning machine, and resisted the impetus toward an industrial revolution in the fourteenth century. China retreated from technology in general after the late fifteenth century.

The political unity of China spelled doom for technology once a single, unilateral decision had been made, versus the fragmented and splintered nature of Europe, history shows.

Now, the same unity ironically was proving a boon for a digital renaissance in China.

Whereas geographic balkanization proved to be a boon for Europe with many discrete centers of innovation, China's geographical unity was a disadvantage, since a decision by a single monarch could end innovation for decades, if not centuries.

Now the Internet was digitally creating islands of diversity throughout the previously impenetrable mass of China.

But history has taken surprising turns; former greatness does not mean future greatness. The network of technology ministries all over China is now bent on ensuring that China's technological future will remain in its own hands. It enters into partnerships with foreign entities only under very strict terms.

If Rupert Murdoch is an iconoclast who traffics in icons, so is his youngest son. Neither can be pigeonholed about their beliefs. And the bottom line is business success—selling the world glimmering images of itself that range from fantasy to tabloid schlock to the highest-quality programming and news.

James appears not overly worried about the possibility of failure (though he does care what people think of him, grilling me about whom I've been talking to, and hoping no one said anything "bad,"), and all too willing to shoulder the blame that might be heaped upon him if he should bungle his mission.

Despite or perhaps because of his extreme youth, James is both aware and unafraid of the enormity of his challenges here.

"I don't think you're going to wake up in the morning and suddenly there's going to be a headline that says 'China Open for Business' ", he says. "China *is* largely open for business and it's a question of being open to partnerships and lining your interests with key constituents in your partnerships and things like that. In the case of China, in particular, very careful consideration has to be given to cultural sensitivities and political sensitivities.

"We're not a political company here in any way, we're interested in providing services and it's pretty nuts and bolts. A lot of people say, well, this is illegal, and that's illegal, but if you've followed the *South China Morning Post* the last two days you see that two days ago foreign investment was allowed and today it's not. It's a process and you just continue to work through it, make sure you keep very good lines of communication with the core ministries you deal with in your sector and just kind of work through it."

Indeed, pere Murdoch acknowledges, "We are a media company, and that is a very special thing. We operate in many countries, all with different cultures, political structures, regulatory environments, and consumer attitudes."

As such, News Corp. finds itself in businesses "that by their very nature interact importantly with local mores and with local politics," he says.

"Our entertainment products are scrutinized for their content: a program or film that is acceptable in one country is not in another," Rupert Murdoch says. "Our news broadcasts seem unexceptionable in countries with a tradition of political openness, and destabilizing in countries that put a greater premium on stability than on dissent."

To say that News Corp. has to respect those rules, says Murdoch, "is to simplify the problem, because we at times find ourselves on a collision course with traditional business practices and the 'establishments' that have a stake in the status quo."

7

PATRIARCHS IN DECLINE

Murdoch placed his son James at the helm of Star just in time to get the company in shape as a key asset to Sky Global. The view from Hong Kong is complex but exciting: James's challenge is to turn an ad-based business gradually into a company offering subscription-based services of all kinds, and delivering information and entertainment to a range of media platforms. James Murdoch was not the only mogul's son in the area trying to make an impact. Rival Richard Li, son of Hong Kong tycoon Li Ka-shing, had made some moves that temporarily startled Star into refocusing its business. Jiang Zemin's own son was also becoming an ace in the technology business, sometimes changing the rules to encourage new markets on the mainland.

From James's window, Victoria Harbor churns in the mist on a foggy morning; tiny wooden boats dart across the paths of great commercial ships. Beyond, an undulating expanse of mountaintops.

"I love you, Dad."

The room falls silent, while a half dozen executives wait for their young boss to hang up the phone. James Murdoch ends the conversation with his father as he often does, unembarrassed by his colleagues' presence in the room. He is leading one of his early Monday morning meetings, and many of the executives present are much older and more seasoned, something he is used to by now. The group settles in before a bank of windows looking out at the Hong Kong skyline, a spectacular frieze of skyscrapers towering over the waterway below.

Entering James's eighth-floor office within the blue glass–and–chrome high-rise that houses Star headquarters, a Chinese woman asks executives, "Would you care for English tea or Chinese tea?" The question—asked of guests in corporate offices, hotels, and all manner of places throughout the city—instantly sets forth the dialectic that subtly pervades most transactions that take place here.

"One country, two systems," is the official mantra and China's explanation for tolerating the liberties enjoyed in Hong Kong versus the mainland since the handover.

The mantra for James Murdoch and his dad, and senior executives scattered over the globe in a bid to secure strategic positions for the company in new markets, is "Be global, think local."

It was a lesson learned after years of missteps in Asia.

Twelve months earlier Rupert Murdoch had no idea that his strategy here would change as drastically as it did. Focusing on Star as the company that promised the most growth in emerging markets, neither Rupert, nor his number two, Peter Chernin, nor COO Lachlan, originally realized the potential of what they hoped would be the most valuable arm of News Corp.

Ironically, it was Murdoch's chief rival in the area, Richard Li, and the activities of his company Pacific Century Cyber-Works (PCCW), that had startled Rupert into a complete revamping of his vision for Star—and moved him to put his youngest son at the helm.

Rupert himself had enabled nemesis Li, who had come into a fortune one day on the deck of Murdoch's yacht *Morning Glory*. The elder Murdoch had inadvertently laid the groundwork for his son's future—and Li's—when he bought Star TV from Li in a two-phase deal in 1993 and 1995 for close to $1 billion. Li would use the money to launch his own new company, Pacific Century CyberWorks.

While Wall Street analysts criticized Murdoch for "overpaying," something they saw as a habit of his, Rupert Murdoch over time was proving to be adept at finding small businesses that represented beachheads he could throw lots of cash into and quickly move into new markets. While the price tag for Star had been more than $1 billion by the time the 100 percent acquisition was complete in 1995, by 2001 it was worth some $6 to $10 billion—by Wall Street's estimates—as the dominant platform in Asia.

(Murdoch had accomplished the same thing with BSkyB, in which he held a 38 percent stake. Back in 1987, he had spent some $40 million on his four-channel satellite service, Sky. By 1989, it was losing $2 million a week. While it still had not turned a profit, by the summer of 2001 it was the United Kingdom's number one pay-television provider, and had signed up 5.5 million subscribers for its digital service. It also boasted a churn rate of 10 percent, half that of its rivals. Analysts were predicting that it would be in profits in 2002, and valued at about 40 times its profits.)

By the winter of 2000, PCCW was knocking the investment community off its feet.* It had announced it would be combining Internet and interactive television services to homes,

*Since that time, the company has faltered, however. PCCW is now in the doldrums.

133

and, partnered with Sony, opening content-creation studios to rival News Corporation's.

Lachlan Murdoch, who sat in for many strategy briefings between his father and brother, acknowledged "the market's reaction to PCCW really woke us up and made us say 'wait a minute.' Here's a company that's doing some small broad-band and Internet deals with this huge valuation on it. We're the number one entertainment/media brand across Asia. We were getting no value for it . . . if you apply the same metrics and valuation to Star that was being applied to PCCW, Star would be the most valuable asset in News Corp."

Rupert took his youngest son aside and talked with him. Even then James might not have been put in the hot seat were it not for the fact that his visit to Hong Kong along with Chase Carey's in January 2000—in search of Internet investment opportunities in Asia—coincided with rumors of manage-ment problems concerning Star's then-CEO Gareth Chang. Chinese-American Chang, it was suggested, was "unwilling to cross swords with Richard Li."

By May, James had been named as Chang's successor, just in time to get Star in shape as potentially the most valuable piece of his Sky Global plans. The move met with approbation in Asia, a continent in which family dynasties are revered, not scorned as nepotistic. In China, says James, the role of family in business is more respected than in the West. "I think it's understood, family connections, because family is so impor-tant and family and business and all that stuff go together. But in our family we all work in the company," he says, and laughs a little, before noting, ". . . or have at one point, so our family life is very business-oriented regardless."

James's task—to turn Star from a money-losing, free-to-air satellite broadcasting company into a powerful distributor of content through a variety of platforms—more often than not in these foreign markets would require partnerships with local companies. James says he had to "dive in, get to know the market, get to know the players, particularly in the Internet space and some of the new initiatives coming out of China that were getting a lot of attention." He notes that "the real push came in March when we really aggressively started preparing for the Sky Global launch and for Star's inclusion in Sky Global."

The existing business comprised 30 broadcast services, in seven languages, reaching more than 300 million viewers across 53 Asian countries. James had to keep on top of it all. Star's channels included the STAR Chinese Channel; Phoenix Chinese Channel (which was recently in profits); STAR Plus, the new all Hindi language channel in India, launched under James's watch; and Channel V, a joint venture music channel between Star and EMI Music, serving Greater China, Southeast Asia, Thailand, Australia, India, and the Philippines. Added to the mix were ESPN STAR Sports; STAR Movies; Phoenix Movies; and STAR News, in addition to distributed channels Fox News, Sky News, and National Geographic Channel.

Rupert Murdoch had high hopes that these channels, largely provided for free in China and delivered to technically illegal satellite dishes that viewers had installed in their backyards all over the mainland, would eventually be the bases for a pay-TV service on the mainland.

Bruce Churchill, Star's president and James's neighbor in Hong Kong, often reminded the young Murdoch that there was a big difference between what is officially approved and what happens day-to-day on the mainland.

"Events tend to anticipate what gets written in black-and-white," he said. "Events transpire and then, because it's their de facto, they sort of end up changing the rules. But they're not typically going to change the rules ahead of things actually happening."

Indeed, things were constantly changing on the mainland. Churchill had first arrived in Hong Kong in January of 1996. Prior to that, Rupert Murdoch had him stationed at Fox in Los Angeles. For a while, Churchill had been going back and forth between Fox and Star, but it was pretty much full-time by April 1996.

In the five years he'd been on the scene in China, the world had changed a lot. The business had grown and expanded. Star originally was a very centralized organization. The head of ad sales for India, for example, reported to the head of ad sales in Hong Kong; and the head of distribution in India reported to the head of distribution in Hong Kong.

By 2000, it was all localized. Having a big bureaucracy with people trying to run the show from remote locations simply did not work. The company had a chief executive in India, Peter Mukerjea, and local executives making the most important decisions, with regular direct reporting to James and Rupert Murdoch.

While it was true that BSkyB was a model for what Murdoch wanted to do all over the world, for the time being Star was operating quite differently. That was a necessity because of local political and cultural issues. "As to where we're headed in the next couple of years, largely Star has been misunderstood," said Churchill. From the beginning, many outsiders believed that the company was simply an Asian BSkyB. In fact, it had never been a direct-to-home business.

In the beginning, Star was all advertising-driven, and offered five channels in English. Over the years, the company developed specific language programming for specific markets, which was largely responsible for its successes.

By 2000, it had encrypted all of its broadcast signals, with the exception of some of the services in China, using NDS technology. The encryption was targeted at the cable head-end, "so that we were then selling that programming and creating a second stream of revenue which didn't previously exist," said Churchill. Star had became the pay-TV leader in Asia.

Early on, Star broadcasts were in analog form and free-to-air, and revenues came strictly from advertising. "So you could just receive it, literally put a dish in your backyard and get Star TV," Churchill said. Though satellite broadcasts were officially illegal in mainland China, there were enough people with their own dishes in their backyards, ignoring the government and receiving satellite programs, that it created enough of a base to attract advertisers.

Once Star migrated to an encrypted business, it could charge a premium to cable operators for encrypted content that they could not receive and rebroadcast over cable merely by having a dish. "If you're a cable operator, that is what happens in Asia, you sell the signal to your neighbors," Churchill said. With encrypted broadcasts, "You have to get a box to decode that signal, and you have to pay us for the right to do that," he explained.

Star's approach was two-pronged. In some regions, where there are sophisticated cable operators, it offered premium content that required decoding and payment to Star; in other regions, there were still free-to-air broadcasts.

In India, however, all Star broadcasts required that the cable operator have a set-top box to decode the signals, which they paid for. This was then rebroadcast to cable subscribers, who, in India, did not need a set-top box but received cable broadcasts directly on their television sets.

Star was now preparing to go the next step—moving increasingly into the direct-to-home business by either creating "addressability" on cable or actually launching direct-to-home satellite businesses—which would be akin to a BSkyB business.

Star's direct-to-home business in Asia was through alliances with cable companies, who received the signals from Star via satellite, and broadcast it via their cable networks to subscribers. That was the setup in India and Taiwan.

In mainland China, while there was a very large installed base of cable, the satellite direct-to-home business was still a ways off. Murdoch and his executives, however, were optimistic that that was opening up, and the government was courting foreign investments in Chinese-run cable companies.

In the near term, the key opportunity would be carrying direct-to-home businesses over cable. But satellite had a huge potential in both China and India because of the land mass that needed to be covered. It would never be possible to lay enough cable to reach everybody in China or India. Officially, both countries viewed satellite as the best way to reach remote rural areas.

"Fine, if that's the entree," Churchill said when considering the limits. Star's approach always had been to slowly get its foot in the door.

"The advantage of the satellite is that it has a national footprint, and therefore a national product you can roll out instantaneously as opposed to waiting for cable being built out," he said. Indeed, Star had been ready for a long time.

Rupert Murdoch was optimistic. He believed the Chinese government itself would soon change its stance on satellite broadcasts, and get into the act itself. "They're going to do their own satellite in a while," he said. "They've got 1 billion 300 million people there. They're going through huge economic changes, which are going to cause varying degrees of prosperity and hardship. And they don't want a collapse like they had in Russia."

Phoenix was another tale of longsightedness for Murdoch.

While Murdoch has owned a stake in Hong Kong–based Phoenix Satellite Television since 1996, it lost some $53 million through the year 2000, but by spring 2000 was suddenly turning a profit. Its broadcasts were still illegal on the mainland, though the Bank of China was a minority owner of the company. Enough people owned satellite dishes, regardless of the government's ban, to attract advertisers, the main source of revenue. Chinese cable companies often down-linked Star's programming, despite government restrictions, distributing it to their customers, who paid little more than a dollar a month for cable service.

Liu Chang Le, the 48-year-old founder of Hong Kong–based Phoenix, planned to launch the first 24-hour Chinese news channel, to be beamed onto the mainland via satellite. Murdoch, with Star, had helped Liu found the original Phoenix Chinese Channel as a joint venture in 1996. Though Phoenix lost some $53 million since its founding, it was now in profits. Star and Liu each own 38.25 percent of the company, with 8.5 percent owned by the Bank of China. Fifteen percent of the company is owned by the public.

By 1999, Phoenix was on the verge of being put out of business because authorities attempted to clamp down on illegal reception of foreign broadcasts. (Hong Kong–based companies are legally viewed in China as being "foreign.") It regained favor with the government with its patriotic coverage of NATO's mistaken bombing of the Chinese embassy in Belgrade.

For Murdoch's part, he had shrewdly teamed up with Liu, a former soldier in the People's Liberation Army and announcer for the Central People's Radio Station. By 2001, Phoenix was offering 42 million homes on the mainland a daily news program that managed not to offend Beijing officials. It also added a movie channel and was distributing its Chinese-language channels to Europe and North America.

Since its public offering in June, the company doubled in value. Ad revenues were rapidly growing and investors were attracted by the huge Chinese television market.

Competition was just beginning in that market. Hong Kong–based China Entertainment Television, known as CETV, which had been broadcasting illegally to the mainland since 1994, earlier in the year (2000) forged a strategic alliance with Murdoch archcompetitor Time Warner. It claimed it reached 33 million households in China, to Phoenix's 42 million.

"When you go into a marketplace like China, you find the extraordinary talent of a filmmaker or a musician. The job of a company like ours is to give them a platform for their voice. It's not about taking American culture and pushing it around the world," said Gerald Levin, Time Warner chairman and CEO, addressing an international conference in Shanghai.

Sales of Time Warner's *Time* magazine were officially suspended in China that week, perhaps because it contained articles by known dissidents and the Dalai Lama. Murdoch's was not the only foreign media company censored here. Bootlegged copies of the magazine, however, could be found at local newsstands.

Indeed, Beijing's Forbidden City was swarming with 10,000 warriors—virtual warriors, that is. China's official terrestrial broadcaster, China Central Television—known as CCTV—had an outdoor studio complex at Nanhai that was beginning to look a little like Murdoch's Fox lot. CCTV was unabashedly a propaganda arm for the government, and competed with Phoenix. (It launched a 24-hour financial news channel in September 2000.) China now boasted 264 million television homes—representing 97.6 percent of the population—up from 36 percent in 1994.

CCTV was founded in 1958 and now offered nine channels to a total of about one billion viewers. CCTV's ad revenues in 1999 reached $1.1 billion.

For CCTV's hit film about a legendary 19th-century Chinese naval battle, staged on a full-scale replica of Beijing's Forbidden City, more than 10,000 extras were hired. Audience members reveled in the slapstick war between soldiers loyal to Hong Xiuquan's Taiping Heavenly Kingdom and the Qing Dynasty army.

The film drew huge weekend crowds; the cost to each moviegoer was the equivalent of a week's wages for a local factory worker.

The power of film and television in China was stunning. In a media market that largely had been dominated by propaganda issued by the ruling Communist Party, the pent-up demand for Western-style entertainment was huge.

Though Phoenix was now a well-known Chinese brand (a Gallup market survey showed that 36 percent of Chinese citizens it polled saw the Phoenix brand as comparable to that of McDonald's and General Motors), Murdoch and Liu were still operating in a gray area. Though it did not seem likely that their company would ever be shut down, they did not expect that their satellite broadcast would be made officially legal anytime soon. Most viewers were receiving Phoenix programs through local Chinese cable operators downlinking the satellite signals (almost 80 million Chinese homes now had cable), despite the fact that Chinese law forbade cable operators from retransmitting these signals.

(Even Microsoft recognized the huge growth in the cable network in China, entering into a deal with the top computer manufacturer on the mainland, Legend Holdings Ltd, to produce cheap set-top boxes running a version of Windows. But acceptance of such devices was deemed to be slow, due to the fact that broadband capabilities were a ways off.)

Still, Murdoch is more optimistic than ever, despite detractors making a point of how much money he's lost in the area over the past decade.

The amazing success of Phoenix is noteworthy. Murdoch says, "It's a pretty remarkable achievement what they've done there. And we plan to have our own channel, quite legally in the short-term in China; it would be purely entertainment, it's not like having news or anything. It would be another Star channel, we might call it Sky or Star or Extra or something."

While James talked to his father on the phone almost every day, his Hong Kong rival Richard Li was dodging his own tycoon father, who was skeptical of some of his activities, according to the Asian press.

Li, 34, is the son of Hong Kong tycoon Li Ka-shing, nicknamed "superman" for his control of numerous industries in Hong Kong. The holdings of Li Ka-shing included the operations of Hutchison Whampoa, which spanned 24 countries in ports, supermarkets, telecommunications, and the Internet. Its net profits for 1999 were just over $15 billion.

In 1990, when he launched Star TV, Li had persuaded his father to pump $62.5 million into the company. The total investment climbed to $125 million. Within two years, it was broadcasting to an estimated 45 million viewers in China and India. While an enormous accomplishment at the time, it represented only a tiny fraction of the market potential, from Murdoch's point of view.

Richard, like his father, was viewed to be a billionaire visionary. Skeptics, however, say he spent vast sums on pipe dreams to inflate PCCW's company stock price. His father's fortune was in old-world businesses; Richard was trafficking in the world of the digerati, and making quite a splash.

Li was actually quite Americanized. He was known to love junk food; he attended high school in Menlo Park, California, and worked at McDonald's and as a golf caddy to earn his own spending money. Li also studied computer engineering at Stanford. Like James, for a brief stint he worked outside his father's company—as an investment banker in Canada. In 1990, his father summoned him to help with the family business. By 2000, Li was building a Bill Gates–like mansion just outside of Hong Kong.

Like James, Richard had an older brother, 36-year-old Victor, who sat in on his tycoon father's board meetings and was the heir apparent. (Victor was kidnapped by a crime boss in 1996, and his father ended up paying a ransom of more than $100 million to get him back!) So Richard and James were in similar positions in lineage within their respective mogul-fathers' empires.

In the spring of 2000, Li stole Cable & Wireless Hong Kong Telecom (HKT) out from under Murdoch's nose in a deal valued at $38 billion, the biggest takeover in Asia. The move derailed a deal Star had nailed with the telecommunications giant to provide television programming for HKT's broadband network. Murdoch had been pushing government-owned Singapore Telecom to make a bid for the company instead. (Months later, however, James nabbed a different deal away from rival Li. Star entered into a partnership with Taiwan's Gigamedia; Li had been courting the company as well.)

While James only recently was introduced to Jiang Zemin, Richard Li and his father have hobnobbed with the Chinese president for years. A photo of Li and Zemin hangs in PCCW's private dining room.

Yes, the sons were rising, and the patriarchs were in decline. While his son James was redefining and carrying out his legacy, and Richard Li was reinventing the visions of his tycoon father Li Ka-shing, no doubt Rupert Murdoch got a kick out of the fact that the son of President Jiang Zemin was making his own imprint on the old empire, forging digital frontiers of his own.

Jiang Mianheng was vice director of the Chinese Academy of Sciences, an organization known for its commercial acumen. He was also helping China Netcom in its plans to become the mainland's largest provider of broadband data services.

Now, under Jiang's oversight, the Chinese Academy of Sciences was playing an increasingly important role as incubator and investor in some of the country's leading high-tech companies. These included the Hong Kong–listed Legend Holdings, the largest manufacturer of personal computers in mainland China.

Ironically, regulatory barriers, largely enforced by his father and other Beijing officials, were standing in the way of China Netcom's ambitions. It was the smallest of the mainland's four licensed telecommunications carriers, and already had an 8,000-kilometer network of high-speed fiber-optic cables, which it hoped to use to provide fast Internet access to multinationals and Chinese state-owned enterprises. A trial of its high-speed Internet service was to begin in 17 Chinese cities in late October of 2000.

The big problem for China Netcom was that it needed foreign investment to survive in the longer term, but the barriers China had placed on foreign investment in the telecommunications sector as part of its agreement to enter the World Trade Organization had the effect of limiting overseas firms to China Netcom's three larger competitors. China Netcom was asking for special permission to allow an injection of foreign capital.

And, indeed, in meetings between James Murdoch and his stepmother, Wendi Deng, News Corp. was able to accomplish an investment in the company that it was told it should "keep secret."

Jiang Mianheng—who attended Drexel University in the United States in the late 80s—was involved with numerous high-tech companies through his role as vice director of the commercially savvy Chinese Academy of Sciences. He'd returned to Shanghai in the early 90s, where he became known as a high-tech tsar, before moving to Beijing to serve in his current role.

During his time in Shanghai, he was chairman of the $240 million Shanghai Alliance Investment Ltd, known as SAIL, and also ran Shanghai Simtech Industries Ltd.

At the Academy of Sciences, he was said to be even more active as a business advocate. The academy was serving as an incubator and long-term investor in some of China's leading computer companies—including Legend Holdings Ltd. The Academy was also a financial backer of companies like Red-Flag Software Corp., a developer of Linux software, the free operating system that rivals Microsoft's Windows.

James had met many times with Mianheng, whose SAIL group had even been in talks with Phoenix TV about investment opportunities.

News Corp.'s big coup with Netcom was made public months after it had been accomplished. It had agreed to keep the deal "secret," as it was technically still against the rules and illegal. Foreigners were banned from investing in basic telecom services, though China had agreed to allow up to 49 percent foreign ownership after its acceptance in the WTO.

In February 2001, News Corp. finally went public with the

news, along with Goldman Sachs & Co. and two Chinese companies, investing $325 million to buy a 12 percent stake in China Netcom. It represented a major presence for News Corp. in one of China's key broadband networks.

News Corp. succeeded by virtue of persistence. It was in the process of liberalizing the China market through the back door. In China, the law seemed to lag behind individual decisions made in local areas on specific issues. Amazingly, the government-backed *China Daily* newspaper applauded the deal as "revolutionary" while admitting that it was not entirely legal under current regulations.

8

FOOTHOLDS

Understanding the Chinese market required that Murdoch station his key executives on the mainland for years, long before he'd sent in his son to close deals long in the making. Murdoch also had personally spent much time cultivating relationships with the new guard of bureaucrats and local business-people, with the help of his wife Wendi Deng. His technologists at NDS had in many ways offered their Chinese counterparts a blueprint for creating new industries where none had existed; the rollout of a national cable network on the mainland was in the works, and, in the spring of 2000, NDS had been chosen as the business partner of choice. If Western media was less than acceptable to some of the old guard, technology offered by companies like NDS and News Corp. was another story; it represented a dazzling opportunity for a new breed of mainland entrepreneurs. While many media companies had given up on China as being too restrictive a market, Murdoch had persisted in doing what no other media company had done before. While his technologists were at work, Murdoch continued to cultivate his relationships with Chinese leaders. Worlds were colliding, and Murdoch at times had an alarming ability to adjust his own values to accommodate less-than-palatable political realities. Still, as is often the case with Murdoch's new ventures, profits were nowhere in sight; the benefits were seen as long-term, and the opening up of the market was being accelerated by a new political environment on the mainland and the prospect of being accepted in the WTO.

The groundwork for James's success had been laid by executives Rupert Murdoch had working in the area for years. A major breakthrough came in 2000, during James's first spring in China, while he was busy cultivating investment opportunities with Chinese companies, assisted by his stepmother Wendi Deng.

While the two were off holding their own tête-à-têtes with mainland business leaders, vice minister Zhang Hai Tao was laying out the state of broadcasting in China, surprising many of those who attended his speech at an industry conference in Beijing.

Three of Rupert Murdoch's minions sat enraptured, not willing to miss a word coming in whispered translation from a Chinese man seated next to them in the front row, one of thousands of local businesspeople in attendance. At stake was a foothold in what would potentially become the largest media network in the world, and the lingua franca was digital technology.

Listening in a front row before Zhang, Laurie Smith (who until James's arrival had been Murdoch's main man on the mainland) had seen it all. He and his colleagues had been pursuing this elusive frontier for years now. Now advances in technology, and the expertise of News Corp.'s technology arm, NDS, were opening doors as never before.

To Murdoch, technology was a double-edged sword. While it had meant loss of control and cannibalization of the old ways (the explosion of the Internet had knocked everyone for a loop), it also enabled greater control than was ever before imaginable—from one-on-one relationships with consumers, to encrypted delivery of personalized content to an unlimited number of individuals on the planet. (The Chinese had been particularly interested in Murdoch's encryption technology, which would provide a modicum of control in an out-of-control world.)

Vice minister Zhang Hai Tao, immaculately dressed in a Western-style suit, was in his mid-40s, surprisingly young for a Chinese official in his position. He had successfully run a provincial television network, and was recently brought to Beijing as one of the country's younger technocrats focused on change. Younger technocrats were being brought in on a "meritocracy" basis and had a mandate to do things differently. There was still much overlapping bureaucracy and duplication of authority. Making decisions was a cumbersome process.

Getting to know the dozens of Chinese ministries and their respective leaders and vice ministers had been like navigating a Kafkaesque landscape at first. But things had changed a lot in almost a decade since Murdoch first arrived on the scene.

For one thing, Murdoch himself, along with his top media experts, were now successfully helping to create new Chinese companies, hiring Chinese talent to run them, and teaching eager young technocrats how to build the devices of the future—on which his own products would run.

Zhang's most important guests whispering in the front row oddly enough were outsiders who promised to help him bring his beloved culture into the digital age. Beside Laurie Smith in the front row, looking up at Zhang, sat Dr. Abe Peled, head of NDS. Zhang, who was now talking fast, had developed a close relationship with Peled over the months.

Peled now leaned his graying head toward his colleague Smith. Beside Smith sat Sue Taylor, NDS vice president for the

Asia Pacific. Taylor was an attractive blond who was once told by a Beijing official who'd entered into a contract with NDS, "I hate you. You're a great negotiator." He'd said it in Mandarin, and she only learned later what he'd said. It was rare for a woman to be in a position of power in China.

Peled, Smith, and Taylor squirmed to hear Zhang's words in translation, whispered by a courteous Chinese businessman. The audience appeared impressed by Zhang's knowledge.

Some of the words coming out of Zhang's mouth were like grenades of surprise for Murdoch's lieutenants, who had been scrutinizing every shift in the landscape for years. Zhang was spelling out his vision for the rollout of a national information network in China.

Change now seemed to be coming in like gales, and News Corp. was poised to catch the wind. A presence in Hong Kong was not enough, and an office had been quickly set up in Beijing several months earlier. To participate in mainland China business, a company had to have offices in Beijing. Mainland China was run out of Beijing, and all its ministries and decision makers were based there.

Back in the United States, while his executives sat perched on the edge of their seats in a Beijing meeting room, Rupert Murdoch and Chinese culture minister Tian Congming ambled under the Los Angeles sun through the back lots of Fox Studios. Workers and messengers in white shorts and baseball caps drove golf carts casually through a maze of parking lots filled with trailers and half-constructed sets. It was hard to believe that the glossiest of Western illusion sprang from this raw site.

Murdoch and Tian Congming are the most unlikely of chums. But it is the spring of 2000, a millennial year, and iconoclastic alliances seem to be the rule of the day. The two men, both dressed in sleek European suits, enter a soundstage on the lot, which Murdoch has transformed for the day into his own mini–United Nations—hosting a range of Chinese culture ministers along with his most fierce rivals.

While his executives are working on a deal in Beijing to supply key technology for a new national cable network in China, the U.S.-China trade bill is going before a divided house, and Murdoch holds forth before his media cronies. He is charming and passionate. Tian Congming is attentive.

"I am fully aware of the opposition, and, obviously, they are quite simply wrong," Murdoch says. "China cannot be bludgeoned or bribed into adopting general policies the Americans may find more congenial."

Greeting Tian and Murdoch is Jack Valenti, megalobbyist and head of the Motion Picture Association. Valenti, like Murdoch, has been canvassing House members to support China in the new trade deal.

"China is getting richer, is getting more confident and is becoming part of the globalized economy." Murdoch said. "They understand that the economic growth and the well-being of their people crucially depend on the continuing flow of foreign investment capital and technology."

Murdoch, Tian Congming, and his boss, China's president Jiang Zemin, had been perfecting their back-patting for more than a year now.

The previous October, Jiang Zemin, a sturdy figure in a European suit with a square jaw and dark-framed glasses, flew to London for a rare visit with the Queen of England—and Rupert Murdoch. Days earlier he'd stood in the back of an old limousine in a gray Mao jacket, inspecting troops and armor.

The Chinese president stood precariously, as did Murdoch, at the fault line between the old world and the new world, the ancient city and the wired city.

Zemin had careened down the Mall to Buckingham Palace in a horse-drawn carriage beside Her Majesty, the Queen of England. Along the way, scores of Chinese flags were flying. Banquets awaited him in Buckingham Palace, Guildhall, and the Chinese Embassy. So did protesters.

That night, the Queen of England entered the Chinese Embassy in London in an ivory evening gown, in time for the Chinese state banquet. The Queen's place, and every other place, was set with chopsticks rather than knives and forks. Across the room were Prince Philip, the Duke of York, the Duke and Duchess of Gloucester, the Duke of Kent, Princess Alexandra and Sir Angus Ogilvy. Also there were John Prescott, the deputy prime minister, and former prime ministers Lady Thatcher and Sir Edward Heath.

The Prince of Wales was missing.

It soon became clear that Jiang Zemin was being snubbed, in protest of his country's numerous violations of human and religious rights.

But there at the table was Rupert Murdoch and his Chinese-born wife, Wendi Deng. Earlier, Murdoch had been at the lunch honoring Jiang at 10 Downing Street, with numerous businessmen and ministers in attendance, talking about the intricacies of trade with China. Rupert Murdoch was there to greet his friend, Jiang, at every event.

It had not been long since the tide had turned for Murdoch. It had started the year before, in 1999, when Murdoch had been welcomed to Beijing by Jiang, who thanked him for "presenting China objectively and cooperating with the Chinese press."

China was a conundrum.

Murdoch had been urging Congress and U.S. businesses to give China a break. Though still politically repressive, China offered more personal freedoms and economic opportunities than ever before, went his argument.

He tended to agree with Henry Kissinger who was against confronting China and thought it should be left alone. Ideology would become meaningless as globalization, driven by the Internet, took hold of the mainland. China would have to evolve quickly enough.

"To get rich is glorious." Those were not the sentiments of Murdoch, but of former president of China Deng Xiaoping. Those words, and other speeches and slogans such as "Some people must get rich first," comprised "Deng Xiaoping Thought," enshrined in 1999 as part of the constitution of the National People's Congress, China's parliament.

Indeed, when Murdoch dispatched his son James to China, it was in hopes that his son would help News Corp. become the media company of choice on the mainland that would "get rich first."

The Chinese government's attitude toward the media and the Internet was actually a far cry from what Murdoch had in mind. But he had to deal with it; he'd even gotten in the habit of rationalizing it.

Now Chinese Internet surfers were required to log on through state-controlled gateways that block hundreds of taboo sites including Amnesty International, Tibetan sites, BBC, and CNN news. Public-access Internet cafes in major cities are reportedly required to hand over lists of their clients to the police.

Mainland leaders viewed it as a *xin shiwu*, or new phenomenon in the potential it offered for propaganda, they proclaimed in numerous statements. (Ironically, *xin shiwu* had been the same term used to describe the benefits of the 1966–1976 Cultural Revolution.) The government stated, through its newspaper the *People's Daily,* that the Internet was the battleground for the struggle between the "correct propaganda" of the government and the "reactionary, superstitious and pornographic" content of the enemies of China.

The paper urged that party members all over China should form troops of web fighters who understand politics and news management, and have a good command of foreign languages, to battle the enemy "at home and abroad."

For Murdoch, finding success in China would require much diplomacy, and incomparable social graces. But Rupert Murdoch was a master of both, especially when he wanted to win.

Murdoch had the ability to change even the most deeply felt allegiances—if doing so would help him competitively. This was sharply illustrated when he abandoned his Australian citizenship in the mid-1980s in order to launch his Fox television network. He would justify his actions, brushing aside criticism. "I am not severing any links with Australia. I continue to have the same emotions and feelings about Australia. If I have to change the color of my passport, then so be it," he said. Indeed, the U.S. Communications Act had left him with no choice; it stated that corporations could not hold a broadcasting license if any officer or director was an alien. Murdoch's ambitions had expanded beyond the rules, as would happen many times in his life; to change the rules he had to change his own personal landscape, in this case.

In China, his ambitions also had expanded beyond the rules, and he had to adjust his own moral sense in order to keep going.

Murdoch, during his years in the region, had also claimed ignorance of China's violation of religious rights and abuses in Tibet.

He'd dismissed the Dalai Lama as "a very old political monk shuffling around in Gucci shoes." He still says, "Privately, many people agreed with me after I made that comment."

At the same time, Chinese employees of Murdoch's have noted that he has been surprisingly erudite about their world. In 1998 Rupert and Wendi, not yet married, came for an international advisors meeting. They were greeted at the Hong Kong airport by a Star vice president, a Chinese woman, Jannie Poon. The three sat in the back seat of an official government car, which took them to the Shangrila Hotel.

Poon, embarrassed that perhaps she was invading the privacy of the big boss and his fiancee offered to find some other transportation. To her surprise, Rupert insisted that she sit in the car with them. He sat in the middle, flanked by the two Chinese women. He was never formal or demanding in how he traveled, and often carried his own bags.

In the car, Rupert was reading all the Hong Kong papers, and demonstrated a thorough knowledge of the local news. Poon was amazed; she, a Hong Kong resident, was not as well versed on the local news as was Rupert Murdoch.

Murdoch, before his guests on the Fox lot, gave a nod to the difficulties of Western media companies breaking into foreign cultures. "We in the entertainment and media industries must realize that unlike many other industries, what we do has important consequences for the political, social and cultural life of the other nations in which we operate," he said. "We have to respect the culture. To act otherwise would be to act as cultural imperialists.

Later, at a dinner, actress Song Chunli floated amid the crowd, past executives from Murdoch archrivals Sony Pictures Entertainment, MGM, and Starz! Encore Group. The somewhat shy Tian Congming is grazed by the fluttering chiffon dress of a woman with silver butterflies in her hair—British fashion designer Zandra Rhodes.

Worlds were colliding.

Back in Beijing, eyes were being opened. Zhang Hai Tao's speech was just the tip of the iceberg.

Peled, who had grown up in Romania, and until age 13 had no indoor plumbing, marveled at how far electronic "plumbing" was evolving, even in China.

The previous fall, the Chinese government had shown off HDTV broadcasts during its 50th anniversary celebration. The State Administration of Radio, Film and Television's Academy of Broadcasting Science ran a prototype of technology it had developed itself. Foreign technologists, however, like Peled, were betting that it would end up using a standard from Europe, North America, or Japan.

"Because analog broadcasting has occupied virtually all terrestrial channels, we'll begin to transfer analog TV to DTV from standard-definition digital TV broadcasting via cable," Zhang said in Chinese, though the words could have come from the mouths of any number of American broadcasting executives. "That not only will push digitalization of the cable TV network but also will create demand for value-added services, digital TVs, and set-top boxes."

Peled nudged Laurie Smith. "I think they're committed to cable distribution," he said, with feigned naivete. At the time there were some 80 million cable TV subscribers in China, receiving mostly Chinese-produced channels, and a 1.86-million-mile network. The new national, digital cable infrastructure was being rolled out, and local and foreign companies were in a bidding frenzy, hoping to be part of the effort.

The Chinese government viewed television as the most important state and party propaganda organ, and was not about to let it be controlled either by provincial cable systems or distributed freely over a satellite that could tune into any other satellite. Cable, for sure, was preferable. After all, a wire could be cut with a pair of shears; satellite broadcasts—like the Internet—could not be as easily controlled.

Satellite was viewed mostly as a solution for expanding distribution to hard-to-reach rural areas. Currently, China's radio reached more than 90 percent of the population, and nationwide TV broadcast coverage was 91.6 percent in 1999. Government officials viewed satellite mainly as the answer to gaining 100 percent coverage in rural areas, through a satellite broadcast receiver project.

With Murdoch's blessing, NDS had been working in China for a year and a half and was eager to participate in the country's creation of a national system. The Chinese government, through the China Information Network Centre, had invited companies to bid for a conditional-access system, electronic program guide, and software for the first deployment of the backbone distribution system.

Indeed, NDS was playing an increasingly important role in Murdoch's global plans. NDS at the time provided encryption and conditional-access services for 16.8 million subscribers in Europe, Australia, and the Americas. It had a market cap of $3 billion.

A China contract meant potentially huge royalties, and would position News Corp. as gatekeeper to the biggest cable network on the planet—larger than the rest of the world's cable networks combined.

Murdoch and his minions well knew that Microsoft chairman Bill Gates had spent the previous three years maneuvering to make sure digital set-top boxes on a worldwide basis would have at their core a version of the Windows operating system.

With News Corp.'s NDS providing the operating system for China's set-top box, the company would gain economies of scale and marketing clout that could not be challenged.

Control of the set-top box used with the network would also ensure that News Corp. was in a position to control customers' online spending, gather mass marketing data, and win a captive advertising audience whether content was delivered by cable, satellite, or other wireless technologies.

NDS had worked for some time with China's Academy of Broadcasting Sciences, a government laboratory, to develop a Chinese version of the cable-scrambling algorithm. It also had shown its conditional-access system working with the scrambling system, something the Chinese were very interested in given their focus on controlling content, scrambling, and access to individuals on a local basis. It was technology that would give the Chinese the control they wanted. It could lock out particular viewers from seeing particular content.

NDS also had been developing, with national Chinese broadcaster CCTV, a Chinese electronic program guide. The State Radio and Film Administration was establishing the backbone for the national cable system and setting up the information network center that would run that backbone. It would distribute all the national content to the individual provinces, to be passed on to consumers via cable. The Chinese government had invested a substantial amount of money to implement a high-speed network that would accomplish this.

SARFT and the Ministry of Information Industry (MII), China's telecom regulator, were also collaborating with digital TV and set-top box manufacturers to design products that would deliver digital cable and direct satellite broadcasting services. China had adopted a European system as its digital satellite standard, and would soon announce a standard for digital cable using some elements of Europe's digital cable standard.

Peled had hosted Zhang when he first took over his position. The vice minister had been on a tour of the world to understand the capabilities of digital television, and Peled subsequently went to visit him in Beijing. He would return again and again.

The vice minister did not speak English and always talked with an interpreter, but with repetition had developed a relationship with Peled. "You see the same person and you come to understand what drives them," Peled said. That was important.

NDS had to be careful about the touchy subject of News Corporation. NDS's office in Beijing was on the same floor and occupied part of News Corp.'s Beijing office, but had a separate entrance. China was averse to content from the company. "We are careful to position ourselves as a technology supplier and focus on technology rather than on News Corp.," Peled would tell his executives.

Peled saw China as a big and proud country, very focused on doing a lot on its own, "which you have to respect," he would tell his colleagues. "And I think you have to understand those things to be able to have a situation where they feel they get something worthwhile and you can do something worthwhile."

The Chinese media was devoting a lot of space to Internet and technology news. Web access had become almost a status symbol for the growing middle class. Indeed, the most exciting prospect for Murdoch, and every other media giant for that matter, was the rise of the middle class in China.

"Because the way they run the country, there is less disparity between the rich and the poor versus places like India, Indonesia, Malaysia and all these other countries," Peled said.

The people NDS hired in China were paid on average $20,000 to $25,000 a year, "but out of that they have probably $20,000 discretionary income because the cost of living is still geared to people who make $2,000 a year," he explained.

Abe Peled had told Smith of the experience he'd had recently in a trendy, expensive restaurant in London, near NDS's headquarters. Sitting at his table with his dinner companions, he'd glanced around the room, only to find that it was not full of the usual Europeans and Brits. "The place was full of young Chinese, like the guys who work for us, having dinner at $75 per person, which they can afford because they have a higher discretionary income."

His hope was that the rising middle class would also pay for advanced television services.

As his speech continued, Zhang offered his view of how China would raise the money to deploy advanced digital services on a national Chinese cable network. It would allow Western companies to invest in the network, which would in turn subsidize set-top boxes offering new services. In return, the investing companies might be able to participate in revenues from the new services, advertising, and other unidentified programming opportunities.

Peled had noted to his colleagues, "They think they can tap into the Western capital markets."

But Zhang was not done. He began rattling off all the valuations of cable companies in Europe and the United States. He knew everything about the AOL–Time Warner deal, and United Pan-European Communications (UPC), Europe's largest cable company. He knew exactly how each company was valued on a per-subscriber basis.

Peled was astounded. He said, "That's kind of interesting for a person who, two sentences earlier, talked about television broadcasting as a key propaganda organ for the state and party!"

A few weeks later, Peled gazed out across the rooftops of Jerusalem. Satellite dishes dot the rooftops of a group of office buildings in a small industrial park, about a mile from the old city. Looking out, the city is white, and the sun reflects the white Jerusalem stone.

Below, a dozen Chinese technophiles are emerging from cars and entering a building in the Hard Hotzvim neighborhood, one of the "silicon valley" sections of town. Neighboring buildings house research centers for a number of American high-tech companies, including Intel, Compaq, and a smattering of biotech firms.

The group, working for Zhang Hai Tao and SARFT, stroll through the sparkling lobby of the NDS research center. Two of the young Chinese men stop as they pass an Emmy Award prominently on display in a glass case, and bow slightly. NDS is plugged into Hollywood, that much is clear, and the younger generation within SARFT—Murdoch or no Murdoch—is duly impressed.

Gee-whiz demonstrations are provided of all of NDS's interactive television technologies. Just think what it could do for Chinese programming. Come nightfall, the Chinese entourage are taken out for brandy, their favorite non-Chinese drink, and to Jerusalem's top restaurants. The Jerusalem tour lasts a week.

In May 2000, James Murdoch received a phone call. It was Laurie Smith, calling from Beijing. The courtship of the China Information Network Centre had been a rollercoaster ride. Smith and his colleague Sue Taylor for weeks had no idea where NDS stood. Their competitors were also courting the Chinese.

Smith was now animated. The China Information Network Centre had made an announcement that had many foreign media companies flabbergasted.

It had chosen a company that would supply the technology that would be the backbone of the national cable system in China. That company would provide a conditional-access system, electronic program guide, and software for the first deployment of the national system, with the potential of serving 1 billion viewers.

NDS had won the bid. But more hurdles lay ahead.

In Beijing, President Jiang Zemin was searching for a man that he branded as an outlaw. Huang Qi had created an Internet bulletin board for missing people in China, which also featured discussions of democracy and human rights. Huang Qi was eventually arrested.

A few months later, a computer teacher named Jiang Shihua was detained in the southwestern province of Sichuan and charged with subverting state power. He operated the Silicon Valley Internet Cafe in the Sichuan city of Nantong.

A character calling himself "Shumin"—which means "common citizen"—had posted a series of articles that the state considered criminal. Shihua had created the persona in an attempt to protect himself. But he had been found out.

9

ON THE PEAK

In their new house in an exclusive area on The Peak in Hong Kong, James and Kathryn Murdoch one evening in December 2000 discuss the dramatic evolution of new media in little more than four years, since 1997 when their courtship began and when James first joined News Corp. to head up new media. A few days later, they travel to Shanghai together, for a lavish party thrown by Star to celebrate its being awarded a rare license there. The lovebirds are starting their life on a new frontier. James's carefree days barreling down the freeways of Los Angeles are a not-so-distant memory.

Tucked away on The Peak, the breathtaking high point on Hong Kong Island where many of its wealthiest residents reside, it is perhaps not so difficult for James Murdoch to forgive the rougher aspects of mainland China's policies. He concedes it takes a "strong stomach" to do business in this part of the world—like eating "dragon," the delicacy at local restaurants comprised mostly of snake.

A glimpse into the private world of the newest generation of the Murdoch family here in Asia reveals that, as is true for pere Rupert, family life and business are one. James and Kathryn are down-to-earth, likable people who say their favorite place here is "home."

Arriving at the ornate wrought-iron gate that stands out-side the couple's rented house, Kathryn has just been dropped off by her driver from her Cantonese class. She enters the spacious house, and is greeted by a maid who offers tea. The newlywed eagerly awaits her husband's return home.

It is the first week of December 2000, and out a balcony window the fading light over the mountaintops has turned the sun into an orange gem. The rooms are spare and aglow. A carved Chinese screen. A simple couch and table. Book shelves. Rupert and Wendi look out over the living room from a picture frame on one of the shelves; on the opposite side of the book case, there is Anna, James mother, and her new husband, American financier William Mann.

James apologizes in advance to prospective guests, "Our house isn't that fancy."

Sydney is leaping for joy. Sydney the Entelbucher, that is. James and Kathryn's Swiss mountain dog, who, in order to accompany them on this sojourn, went through weeks in captivity (while Kathryn spent weeks on paperwork). Finally, an identification chip placed under his skin provided him with proper credentials to become a canine ex-pat living in Hong Kong.

A magazine photographer is to arrive shortly to capture the couple at home, and golden-haired Kathryn, wearing a pair of black slacks, a sweater, and no makeup, takes a seat on a small living room couch.

She laughs, remembering her early courtship with James in 1977, when she lived in Australia. They both had become keenly interested in developing Internet-based businesses. "Everyone commented that suddenly James had a lot of busi-ness in Australia," she says, chuckling. At the time, James was liv-ing in New York and had just begun working for News Corp. in new media. The two had a long-distance courtship for awhile, but Kathryn had been pondering moving back to the states.

After meeting James, the choice was easy, she says. In late 1997, Kathryn moved to New York and worked for *Gear* magazine for awhile, before working in PR at a publicity company. It was a hot time for Internet companies; the president of the PR company launched fashionwiredaily.com, and Kathryn for awhile was doing two jobs, handling PR for the Internet startup as well.

"I found out I was more interested in marketing, and the Internet thing came along, and it was a huge opportunity," she says. "It was exciting to be part of all that. It just took off. I was working crazy hours, and in the middle of New York. It was great, a lot of fun." James likewise was focusing intensely on Internet businesses at the time, at his job as head of News America Digital Media.

Since that time, of course, the dot-com bubble has burst. But James cut his teeth at his father's empire, guiding the mammoth's way into new media ventures.

James and his bride had come a long way from the time he headed up News America Digital Publishing, the predecessor to News Digital Media. James came to the company fold in 1997; prior to that, he had worked as a part-time intern for the company as early as 1993, while he was still at Harvard, doing design work and screen savers for some of the earliest Internet applications.

Screen savers were a big deal in those days prior to the explosion of the Internet. They were viewed to be "supercool," he said, and in fact James had brainstormed with his friend Matt Jacobsen, a senior vice president of the News Technology Group, for a way to create a screen saver that would also provide weather reports, horoscopes, news, stock quotes, and all types of personalized information to your computer screen. In essence, he'd invented Pointcast, but never acted upon it. Two years later, News Corp. would make a failed bid to buy Pointcast. The company would reject Murdoch's offer, only to later sell the company for a tiny fraction of what he'd offered.

In his early days at News Corp., James had an office in Los Angeles as president of News America Digital Publishing. Like his father, he'd commute between offices in New York and L.A., and loved letting loose on the California freeways behind the wheel of his 1976 Cadillac Eldorado convertible, which had originally been owned by his uncle. (He loved old cars. He also had a 1960s Alfa Romeo.)

Just four years later, in 2001, his life was markedly different, punctuated by state dinners with the likes of Jiang Zemin. Clearly, his freewheeling days were over, and even his closest friends—and his wife—remarked at the difference. "His creativity goes into work now," said Kathryn.

James appears slightly embarrassed when reminded of his former adventures. One occasion during his first year at News Corp., driving at an ungodly speed between Los Angeles and Laguna, California, where he was due to give a speech at an entertainment technology conference, was legendary. The wind was blasting through James's hair and that of his two colleagues seated beside him in the front seat, one his public relations expert and the other a News Technology Group executive vice president. James didn't drive much in Manhattan, so hitting the open road was always a blast.

That time, it was a three-ring circus. With cell phone in one hand, cars dodging all about him, wind blowing, he was being interviewed by the *Los Angeles Times* but could barely hear a word, and the phone kept cutting out. Next to him, his publicist was helping him redo the speech he was about to give.

When he finally made it before his audience, the young Murdoch launched into his tirade, cursing joyfully and profusely, and describing many of the efforts of old media companies as "bullshit."

Yet, he and his colleagues described what they were doing

at News Corp. back then as "triage," as they attempted to fix some of the old empire's missteps during its fledgling forays into digital media. Amazingly enough, back in 1994 Rupert Murdoch had acquired the online service Delphi at a time when it had more subscribers than AOL.

At the time that News Corp. was attempting to make a go of it with Delphi, traditional media companies thought the Internet was a technology business, not a media business. So they brought in technologists to run it. In the end, it was a lesson for Murdoch to stick with his strengths. Around the same time, even Hollywood's Creative Artists Agency hired AT&T's Robert Kavner to head up its online entertainment endeavors. He was eventually booted out when it was clear that he—a technologist at heart—hadn't a clue about the entertainment business.

Likewise, Murdoch had hired a technologist from IBM to run Delphi, as though it were making widgets. Murdoch and other News Corp. executives realized after the fact that that was like having the guy who runs the presses run a newspaper. It was a ridiculous prospect.

Like his father, James also had great irreverence for the established media. In Cannes, France, shortly after he joined the company, he was at Milia, the high-tech conference. James sat jet-lagged at the Majestic Hotel with another News Corp. executive.

At 2 A.M., the two executives watched Lou Dobbs on *Moneyline.* Dobbs was talking about a recently announced alliance between Yahoo! and Fox as if it were a grand alliance, the Fox logo and the Yahoo! logo emblazoned dramatically on the television screen. The deal, in fact, had been nothing but an advertising pact, no big deal really.

James turned to his colleague and burst out laughing; it was an ongoing joke how the media always missed the boat. "We better go gamble," he said, and the two headed for the blackjack tables at the nearby Carlton.

Both of Rupert Murdoch's sons had an intuitive feel for the media that they seemed to have inherited from their father. James was known by his colleagues for his habit, first thing in the morning, of reading all the newspapers he could get his hands on before starting work. It was a cathartic experience. It always had to be the physical paper in his hands, despite his digerati status. It was a custom both sons had observed in their father, as though the feel and texture of newsprint was an original event in their lives—which, of course, it was—as well as a tactile experience that launched them into every other reality that unfolded each day.

James never would have landed in Hong Kong working for his father at all, if it had not been for pere Rupert's urgent pleas in 1997, after he'd failed in an attempted Internet venture with MCI. That failure moved him to convince his youngest son that his skills were urgently needed at the company.

Anthea Disney, executive vice president of News Corp., headed up iGuide, a Yahoo-like portal Murdoch hoped would—in conjunction with Delphi—become a platform for all manner of News Corp. content, as part of the failed MCI venture. MCI would provide the "access" component, and a database of millions of potential subsribers.

Scott Kurnit, chairman of About.com, who headed up the News Corp.–MCI joint venture at the time, says, "Rupert had the vision and the commitment. He's smart, and got the 'net very quickly and understood it. I remember in our first meeting when we started talking about what the product would be, he was a quick study and very engaging. We sat around a table of computers and looked through the Web together. It's not accurate that he only recently got the Internet and bailed out fast. Rupert had a vision for it before the market recognized it. He bought Delphi early, it was a savvy buy, and relatively inexpensive."

According to Kurnit, the MCI joint venture did not pan

out because, unbeknownst to News Corp., MCI was preparing itself to be acquired, it was not putting up its end of the financial investments, and its interests were only short-term. The deal fell apart when MCI formed a separate joint venture with Microsoft in 1996. "It didn't pan out because partnerships are hard," Kurnit says. "But at the time it was a good move. Had that stuck together, he would have had himself a major asset."

James and his father hope the second inning of the "Internet game" will be different. So do other media executives. Says Kurnit, "The linkage to traditional media companies at least in the first inning of the Internet has not been all that powerful. If you have the wherewithal and the model to run a business in a soft economy, you're going to really be well positioned when it brightens, and we know it always does."

For News Corp. and other media companies that were still in the investment mode of these businesses, there were tough decisions: They needed to balance short-term cash use and investment against the long-term rewards. The markets turn sour quite quickly, in terms of the value the world places on both an Internet company and on the ad market in general. Media companies are ad-supported companies by definition. While ads on the Internet made perfect sense, it was still early, and the ad models hadn't been fully defined. There was still optimism that they would be.

Traditional media companies would either buy their way into digital media businesses, or they'd create from scratch. They've been more successful buying than building because the culture of Internet companies has been very different from traditional media companies—faster and more aggressive, and far less risk-averse.

Nevertheless, for the first generation of Internet applications, Anthea Disney said James "helped his father understand those new media opportunities in ways that enhance the company. He was quick to understand it, he's part of the generation that grew up using the Internet, his father wasn't. His father had to learn it. He played quite a role in that."

James was also the first to say, however, "if we can't figure out how to make money on this, we have to limit how much we spend."

It took some convincing to get his younger son to leave his job at Rawkus Entertainment, the hip-hop record company he had launched with a few of his high school friends after dropping out of Harvard. Rupert eventually bought the company, once James agreed to work for him instead. He'd managed to convince his son that he was taking electronic media seriously.

"I didn't want to initially. I thought, well, I've got a job," says James. "But then it seemed like a good thing to do and we managed to put Rawkus together with this company we had in Australia for like 30 years, Festival Records. So I had to look at that as well, and take on a variety of projects. That was pretty interesting, so I said yes."

While heading up News America Digital Publishing, those who worked with James say he was still an artist at heart, known for doodling caricatures of other executives during business meetings. He oversaw the creation of Internet sites for many News companies, including Fox Sports.com, Foxnews.com, and Fox.com on a global basis.

Those who worked for James enjoyed him and also knew that, like his father, he did not suffer fools gladly. You had to be on your game. Those who didn't survive or disliked News Corp. were usually those who were "political." Current and former executives say that, surprisingly, News Corp. was not a political place. It was entrepreneurial. Talent succeeded.

Others, however, reported if pere Rupert intensely disliked the results of a project aesthetically, one could be fired. (In the spring of 2000, for example, Bill Mechanic, the former head of Fox Film, left his position allegedly because Rupert was disgusted and infuriated by his film *Fight Club*. He personally found it repulsive.)

Nevertheless, other media companies often had narrow career paths their executives would walk down. Said one former Disney executive who worked for Murdoch for years, "At Disney, it's like you're an electrician. You're told 'stay within the plumbing.' I was a TV guy, and that's all I did. It was like 'shut up and row.' And at News Corp. you do what you do, but you can do a little of this and a little of that, and your ideas can have an impact all over the place."

Executives described receiving a "psychic income" from the place: the creativity and lessons learned from the entrepreneurial attitude that permeated the company.

What's more, each of the Murdochs had their preferred source for a "pure information stream," as one News Corp. insider put it. Rupert relied on his top man, Peter Chernin, who had worked for him for thirty years, as well as the word of James and Lachlan. He trusted them implicitly, despite the youth of his sons.

James proved to be prescient on many occasions. In the early days of the Internet, James promoted the value of integrated media sales, not just using the company's inventory on television to promote web sites, but actually selling things together, creating cross-media platforms and building convergence.

In 2000, those were all buzzwords, but upon James arrival at News Corp. in early 1997, no one was doing it. James recognized early on that the Internet on its own would never be a business; it was part of the business. He used to say that just because in Australia and in Britain News Corp. owned trucks, it didn't mean it was in the trucking business.

The Internet was a distribution tool, a way to get media

from one place to another. The medium, however, was also the message, as Marshall McLuhan said. It would also create opportunities for completely different forms of expression.

Some of James's physical habits were almost a metaphor for how he and his family went about life. One of the first things that mystified his colleagues when James first set himself up in his Los Angeles office as president of News America Digital Publishing was the rate at which the man would go through shoelaces. It was as though every day was a long-distance trek through rough terrain, so that he was barely able to keep his shoes on his feet.

One of the first things he had said to his secretary was, "You have to have enough shoelaces here for me. I want you to stock up on shoelaces." A News executive who was one of his closest friends would laugh and puzzle over this, out loud, to his friend. "Who blows through shoelaces?" he would ask. Nevertheless, James never had enough, and would often send out for a pair. For whatever reason, he tied his shoelaces with a vengeance, causing them to break in his hands.

James, unlike most of his generation who seemed to prefer wearing jeans and gym shoes to work, loved beautiful clothes. One of his father's executives introduced him to "the Prada lifestyle." In Hong Kong, James had all sorts of exotic suits made for himself.

Those who worked with James since his early days at News Corp. were impressed by his loyalty and esprit de corps. He stuck by them, whether things were going good or bad. He was willing to take a punch for someone else if things were tough, and often gave credit to other people for accomplishments. "It was a sign of security, and it's rare in business, and it's superrare in the media business," said one former News Corp. executive. "A lot of people will hang out and see how things are going with their finger in the air to see which way the wind is blowing before they commit to anything. They don't want to take the fall if things don't go well. Not James. That was a function of the integrity of his father, and the family, and the history of the company."

Both sons, James and Lachlan, had an intimate understanding and appreciation for the business their grandfather had started. Work was part of the rhythm of their lives. Other News executives were known to get a phone call every day of the week from James, even on Sundays.

Lachlan, very supportive of his brother, says James's performance has been stellar, pointing out that the dismantling of News Digital Media and unloading of Web MD—two earlier efforts of James's—were more a reflection of changes in the market that were affecting all media companies. Lachlan says, for example, his brother's vision about Gemstar's strategic value was prescient.

The pact between News Corp. and Gemstar TV Guide had come about after pere Rupert sold TV Guide, initially not recognizing its value in an electronic television world. James pushed the strategic value of the interface when paired with the powerful electronic patents owned by Gemstar.

Still, contrary to the young Murdoch's earlier vision, Rupert had always felt that content-driven sites that relied solely on advertising for revenue were not viable businesses.

Instead, James's father saw the Internet as a great distribution vehicle, "but couldn't figure out how to get the revenue out of it." Anthea Disney mused over the predicament: "When it's clear there's no way to monetize it and Wall Street does not appreciate it, and when he's having a hard time figuring out what the business model is, then he says let's slow down, let's wait till we can figure out what the business model is. Undoubtedly when we do figure out what the business model is, that will be when he 'gets it' again."

Vladimir Edelman, a former program development executive at News Digital Media and current chairman of New York—based Filter Media, has worked for all of the networks at one time or another, but notes that News Corp.—despite being in the media for scaling back its Internet ventures—was way ahead of the game, in a world where digital media is the "red-headed stepchild," and getting resources to start new media businesses is like pulling teeth.

Edelman says that during his time there, James was regarded as "a smart and aggressive guy, very sharp about digital media." Employees, after meeting him, did not ever feel he was in his job "just because of family ties."

"He was very single-minded in his mission," Edelman says. "The family is amazingly driven and focused, and you never see derisiveness. It was a great place to work." Edelman left to form his own company, Filter Media, a strategic consultancy for interactive television.

"Overall, News Corp. was probably the most flexible and aggressive company I worked for," Edelman says. "But they faced the inability in the short term to monetize what they're doing, like many new media endeavors."

Needless to say, James was not then the polished executive he is today. At one 1997 event in Los Angeles, according to one former News Corp. executive, James spoke of the role of media and described as "bullshit" the "sacred Internet cows" that had suddenly become the darling of the media world.

Still, while soft-spoken and even shy in personal encounters, before industry audiences James remains wildly expressive, creative and outspoken. While still making public comments that often cause outrage, he says he regrets comments he made during a speech in Edinburgh, Scotland, the previous summer, during the Edinburgh International Television Festival (a conference his father often used to attend), criticizing the business of rival Richard Li, mostly because of the ruckus made of his comments in the press.

"PCCW . . . is arguably the worst offender of paying lip service to the notion of globalism," James had said. "I fail to understand how one can define a free-to-air, English language rehash of circa-1980 MTV as a global multimedia-broadband-interactive-TV service."

During the Edinburgh speech, James asserted that other media companies did not recognize the importance of offering local programming in the four dominant language groups—Mandarin, English, Spanish, and Hindi. Star, on the other hand, was now broadcasting in seven different languages to more than 53 countries. It produced and commissioned 11,000 hours of original programming in India and 9,000 hours of Chinese programming. James still does not believe that English will be the universal language of the future. "Apparently Mr. Li still hasn't learned these lessons, producing English language programming out of England for supposedly core markets in India, Japan and China," James said. He applauded, on the other hand, Spanish telecom giant Telefonica, which built bridges to Latin America and branched out into English through the merger of its Internet arm Terra Networks and Lycos. (Kathryn, who is turning out to be his best personal PR person, says the media seized on a few sentences of James's out of everything he said in a 45-minute speech.)

A few days later, Richard Li fired off some salvos of his own. His managing director Alex Arena told an audience of 200 business executives at the Credit Suisse First Boston Technology conference in Hong Kong, "There seem to be some people who think PCCW operates with one facility and in one language." Of course, "some people" was James Murdoch.

Like his father, James seemed to have a propensity for agitating his competitors to compete more aggressively. "As those who know anything about our company are aware, that's not true," Arena said, adding that the company planned on focusing programming on local markets, and "English is the world language and that's what we are using initially."

As far as his own language is concerned, James is baffled at reports that he speaks in profanities, and cannot recall ever doing so. "I don't know where that came from, it's bad," he says. "Somebody said I was vulgar. And I thought that wasn't very nice." Indeed, those close to him note that in the course of a week, both in formal and informal conversations, in person and on the phone, he was observed to have cursed only once—and self-consciously—during a discussion of the press's reaction to News Corp.'s announcement that it was cutting back News Digital Media. "Reporters who are saying oh they fucked that up . . . were the same reporters who two months before were saying we weren't spending enough," he had said, and then paused to note, "there you go, that was profanity." He then laughed.

Since moving to Hong Kong in 2000, Kathryn and James have not seen family members as often as they used to, though Anna Murdoch, on her return from the Sydney Olympics, had stayed with the couple in their new house. James had informed his assistant at Star TV to cancel all his appointments because "Mom is in town," and had even turned down a meeting with the head of Taiwan's Gigamedia, who had called on him that week, and with whom he had just completed a mammoth partnership. James was quite devoted to his mother, and spoke of her glowingly and with much admiration.

Those close to him say that James is also very protective of his mother, making sure that there is no thought of comparing her to his new stepmother, Wendi, though he says his relationship with Wendi is strong and "solid."

Wendi had also visited James and Kathryn at their new home, while on a trip to China. Rupert and his wife would not arrive until after the New Year. His plans to visit in late summer had been canceled due to his cancer treatments.

Kathryn does not remember exactly when she met Wendi, but it was after James's parents had separated, she says. "The whole year was a blur for me. My mother passed away the same year the Murdochs got divorced. It all sort of happened at once."

According to Kathryn, the Murdochs are an astonishingly close-knit family, even after Rupert and Anna's divorce. Though competition may be high, those close to the clan—including Kathryn—say jealousy and backbiting are rare, despite mythology in the press regarding the succession wars.

Kathryn indeed was surprised at the closeness and loyalty of Murdoch family members, and had originally approached meeting the clan with trepidation.

In the summer of 1997, when Rupert and Anna Murdoch were still together, Kathryn was invited to meet the family during a 10-day sail around Australia's Great Barrier Reef, aboard Rupert's yacht *Morning Glory*.

Kathryn had been nervous about the prospect of meeting Rupert, she had read so much about him. And she faced being held captive aboard ship for ten days. "It's a good thing we got along really well," Kathryn laughs. "I had so many preconceived notions, especially about what James's father was going to be like. I was terrified. And he was such a nice guy. That's when I started learning 'don't believe everything you read'!"

Kathryn dismisses rumors that Rupert Murdoch's chauvinism stymied his daughter Elisabeth's ambitions. Regarding James's "father's attitude towards women," she says, "while he is Australian and of an older generation, I have never known him to disregard someone because of gender (or race, for that matter). He makes immediate, instinct-based decisions about people that are entirely of his own judgment, not society's."

Kathryn adds that to get attention in the Murdoch clan, one must be "a little pushy." She says, "One of the first things I learned when joining this family was that if I wanted to get heard in a discussion, I needed to say my piece quickly, efficiently, loudly and with the conviction and ability to back it up. Even wildly different viewpoints, and we all happily disagree about politics, etc., will be heard if presented well, but conversely, anyone in the office or at dinner too timid or irrational or with bad timing will be drowned out.

"I also note that neither Anna nor Wendi are the purely decorative women that one might expect. They are both intelligent, strong and informed—things a male chauvinist does not want in a wife. As far as Liz is concerned, she is battling what all working mothers battle: the war between your job and your children for your limited time. Putting in those long hours with three small children is extremely difficult, and while I think the family were all sad to see her change careers, we understand how hard it is," she says.

James and Kathryn had been moved into their house for only a couple of months, and Kathryn, though very busy getting settled, at times wondered what she would do with herself. She also missed James fiercely when not traveling with him.

"There are actually a lot of people in similar positions, where they came out for a great job, and the wife has given up her job wherever she was. And so she's like, OK, what do I do with myself now? Some people come up with some great exciting careers, and it seems a lot of people get pregnant actually," she says.

James's Mom on her visit had actually been encouraging the latter. "She's definitely cheering for that," says Kathryn, who seems a little more eager at the thought of a fascinating career—at least for the moment. (A few weeks after our interview, Kathryn landed a job as a marketing executive with the Hong Kong office of Louis Vuitton Moet Hennessy, the French luxury goods company.)

"James is romantic in the classic sense of the word," Kathryn confides, her eyes sparkling mischievously. "He's romantic as a husband of course, but there's a much bigger part of his personality that is romantic."

She goes on. "He loves to wear—and loves the *idea* of—seersucker suits, a Panama hat, and a mint julep," she says dreamily.

His sense of wonder of the world at first startled her, she says, and threw light on the general cynicism of their generation. "If you think anyone was going to be jaded or cynical or worldly or whatever, that it would be him. It was always something I was so impressed with when we first met."

Her recent unemployment, with the move to Hong Kong, allowed Kathryn to accompany James on his business trips for the first time. "It's been such a treat the last few months to be able to travel with him, because I was never able to do that before when I was working all the time," she says. Otherwise, his intense schedule is sometimes hard to take. "It is hard, when he was coming out here January till June basically before our wedding, he'd be here three weeks and then back in the states, and that was really hard, especially when you're planning a wedding."

The doorbell rings, and James has arrived home. There is

much leaping from Sydney's direction. James then turns to introduce himself to the magazine photographer, who has been waiting patiently to do his photo shoot with James.

Kathryn is talking quietly to her husband now, her hand on his shoulder. The photographer is getting restless as the spectacular light on the balcony is slowly fading.

In the first several months at Star, James, with the help of his stepmother, had aggressively nailed investment opportunities in mainland China and Indian Internet portals and services companies, including netease.com, renren.com, and indya.com.

He had also completed a round of successful meetings with government officials at Beijing's State Council and Information Office, and at China's State Administration of Radio, Film and Television, in an effort to encourage Shanghai officials to allow Star to open a film studio and sales office there.

Though James was achieving a lot (his brother Lachlan considered his activities to be "very aggressive"), like his brother he was still only a CEO in training; nothing could have been achieved without Rupert providing the opening sally in a one-two punch. James was following up on deals both Rupert and his wife Wendi had set in motion months before, in both China and India.

Deng is useful, James agrees, though not as useful, he is quick to point out, as some have tried to portray. "I mean, she's in New York and she spent most of the summer in California with my father who was undergoing his cancer treatment," James said. "It's a good relationship, we worked together on some of these things and she has a lot of insight into the market."

Bruce Churchill, who had hired Wendi as a summer intern between her first and second year at Yale School of Management, says, "Certainly she has been involved in some of the work we've been doing in China. Again it comes down to a little bit about Chinese understanding of the family and the importance of the family in the business. There's nothing sinister about it." Still insiders say that having Wendi in the middle also caused some communication problems for James.

"To be honest, having Wendi can be helpful and it can be an added complexity. It's helpful in that she speaks the language and people will say things to her that they might not otherwise say because of the language and the human connection and the fact she's a member of the Murdoch family," the insider said. "The unhelpful part can be of course that she then has a direct line to the chief executive of the company. And I think it creates problems for James because sometimes conversations are going on about the China business that are really Star business but they are going on back in L.A. with Rupert and it doesn't all get communicated properly. It does cut both ways and that's just something we have to manage."

While most News Corp. employees and senior executives responded well to his arrival at his new job, James acknowledges that on occasion he has been treated rudely by those who seem to be thinking, "You got where you are just because you're a Murdoch."

Says James, "Yeah. Some people might have that attitude. That's why it's important to stay as centered and buttoned-down as possible and try and do good work. You have to earn respect, and hopefully you can do that more times than you can't do that."

Most mere mortals will never know what "going to work" means for a Murdoch. James acknowledges not only the challenges of his job, but the difficulties—and benefits—of being a Murdoch. The crossover between family life and business life has always been evident. "That," he insists, "has been a good thing."

He is familiar with, but brushes off, the notion that some on Wall Street view him and his brother as upstarts. "I think it's pretty obvious what my job is and what I have to do. If I can't do it, people probably won't like me, ya know?" he says, and then laughs, musing over the scrutiny he is receiving. "But if I can do a good job I'll be fine. So I don't really worry about that stuff."

He is far from indifferent, however, about how he is being evaluated. One of the first things he says during an interview is, "I hope no one is saying anything bad about me." And who can blame him?

His father Rupert has been the subject of much bad press over the years—especially in the United Kingdom—though he has heaped his share of it on others via his numerous newspaper and television properties around the world. (James points out that some of this is because, unlike other large companies, his father—until very recently—never bothered to appoint a public relations executive for News Corp., so "wrong information" never got corrected and was spread in the media for years.)

Still, like his father, James responds to inaccurate and critical press reports with humor. In London, when the *Observer* wrote hostile accounts of his father, Rupert was known to throw the paper on the floor and burst into gales of laughter, exclaiming "the bastards!"

James likewise laughed over a "very inaccurate" article that appeared one November morning in 2000 in the *South China Morning Post*. The article, among other things, depicted him and archrival Richard Li as sumo wrestlers, pasting their heads on the rotund bodies. Kathryn found "at least 12" factual errors in the article. James, self-deprecating as usual, grins ear to ear and says, "the only thing they got right was the body!" (James is handsome and fit, though apparently not to the degree he'd like to be.)

Are you dressed? Are you going to wear that?" Kathryn whispers to James.

There is no time to change. "I was just told as soon as possible," James replies.

As the photographer, a compact British fellow, urges the couple to the balcony and the red cinder that is the last remains of the sun, Kathryn says to her husband, "Sydney is being unbelievably bad."

"Really?" James asks, staring at Sydney. "He's being unbelievably bad?"

"Well, he just can't handle not being the center of attention at all," says Kathryn.

James Murdoch does not seem to like being the center of attention.

When you ask him to talk about himself, his eyes turn downward and he changes the subject. He wonders why anyone would want to know about the Murdochs' personal lives and opinions, and prefers talking about business.

Photos make him particularly uncomfortable, and Kathryn has taken to tickling him to get him to lighten up. While the photographer adjusts his lighting, the couple begin whispering to each other, and James becomes animated, telling his wife about a "$22 million contract" he has in the works. They have melted into each other, Kathryn snuggling against him on a divan with a Chinese carved canopy. Everyone else in the room has apparently disappeared.

The photographer begins shooting frantically and James breaks the spell, looking up, exasperated. "Is it over yet?" he asks. Kathryn frowns at him. He smiles at her and says, "I won't be rude."

"I told you, it's not glamorous, it's boring," Kathryn, a former model, says to her husband. "Now you'll believe me." This is one of the first times that the lens has been turned on James. And it's just the beginning.

Beginning with his taking the helm at Star in 2000, the business world has been keeping an eye on James Murdoch.

On a Tuesday morning in early December 2000, Shanghai is bathed in smog, giving a soft impressionist quality to its futuristic-looking skyscrapers that city officials now proudly brag outnumber Hong Kong's.

Not far from the Bund, Shanghai's downtown riverfront famous for its 1920s- and 1930s-style architecture, a ballroom at the city's new Grand Hyatt is becoming packed.

James is in the midst of a lavish party, being teased by a dancing Chinese dragon, a spectacle staged to please more than two dozen government officials and hundreds of local business executives who'd shown up to toast the young Murdoch for his activities in the media market on the mainland. The Chinese guests stand agape when James enters the room, and nudge forward to get closer to him. He moves through the room shaking hands and conversing with the ease of a film star.

James gets up on stage to speak before the crowd, and he is as smooth as a Hollywood celebrity, speaking clearly and dramatically, completely at ease as if he's been doing this for years. (This is surprising, given that, on a personal basis, he is soft-spoken and even shy.)

Afterward, looking very relaxed in his conservative gray suit, James—with Kathryn at his side—works the room with many handshakes and photos with Chinese film studio heads and government policy makers. Images of Gillian Anderson, Sean Connery, and other Fox stars are flashing across a huge video screen before the rapt audience. Rupert Murdoch flashes by, shaking hands with Chinese president Jiang Zemin, and there are whispers of "Murdoch" in the crowd. James and Kathryn have a kiss.

In recent months, having the "son of the owner" at the top of Star has proved to be a boon rather than a detriment.

"I think putting James in has been smart on a couple of levels: One, it has shown the company's level of attention and commitment to Star in the sense that it's now very much on the radar screen. Also, putting in anyone else but James would have been 'here we go again,' " said a top ranking Star executive.

Indeed, there is a buzz about "Rupert Murdoch's son."

Amid the company fete celebrating Star's becoming the first and only foreign media company to be awarded a license to operate here, the petite Madame Jaio Yang stands demurely in a dark blue suit. She is vice director of the Shanghai Municipal City Information Office, and, along with other high-ranking local officials—the watchdogs when it comes to the presence of foreign business—sports a corsage on her lapel, a gift presented by the young James. It is a flattering formality much appreciated at honorary meetings in greater China.

Says Madame Jaio, after toasting James before the crowd, "James Murdoch in Shanghai is a great thing. He and Star TV will help build the media industry here, and he has honored our culture and traditions."

It was a startling gesture, given that a little more than a year earlier, Rupert Murdoch was still viewed in many areas of Asia as a Western devil, his endeavors demonized to the point that one hotel proprietor stationed an armed guard outside of Rupert's room to prevent his illustrious guest from being murdered. ("I don't think I need a guard," Murdoch said. "Sometimes you're traveling and local managers overreact, they think they have a visiting head of state and they put in armed guards and things, which is very embarrassing.")

In China, James is far more than just an extension of his father, say observers. His colleagues say that due to many changes around the country, James is much better suited than his father to communicate with the young guard occupying government offices these days.

Says Laurie Smith, "There's actually an easier communication there than you'd expect. There are local, born-and-bred entrepreneurs in their late twenties and early thirties, and James connects with them."

In September, after formal meetings in Shanghai, James was taken on a whirlwind tour of electronic media, visiting station chiefs at Shanghai TV, newspapers, and radio, all who were about his own age. "He had a lot more in common with these people than he expected," Smith says.

James's natural inquisitiveness has served him well in China, say his colleagues. "James is interested and engaged in the local culture. He wants to get behind everything, to read and talk and hear about what lies behind the businesses here and the people. He always wants to get a better understanding," Smith says.

Local Shanghai businesspeople report that while Rupert Murdoch's visits these days are treated like "a state visit, he is so admired," James is more on the same level of young entrepreneurs and officials flourishing since Jiang Zemin's restructuring of the country's ministries.

"He has different skills than his father," says Gary Walrath, senior vice president at Star. "His father is ambassadorial when he meets with important people here and discusses the big issues. James gets into the detail, knows the minute details of the business, and is a risk taker."

News Corp.'s Star TV being awarded a license to open an office in Shanghai was "another milestone in the march toward legitimacy," said Bruce Churchill, Star president.

Star had yet another "win" around the same time, but this time it decided the investment was not worth proceeding further.

Ironically, though Star had actually won a pay-TV license in Hong Kong—where the market was much different than it was on the mainland—in late November 2000, after much internal debate, it decided not to use the license after all.

The broadcasting industry in Hong Kong was finally being deregulated. It had been a monopoly, and when, more than a year earlier, the government had been in the process of issuing new licenses, Star applied for one.

Since that time so many other opportunities had come along, in Taiwan and India, that Star had backed off in Hong Kong. It also was not as attractive a market, given that some five other licenses had been awarded, and the size of the market was not large enough to support that many competitors, in Star's estimation.

In addition, Hong Kong was a Cantonese-language market. If Star was going to invest in Cantonese-language programming, it would be difficult to justify the cost, over the small base of two million homes in Hong Kong.

"In reality, Star would do it only if it believed it had a good shot at, within a reasonable time period, being able to sell that service to other parts of Southern China," said Churchill.

While Mandarin was generally the language on the mainland, just over the border from Hong Kong, large populations in Southern China all speak Cantonese. In fact, the market was huge, estimated by Star to consist of 40 million homes, as compared to the two million in Hong Kong.

The attraction had been to migrate a business that was Hong Kong–based to Southern China. The question was, was it necessary to launch a Hong Kong business immediately in order to take advantage of that opportunity? Star decided it wasn't, and would apply later for another license.

191

In early December, it announced to the public that it would not use its Hong Kong license, to much surprise from the media. James Murdoch and others declined to comment on their decision.

Compared to the enormous immediate successes it was having in India and on the mainland in recent months, the Hong Kong opportunity looked less exciting.

Indeed, the market in India was opening up so rapidly, News Corp. and Star could barely keep up.

10

RUPERT AND RUPEES

In India, as in China, the media business was a protected industry, and ter-
restrial broadcasters were all government-owned. Although there still
remained strict regulations regarding foreign ownership, the pay-TV market
was exploding and opening up far more quickly than that in China. Once
again, the mythology and paranoia about Rupert Murdoch was larger than
life. An outspoken guest on a Star-broadcast Indian talk show inadvertently
outraged some viewers, inspiring an arrest warrant to be issued against the
man who was held responsible for beaming in such programming: Rupert
Murdoch. But India was an unpredictable place, and while one county
labeled the media mogul an outlaw and fugitive, Prime Minister Vajpayee
was inviting him as his guest to the palace. By 2001, by tailoring new Hindi
programming to local tastes, Murdoch managed to ascend to become the
number one broadcaster in the country.

ince taking the helm at Star in the spring of 2000,
James had been visiting India every six weeks, which
meant a "regular inflow of James's input," a very powerful ingredient catalyzing all the diverse activities in which
the company was engaged in India.

The broadcast industry in India was very young, and the
government was quite cautious about the level of foreign own-

ership they would allow. James found the place more unpredictable than mainland China.

Nevertheless, liberalization was going on throughout the economy, and the media was getting rougher treatment than some other industries. Peter Mukerjea, chief executive of Star TV India, said, "It's historically been a protected industry, with the terrestrial broadcasters owned by the government." The ownership and control of television by the government was similar to the situation in China.

The groundwork for James's surprising success with Star in India had actually been laid by a risky tour Rupert Murdoch had undertaken during the spring of 2000.

He had not been in the country at all for four years, and it had changed dramatically in that time. India had viewed Murdoch as a threat, and there were court cases against News Corp., by "people who had a particular axe to grind as far as News Corp. was concerned," according to Mukerjea.

Indeed, the trouble started back in the summer of 1995, when an arrest warrant was issued for Murdoch by a Bombay magistrate, making the media mogul personally responsible for an off-the-wall comment made by a guest on a program broadcast by Star. The man had insulted the most revered of all Indians, Mahatma Gandhi. Murdoch's bail had been set at just 100 pounds.

The program, beamed in from Hong Kong, was a racy chat show known as *Nikky Tonight,* which usually featured gossip about the Bombay film industry. The guest, Ashok Row Kavi, was a gay activist and well-known Bombay gadfly.

On a program that aired May 4th of 1995, hostess Nikki Bedi egged Kavi on to repeat comments he'd made years earlier in the press, calling Gandhi "a bastard bania." Gandhi indeed was a *bania,* a Hindu born into the merchant caste. But the word denoted miser and wheeler-dealer, which was absurd as peasant Gandhi was unconcerned about money. The hostess laughed as if it were a salacious joke. The show was inane, but by chance a great-grandson of Gandhi happened to be channel-surfing when he came upon the remarks.

Once Mr. Gandhi voiced his objections, a firestorm of outrage ensued. Parliament denounced hostess Bedi as well as Star TV, with some demanding that it be banned from India. What's more, some Indians already felt under siege by Western culture, with shows like *Baywatch,* distributed by Murdoch, and MTV being pumped in and attracting large audiences.

Star took the show off the air and apologized. But the show's producer, Bedi, and Kavi were wanted by the police and forced to leave the country. An arrest warrant for Murdoch was also issued.

By late 1998, a Delhi magistrate was still trying to have Murdoch arrested. He ordered a list of Murdoch's assets and properties in India be drawn up, in a move to have them attached and sealed. Murdoch, who was clueless, was being charged with distributing obscene movies—*Big Bad Mamma, Dance of the Damned,* and *Stripped to Kill*—which were big hits all over Asia at the same time they were being shown in India. Murdoch had no idea what the movies were, or that they were being shown. They were standard fare in Asia. But the witchhunt was on again, and more warrants were issued for his arrest.

Indeed, India watchers noted that if the country's Indecent Representation of Women's Act were to be applied uniformly, not a single Hindi or any other Indian-language movie would ever make it to the big screen. Indian movies often displayed Indian women being chased, fondled, and raped—and often sadistically. There had been objections, but never so vehemently as when Murdoch happened to be distributing them.

CNN founder Ted Turner, who is said to despise Murdoch and resent his global expansion worldwide, at the time laughed gleefully over these developments. "If he steps off the plane in India he's goin' straight to jail," Turner guffawed, getting a huge kick out of the image. "Jeez, they got a sub-poena out for him—an' they don't have one out for me."

Turner had an ethical sense that was homegrown. "Own-ership should be restricted to locals—even if they are bums. It's better to have a local bum, then at least you can do some-thing to him if he steps out of line—like spit on him, or punch him in the nose," he said. "But if he's holed up in California, like Murdoch, you can't get near him. The Indian govern-ment can't even lock him up, because they can't catch him and he won't come to India."

By September, India's foreign ministry told a local court that it could not bring Murdoch to trial on obscenity charges in India because the extradition treaty between the two coun-tries didn't cover such offenses. And nothing further came of the charges.

It was no wonder Murdoch's return to the country in the spring of 2000 was viewed to be a bit "scary"—no one was sure how the Indian government or the media would respond.

T he Ashioki Hotel in Delhi was brimming with celebri-ties, politicians, and heads of state the night that Rupert Murdoch showed up in the spring of 2000.
Prime Minister Atal Bihari Vajpayee sat rapt beside Murdoch's side at the lavish dinner. The premise for the grand fete was the seventh anniversary of one of India's most popular television shows by Star, a chat show that featured politicians, film stars, and all manner of rich and famous per-sonalities. By that time, about 300 episodes had been aired.

Guests included those who had been featured on the show over the years. Now Murdoch was being treated like royalty.

During the visit, while son James was back in China work-ing closely with his stepmother, Wendi Deng, identifying investment opportunities in promising companies there,

Murdoch and Mukerjea went about identifying promising Indian companies they hoped to partner with.

"It gave me an opportunity to present to Rupert a perspective of India that made him feel comfortable that it was a market that would grow at a rapid pace; News and Star needed to have a strong foothold in this country," Mukerjea said.

Simultaneously, Star was embarking on perhaps the wildest ride of its history in India. Mukerjea and Star programming aces Steve Eskew and Samir Nair presented to Rupert Murdoch a view of the state of the nation, and how Star could be performing in relation to its competitors and the rest of the market, in terms of growth.

The company had just come away from its relationship with Zee TV, and had the opportunity to launch a 100 percent Hindi-language television channel, which had not been possible until the Zee partnership ended.

The seemingly outlandish notion was to create a Hindi version of "Who Wants to Be a Millionaire?"—better known as Kaun Banega Crorepati, or KBC, in Hindi—and to use that as the launching pad for Star's first Hindi channel, which it needed to be a smash success.

Around a conference table at Star India's headquarters in Bombay, after hearing the proposal, Murdoch was worked up and pounded the table with his hand, according to those present. "Listen, we've got to be the number one channel in India, and if it needs a certain amount of investment to get this show going, I want you to offer the largest amount of prize money and make it the best television program ever."

Mukerjea and his colleagues suggested that Star should offer 100,000 rupees as prize money—about $2,500 U.S. dollars.

Rupert was appalled. "I think you guys need to raise the stakes," he said, his gambling instincts surging like they had at the blackjack table during James's bachelor party.

Mukerjea needed Murdoch to make a decision on the spot. It wasn't often they had the chairman's full attention and authorization on the details of a strategic project. Some bantering went back and forth. Finally, Murdoch said, "Hang on a minute, I think you really have to leapfrog into a leadership position, and the only way you're going to do that with this program is to really put your money where your mouth is. Do it well, and I'll sign off on the budget."

The team again presented Murdoch with assurances that the production would be the best-quality television that could be offered anywhere in the world, and plans were presented to create the prototype in the original London studio where the British original had been produced.

Murdoch commanded, "Forget a hundred thousand, put on the table *ten million* rupees as the prize money," he said. A few jaws dropped around the table. India was nothing like the United States, where a million-dollar prize was par for the course. One hundred thousand rupees would have been considered quite a handsome prize by members of the Indian middle class. Now, the new sum was equivalent to a quarter of a million U.S. dollars.

There was a mixture of excitement and trepidation. "With that sort of prize money and that level of commitment from the boss, there was no doubt in anyone's mind what the task entailed. There was no question of being second best," Mukerjea said.

Getting Star from a zero presence in Hindi programming to number one was a formidable task, and now the big boss was watching closely. His son James would check in from time to time to monitor progress.

In Bombay, as in many cities in the world, there are millions of people commuting in and out every day. Following the mantra, "be local, think global," Murdoch, Mukerjea,

Eskew, and their colleagues knew that cracking the Hindi television market would require intimate understanding of the everyday lives of local citizens. They also knew, from News Corp.'s and Star's experience all over the globe, that each geographical market had its own quirks.

A fact of life was the need for lunch. And one of the preferred ways of getting lunch in this city was through a particularly popular lunchbox service for office workers that delivered lunchboxes by bicycle to literally millions of people all over the city.

On the afternoon of the day that Star was to air its first episode of KBC, workers all over the city opened their lunch to find a surprising message. In Hindi, it told them when they returned home that evening, they should be sure to watch KBC, promising that it would be the biggest show in the history of television in the country.

In India, the game of cricket is a passion as much as the NFL finals are in the United States. It drives people "insane," Mukerjea said, because the playoffs, in India, are with its rival neighbor, Pakistan. In India and Pakistan, a cricket match is something that gets the highest television ratings on a fairly regular basis. This is fueled by the territorial and religious rivalry between the two countries, "combined with the fact that both countries absolutely love their cricket," Mukerjea says.

Mukerjea had asked his marketing and programming executives to launch the first KBC program on the third of July, in a way that would ensure that it got higher ratings than an India/ Pakistan world cup final. If they could manage that, Mukerjea was sure that the show would have sufficient staying power.

Star's success with that show exceeded that original goal, causing it to rocket to the number one position in Hindi television programming, and fueling a barrage of other Hindi programs it would launch.

By the summer, the top 15 out of the top 20 shows in India were all Star channel shows. As Rupert had done with Fox in the United States, his television presence in India had gone from nothing to the number one network.

Kaun Banega Crorepati shattered ratings records and spawned several copycat game shows. It destroyed the assumption that only "Bollywood"—the nickname for the country's film industry—worked in India.

The show was a homegrown hit, and catapulted Star to the number one pay-TV channel in India. A non-Indian programming concept had been tailored to Indian tastes.

In India, there are two sides of the broadcasting market: terrestrial broadcasting, available to 70 million homes; and cable and satellite broadcasts (which are delivered through cable), available to 35 million homes. Star had become the leading channel in the 35-million-home universe. Satellite channels were delivered through cable operators, so they were one and the same.

The upside was huge, and this fact fueled Murdoch and his sons' optimism about their fortunes in India. In fact, while there were some 300 million households in India, only 17 million television sets were in use. More than half of the country did not yet own a television set. Out of the 17 million households that had one, about 50 percent were still black-and-white.

"The opportunity in that is immense," Mukerjea explains. "If you can imagine the scenario over the next 2 to 3 years, as new brands arrive on the market and prices come down and people's level of affluence starts to grow, one of the first items in their hierarchy of purchase is a TV set."

Star, he said, is poised to take advantage of this market growth. And the presence of those television sets in the households of the growing middle class in India makes Star's rollout of a direct-to-home business even more urgent. To have access directly to customers who will buy premium services will require the addition of a set-top box.

Murdoch and his sons were bullish on India.

But the numbers were a bit different from what most people imagined. Though the population was a billion, the market was only 50 to 60 million middle-class homes—which was still a very large market by any measure, basically the same size as the middle class in America.

Of India's 70 million homes, less than half have TVs in use, and there are about 28.5 million cable homes, making India the number three cable market in the world, after the United States and China. The middle class in India was also growing rapidly, and lots of new wealth was being created. The broadcast market was entirely terrestrial or cable, despite News Corp.'s early attempts to be the satellite pioneers.

In November 2000, however, a major breakthrough came when the Indian government announced that it had approved a regulatory framework for introducing direct-to-home satellite. Though the terms were that foreign companies could only own up to 30 percent of any satellite business in the country, Murdoch and his executives believed the situation was not onerous; the Indians had been flexible before, and they would be again.

ISkyB was the brand name for the direct-to-home business in India that News Corp. had tried to launch back in 1995. The market was completely unregulated and the company was about to jump in with a high-powered direct-to-home satellite business.

At the time, "there was just no regulation," acknowledged Star president Bruce Churchill. "In that sense it was legal." At the moment the business was about to launch, after the company had signed up millions of subscribers, the government put a halt to it all.

Churchill said the company was told by government officials, "We'd like to regulate it, but we don't know how so we're just going to ban it." And that's what they did. The whole effort got put on hold for three years.

In the fall of 2000, with the regulatory environment defined, at least preliminarily, News Corp. was ready to try it again—this time with Star India. And this time, it would also require an Indian partner. Murdoch was expecting that it would have more than one.

Hathway was one of the largest cable operators in India. News Corp. executives assessed it was clearly the most professionally managed. It was also strong in a number of strategic metropolitan areas—particularly Bombay and South Bombay. Murdoch liked to refer to it as the Manhattan Cable of India, in that its strongest position was in the best neighborhood.

In late 2000, News Corp. decided to make an investment in Hathway, taking a 26 percent equity stake. The money it invested was actually meant to be used to upgrade the network to provide direct-to-home premium television services, as well as enhanced and interactive television services.

At the time it made the investment, there was no "addressability" anywhere in India. That is, set-top boxes were not present in homes, and so no company could tailor their offerings to individual preferences. Cable came into the home, and connected to the back of a cable-ready TV, where viewers received all channels for one flat price. To increase revenues per household, cable providers and broadcasters needed addressability in order to provide premium offerings. The answer was the set-top box, and Star had an ambitious plan to roll out its World Box in India during the first half of 2001, taking advantage of the economies of scale it would enjoy from its global manufacturing capabilities and the float of Sky Global Networks. In India, the boxes would be cobranded with Hathway. For its part, Star would provide the premium services, the broadband portal, and all the enhanced television applications.

In India, as in China, a big issue was what consumers could afford to spend on a set-top box, if they could afford one at all. In these markets, viewers had historically paid relatively little for what they obtained in the area of pay-television.

In China, in fact, the price was regulated—$1.25 for all the basic channels, and they were all local Chinese channels. Premium offerings, however, were not regulated.

In India, because viewers could not choose their preferred offerings, broadcasters simply made all their channels available. At the moment that addressability became possible, Star expected that, as in the United States, certain programs would get tiered. Viewers would pay extra for the equivalent of HBO, which in that market was Star Movies.

In India, the fact that people hadn't yet paid for these services didn't mean they couldn't afford them. Substantial sums were being spent on mobile phone bills, for example. "There's evidence to suggest that people can afford it, it's just the premium services haven't been offered," Churchill said.

Besides, in the past eight months, there were other reasons for optimism about the market. Murdoch had made many new friends in the country.

His visit the previous spring was coming full circle.

A failed partnership with Zee Telefilms in India had taught Star TV much about when and when not to trust its supposed partners. Prior to that, News Corp. had spent three years and millions of dollars, all for naught, on early attempts at a direct-to-home satellite business with ISkyB. The government had outlawed satellite broadcasting just as the company was ready to go to market.

In the winter of 2000, James and Kathryn traveled to Bombay, meeting dignitaries and making substantial progress with respect to breakthrough business opportunities for Star. Rupert had laid the groundwork well.

But it was still a surprising and potentially perilous terrain. At about 8:00 P.M. on Sunday evening, November 19, as James and Kathryn entered the lobby of a Bombay apartment house they had never visited before, the lights went out.

Kathryn, a bit startled, was reassured by James that this is a common occurrence in India. The elevator was not working, and they were in complete darkness, so they headed slowly up a dark stairway, feeling their way to Peter Mukerjea's fourth-floor home, where they'd been invited for a cocktail reception. Mukerjea was the chief executive of Star India.

While Mukerjea was frantically searching for candles, hoping that he could at least make the place look romantic, James and Kathryn were at the door.

"It was unfortunate, but we found it funny. It was so very *India*," Mukerjea laughs. The lights came back about 15 minutes later.

Later in the week, the couple traveled to Delhi for a rooftop party at the Oberoi Hotel with India's ministers and policy makers.

It was a pleasant November evening in Delhi, and Kathryn arrived shortly after James, in an elegant sari, looking like a northern Indian woman from Kashmir, with her fair skin and blond hair.

Among those impressed by the traditional Indian specter of Mrs. Murdoch was a couple known as Mr. and Mrs. Shah, the head of India's terrestrial broadcaster, known as Doorbarshan, and his wife. Star was in the midst of secret talks with Doorbarshan about a joint venture that would allow Murdoch's satellite business into the country for the first time. James, however, was also vying against a similar bid by Richard Li and PCCW.

Across the room was the owner of India's largest-circulating news and current affairs magazine, *India Today*. Two other bigwigs from the publishing world were also there, the editor and owner of Delhi's *Hindustan Times*.

Though no deals were made during James and Kathryn's November trip to India, the goal was to "concretize some of the earlier discussions we had when James was last here, and a whole lot of things that happened in between needed to be finalized," Mukerjea explained.

Much meeting time was spent working with Star's Indian partners on the new direct-to-home regulations the government had just announced. Representatives from Merrill Lynch and Arthur Andersen were present to help figure out regulatory framework issues related to the percentages allowed for the participation of foreign companies.

James would return again to India in January, and hoped he would be accompanied then by his father, whose last visit to the country had been so fraught with controversy, a hotel proprietor had stationed a guard outside the elder Murdoch's door.

The broadcast industry in India was at a critical point, and the government was quite careful about regulating foreign ownership. A decision in November 2000 to legalize satellite broadcasts, and allow foreign companies to have up to a 20 percent stake in local businesses, was an enormous signal to James that things were about to open up as never before. Still, he found the place more unpredictable than mainland China.

Peter Mukerjea said, "It's historically been a protected industry, with the terrestrial broadcasters owned by the government." The ownership and control of television by the government was similar to the situation in China.

Star had been eyeing an additional investment of some $400 million in a new direct-to-home business in India. James had already spearheaded new strategic partnerships with such companies as Hathway, one of the top cable operators in India. He was in the midst of meetings with dozens of Indian and Chinese government officials, business leaders, and made the rounds to Shanghai, Beijing, Bombay, and Delhi every few weeks.

He helped Star India chief Peter Mukerjea to identify Indian companies which they might partner: indya.com; fab-mart, a shopping portal; Baazee, an auction site; and Expocity, a city guide portal. At the same time, Star had won a slew of new FM radio licenses, and Rupert Murdoch was on his way to approve the new business plan in India.

Mukerjea says that James's presence had a major impact on Star's success in India. "It's been a sense of a huge amount of energy he's brought in. In terms of responsiveness, it is a much more pragmatic approach to doing business here. In terms of specific issues, he has a lead role in activity in new media and new technologies—particularly the Internet. As a result over the last few months, we've had a far greater focus on the development part of new media. We've made some investments, pretty significant ones on the order of hundreds of millions of dollars."

But Murdoch's enemies were not thrilled about the success he was having in foreign markets. CNN founder Ted Turner, the son of a Southern billboard mogul, had a legendary hatred for the News Corp. chief, and made no bones about it. His raging outbursts against Murdoch were not the only times the colorful side of his personality revealed itself. Turner was a tabloid headline writer's dream. Even *60 Minutes* had broadcast images of him lying prostrate on the floor, when, upon winning the America's Cup, he slid under the desk at a press conference after one too many toasts.

Turner liked to brag that his media visions were way ahead of Murdoch's. Twenty years prior to Rupert's attempt to buy the British soccer team Manchester United, Turner recognized the value of owning sports and movie rights. In the mid-1970s Turner bought Atlanta's baseball, basketball, and ice hockey teams—the Braves, the Hawks, and the Flames.

Murdoch's continued international expansion brought its share of vitriol. "Murdoch really wants power, to control governments and build up the kind of media monopolies all over the world that he has [in the United Kingdom]," Turner told the U.K. paper *The Guardian*.

Turner liked to repeat what an Indian television executive attending the CNN World Report conference in 1997 allegedly said to him. "His country didn't fight to get its freedom from Britain for 100 years just to turn it over to Rupert Murdoch," Turner recounted. In the United Kingdom, Turner's CNN vied with Murdoch's Sky News and BBC News. Its prowess in the United States however was uncontestable—until Fox News started making inroads.

Now, even in the impossible market in India, Murdoch was making enormous strides. Not only was Murdoch in India, but he was being treated like royalty.

Things had changed even for rival Ted Turner. CNN had been swallowed up in the mid-90s by Time Warner and Turner was out of the thick of it. A vice chairman of the AOL Time Warner behemoth, he did not take Murdoch as personally as he once did. He was overseeing some 30 magazines including *Time, Fortune, People,* and *Entertainment Weekly,* and, ironically, with the AOL merger, had some worry about the future of newspapers and print because of so much media being online.

Murdoch was unfazed, and had been relatively nonchalant about the impact of the Internet, compared to his rivals. "The proliferation of new media is not the death knell of the old. When talking films came along, everyone predicted the death of radio; when television came along, everyone again predicted the death of radio, and the demise of the newspaper and film industries as well; when cable came along, everyone predicted the death of network television in America. And now we have the Internet, which some see as the technology that will kill off all the others," Murdoch said. "Well, it hasn't worked out that way. All of these industries are doing quite well. They may miss their old monopoly positions, and they may be struggling harder to give consumers what they want, while earning a reasonable return for their shareholders. But with good management, media companies in all of these industries can continue to survive and prosper."

But the two men did have some things in common. Both had an intuitive sense for what sells. Among CNN's editorial policies, led by such newsroom legends such as "Mad Dog" Kavanau, is "If it bleeds, it leads."

While Murdoch liked to brag about his immortality following his successful cancer treatment, Turner was also known for his braggadocio: "I know for a fact that Clinton had a TV put in his bathroom so he could watch CNN," he said in one interview, pounding the table with unrepressed amusement.

Unlike Murdoch, who is sanguine about his longevity, Turner, whose father died at 53, says he does not bet on being around more than one day at a time.

The whole India controversy is puzzling to Murdoch, "I wasn't disliked. I had no enemies in India. No, no, no, it's all bogus," he says. "Mysteriously a warrant was put out for my arrest. Some trumped-up thing which got headlines all over the world."

Murdoch laughs, recalling that "when there was a warrant out for my arrest, the president of India asked me to be sure and stay at the presidential palace when I'm next back there," to protect himself in case there's any problem with the police. "The warrant had been issued in one province of India, it was not nationwide, but it got international headlines!" He bangs on the table. "It was trumped up."

"I dunno, there's someone on a talk show at one in the morning that called Gandhi an old bastard or something, ya know, this is like sacrilegious, ya know, I don't know what it was. Porno is on at one in the morning," he pauses, and then blurts out, "But all Indian films are close to porn, I think." A big laugh.

Murdoch continues, "I really don't know what it was. Certainly I didn't know anything about it. Certainly we don't have a porn channel or anything like that. Or anything even approaching an adult channel."

Surprisingly, India seemed a lot like the American market in the early 1980s, when cable television was unregulated and growing at a breakneck pace.

Cable programming—delivered by satellite—came to India in 1991, pumping CNN news reports of the Gulf War, and the Indian government did not interfere as a new industry developed.

Still, in a country of more than a billion people, only 70 million homes had television sets. Of those, about 28.5 million had cable. India was the third-largest cable market, behind the United States and China. Indian viewers received up to 85 channels for a monthly rate of 150 rupees, or $3.26.

As Star soared in the ratings, Murdoch increased the company's distribution plans. While James was authorized to invest in 26 percent of India's third-largest cable system, Hathway Cable, for $70 million, Mukerjea planned to upgrade Hathway's network to provide broadband service to its 2.5 million subscribers.

But competitors were also scrambling for the market.

More than 30 new channels had been launched over the previous year, but advertising had slowed to an annual growth rate of 15 percent, down from 25 percent.

Murdoch, however, was showing no signs of scaling back. He was investing more in India than anywhere in the world.

By mid-December of 2000, James was pretty worn out by the globe-trotting mission his father had launched him on. On December 13, his birthday, James turned 28 and was named to the News Corp. board. The day before, he'd arrived in New York with Kathryn for his first official board meeting and his father's announcement to the world that he'd been given a seat.

But on his birthday, James was too worn out to celebrate, or to attend the News Corp. Christmas party scheduled for that evening.

In an e-mail message on the morning of December 14, Kathryn, his wife, wrote: ". . . we just arrived in New York a couple of days ago and have been quite hectic, catching up with all of our friends and getting ready for Christmas, as you can imagine. It was also James's birthday yesterday and, as you probably read, he is now on the board of News. E-mail is still the best way to reach me as we are running around a lot right now."

That same evening, she gave an update. "We're in New York until tomorrow, when we head to the country for some well-deserved rest (at least for James). We didn't make it to the party last night as James was ill from exhaustion/jet lag/fever. Not a very exciting birthday for him, I'm afraid. James's mother is working like crazy to get her house renovated before Christmas. . . . James and his dad will be in Hong Kong in January."

Indeed, while James and Kathryn prepared to visit his

mother Anna Murdoch and her new husband at her renovated house on Long Island the morning after his corporate Christmas party, Rupert Murdoch boarded a plane for the Australian outback, to spend some time and the holiday with his mother, Dame Elisabeth Murdoch, at his boyhood haunt, Cruden Farm.

Lachlan would join his father and grandmother, and also oversee an executive strategy session at a remote sheep station in the outback owned by his father.

By the New Year, James and Kathryn sat side by side on a plane from New York. It's a very long trip to Hong Kong, and as the plane takes off, James turns, as he always does when they fly together, and pokes Kathryn in the shoulder.

"Look, look! Look at the clouds, they're so beautiful!" he says, sounding like a young boy. As she usually does, Kathryn laughs and kisses him. He presses his nose up against the window again, and begins all over. "Look at the sky!" On a night flight, the skyline of New York is all aglow. "It's so beautiful! Is that the greatest city on earth?" he asks, not needing an answer. "Is that the greatest city on earth?"

James has a startling innocence that is disarming when one likewise considers the savvy deals and complex political environments he traffics in these days.

Kathryn herself says at first she was in disbelief that her husband could get so excited *every* time he saw the world from the air. "He didn't do this just once! He does it every time!" she laughs. "I had to repress my natural impulse to go, 'Yeah yeah yeah,' and instead realize, 'You're right, you're absolutely right!' "

"It's such a great way to be," says Kathryn. "I wish I was more that way." She then becomes quiet and thoughtful. Her voice is soft. "I think our generation thinks cynicism is intelligence," she says. "It's really not actually, it's just cynicism."

James's favorite place in the world is New England and,

perhaps understandably, he's already daydreaming of retiring there. "New England is God's country, it's so fabulous. I'd like to retire in New England or something. When I'm like 80 or something, live by the sea," he says. "It's so beautiful there."

It was the one thing he misses most about not living in New York, that he can escape on the weekend to his Connecticut retreat on the river. "My dog misses that, too. You can't really take the dog, there aren't places you can go and let the dog just run here in Hong Kong. It's sort of sad. He'll be OK."

James's boyishness is unleashed when away from his business wranglings. Yet he does not have to think long or hard when asked who his mentors are in life. "On an active basis, my father. He's really the most influential figure," he says, pondering this a bit. "My father and my mother—my parents."

What are his childhood memories of his father? There is a silence, while James plumbs some depths. Then he says, "I don't know. There was a lot of work." And he laughs. "A lot of work."

11

IN THE LAND OF
THE GIANTS

While Murdoch was making great leaps and strides in the pay-TV and inter-active television arenas, Microsoft mogul Bill Gates was salivating for a pres-ence in the living rooms of households all over the world by putting a version of Windows on interactive television sets. In the early days of the software industry, he'd provided the solution for computer giant IBM's entrance into the PC world. Now he was in the position of having to turn to Murdoch for his chance to be a player on the platform of the future: the interactive TV.

The opportunities for Asia to become a driving force behind the digital economy on the global stage are tremendous. . . . Windows 2000 makes it possible for companies of every size to realize that potential."

The words of Microsoft chairman Bill Gates were particu-larly grating to some News Corp. executives who had been pounding the pavement in China for almost a decade.

Bill Gates was disliked in China far more than Rupert Mur-doch ever had been. At least that was consolation. Gates, like Murdoch, was aggressively courting Asian business leaders and government officials.

At a Korean summit with leaders from all over the Asia Pacific region, Gates said he considered Asia the fastest-growing area of the world in terms of adoption and consumption of new technology. He predicted that by 2003 there would be 63 million Internet users in Asia generating some $32 billion in e-commerce, largely through broadband services.

"We are incredibly optimistic about the future of Asia, because its countries are rapidly increasing their investment in the technologies and infrastructure needed to connect businesses, governments and educational systems," Gates said.

Gates went on to point out that, by the end of 2001, China would rank as the world's third-largest market for personal computers, and its Internet usage would double.

But in terms of the entertainment market and interactive television—where the big explosion was expected in Asia—Gates was far behind.

Microsoft was in fact in the midst of an interactive TV disaster that left the company in a position similar to the one IBM faced during the early days of PC market: Use someone else's software to play catch-up in a hot new market.

The software giant had turned to NDS to license an operating system for set-top boxes that would become the new personal computers of the interactive television world. What's more, Microsoft was paying royalties for the technology. Gates had been in the position of gatekeeper for more than two decades now, collecting royalties from virtually every PC maker on the planet for the right to ship his Windows software on their computers. Now the tables had turned. Gates didn't have a clue about the television world, and television sets with the ability to act like PCs had him worried. These devices had Rupert Murdoch salivating.

The huge potential mass market for digital television—and the accompanying interactive services it will enable—Gates likewise had savored for some time.

Microsoft had hopes of turning its operating system dominance on personal computers into a leading position in digital television and other interactive consumer devices that would be used to do everything from surfing the Internet to home shopping, banking, and playing games.

Microsoft so coveted the emerging interactive television market that it invested some $10 billion in cable companies in an effort to secure a position. However, despite these moves, the software giant still lagged behind.

NDS's partnership with Microsoft actually began with a series of tête-à-têtes at Microsoft's new Mountain View, California, campus in the fall of 1999. At that time, Microsoft was formulating a plan—with some 200 developers in its consumer group focused on the problem—for placing Microsoft software at the heart of television set-top boxes around the world.

Microsoft was telling would-be customers that its TV Platform was a "comprehensive software solution for the television industry that makes television more useful, fun, and engaging for consumers today and in the future."

In reality, the company was struggling to deliver the software. Yet, it pitched its customers on a technology it hoped would allow TV network operators to offer consumers an array of "new and engaging enhanced TV programs and services on both today's digital set-top boxes and next-generation TV-based devices."

Microsoft's hope was that this software would not only address current digital television services such as pay-per-view programs and electronic program guides, but would enable advanced TV services for consumers. "TV can be a household's entry point into new forms of entertainment, communication, information, and e-commerce," the company said in promotional materials.

One category to emerge, Microsoft and many other companies predicted, would be "Personal TV," which would enable viewers to control and customize content.

But the future was turning out to be a little more complex than the company had imagined. The problem: Advanced TV services using Windows technology required a lot of processing power and memory. Microsoft did not have an answer for the current generation of set-top boxes that used much less memory.

NDS, on the other hand, had been selling its software to set-top-box manufacturers for some time, including its conditional-access software that enabled cable and satellite networks to encrypt data securely for delivery to millions of subscribers.

Microsoft's longer-term strategy, recognizing broadcasters require sophisticated software to offer interactive services, was to combine these interactive TV functions in a future version of Windows, code-named Whistler, hoping to extend its operating system franchise to the television world.

But the software giant had to act fast. Analysts were projecting that television networks and Internet providers would invest more than $50 billion over the next five years to launch new digital broadband networks featuring interactive content for their subscribers.

Twenty miles south of San Francisco, at Microsoft's new Silicon Valley campus, a group of programmers and engineers congregated in fall 1999. Phil Goldman and key members of the Microsoft Television Platform group, an effort high on Bill Gates's list of strategic projects, greeted a team from NDS led by Jas Saini, VP of consumer devices.

Goldman, Microsoft's general manager of Television Platforms, had founded WebTV as a tiny startup in 1995. The company was subsequently bought by Microsoft, and Goldman joined the company and became a member of Microsoft's executive board.

Microsoft folded together WebTV, Microsoft TV, and Microsoft TV Server as components of its software platform for interactive television. Over time, WebTV had gained a foothold in over a million households across the United States, and was one of the largest Internet service providers. But it was stalled, and could not get beyond its installed base of one million, largely because of lack of applications and programming.

Goldman, along with Microsoft business director Tony Faustini and Steve Wasserman, better known as "Wass," the key technical architect for Microsoft TV, sat across the table from Saini. Accompanying him were Ira Reznik, a female executive who served as director of U.S. sales for NDS, and Michael Dick, NDS vice president of systems integration. Occasionally, Microsoft Senior Vice President Jon DeVaan would poke his head in.

The discussions commenced regarding Microsoft's interest in NDS's conditional-access software, and informally meandered to the idea of fully licensing the smaller company's Core middleware. It would be the quickest way to get to market.

The two groups continued to meet over months and put the final touches on the deal in Las Vegas, during the Consumer Electronics Show. A number of items were still being wrangled over, such as who would support Microsoft TV customers, and how Microsoft would commit to developing interactive applications for the Core middleware, now branded as Microsoft TV.

Finally, Microsoft agreed it would essentially brand NDS's software as its own Microsoft TV Basic, and the companies would jointly "extend" the technology for more advanced features.

While not yet sure of how it would accomplish this, Microsoft planned, with Microsoft TV Advanced, to enable advanced set-top boxes, integrated television sets, personal video recorders, and combination devices with interactive broadcast and Internet services. With that middleware software, it planned to combine both analog and digital TV technologies, and to offer such features as an advanced electronic program guide, digital video recording, and live TV pause.

Microsoft hoped to eventually develop an advanced version of the software on its own, but was counting on NDS to continue to extend the software for more advanced functions, for the time being.

Of the Microsoft TV efforts, Goldman said, "I think working on the Microsoft TV platform right now must be what working on the PC was like a decade ago. Everything that has been simmering in the background is suddenly all coming together, and the result will be revolutionary yet inevitable." More than 200 people are building the Microsoft TV platform at the company, combining Windows technology with NDS technology. Goldman said, "It still feels like it did in the old days when there were twenty of us sitting around trying to figure out how this thing should work."

Microsoft is relatively quiet about NDS's ongoing role. In press releases and on its web site, Microsoft brags its Microsoft TV software is "used in over 1.5 million set-top boxes across Latin America, Asia and Europe, delivering enhanced pay-TV functionality on satellite, cable and terrestrial networks." In actuality, it is the NDS software that is used in 1.5 million set-top boxes.

Microsoft has never had a presence in the TV market. And its biggest wins in that area—UPC and AT&T—have had some setbacks recently, while Microsoft readies software that will work. Analysts say the company's problem has been its

Windows-centric approach to every market. Software from outsiders does not have the burden of existing Windows code.

While the deal with Microsoft was lucrative, allowing News Corp.'s NDS to collect royalties on an ongoing basis for every Microsoft TV set-top box, NDS was also in the tricky position of competing with, while supplying technology to, the software giant.

Ironically, Murdoch, like Gates, has recognized that control of the set-top box used with any broadcast network—be it cable, satellite, or other wireless technologies—would put his company in a position to control customers' online spending, gather mass marketing data, and win a captive advertising audience.

Through NDS, News Corp. itself is vying for major interactive television deals around the world. NDS's technology, in fact (combined with Henry Yuen's Gemstar), will be the strategic glue binding many of the new ventures being targeted by Murdoch's new combined satellite platform company, Sky Global Networks.

"If you take what Microsoft and Bill Gates did to IBM, that's basically what the situation is," NDS's Saini would tell his colleagues, enjoying the irony.

IBM was in a similar situation in the early days of the PC industry. The company didn't have the operating system that was of the right size and power for PCs.

Like IBM, Microsoft now had no choice but to license what it needed from a smaller, innovative company. "Our aim is to have an arm's-length relationship with Microsoft," Saini says. "Although we are working with them to enhance this middleware, we see in the long run they will run it themselves and we would get the revenue stream from it. . . . If you can take the parallel with IBM, when Microsoft sold them the operating system, Microsoft got the royalties."

NDS president Abe Peled would inspire his troops. The position the company was in was something to be held onto. In the spring of 2000, he was still saying, "Today Microsoft does not have any of the technologies NDS has, and we hope to keep it that way."

Microsoft had been dealt a series of setbacks. In the fall of 2000 UPC disclosed that it would put off plans to use Microsoft TV software because the software giant missed deadlines for delivering the finished product. Instead, UPC is using software for digital set-top boxes from Liberate, a company in San Carlos, California—despite Microsoft's move to increase its equity stake in UPC to 8 percent just three months earlier.

Microsoft's deal with UPC would have done much to establish Microsoft's reputation as a reliable provider of interactive television software that integrates an electronic program guide, Internet services, and video-on-demand with traditional broadcasting.

Also at risk is the partnership, inked the previous spring between Microsoft and AT&T Broadband, to bring advanced broadband television services to consumers, according to analysts.

The two giants demonstrated AT&T's interactive platform on advanced set-top boxes using Microsoft TV Platform software, and said AT&T would license the software, for both client set-top boxes and television servers. AT&T planned to integrate its interactive TV platform with the Excite@Home backbone, allowing AT&T to take advantage of Excite@Home's broadband applications and services.

Jon DeVaan, senior vice president of Microsoft's Consumer Group, who orchestrated the deal, was optimistic. "We are pleased to report excellent progress on all fronts in our work with AT&T," he said.

But AT&T now seemed to be backing off from that pact, with concerns about Microsoft's ability to deliver the product. AT&T is also using software from Liberate. Company executives confirmed that Microsoft was late delivering its promised software, and that software from Liberate would fill the gap.

While rivals like Liberate and OpenTV believe Microsoft is trying to buy its way into the interactive TV market by taking stakes in several European cable companies, so far these stakes have not solved its lack-of-product problem. (So far, Microsoft has spent some $10 billion on cable stakes. In June 1997, it put $1 billion into Comcast, for an 11.5 percent stake in the company. That was followed by a $5 billion investment in AT&T; $2.6 billion in Telewest; $500 million in Britain's NTL; $400 million in Rogers in Canada; and $353 million in UPC, based in the Netherlands.)

News Corp.'s strategy, however, has not been dissimilar. It has invested in numerous cable and satellite TV operations and most recently bought a 26 percent stake in one of India's largest cable networks, Hathway Cable and Datacom Pte. Ltd.

The anticipated explosion in digital television is creating new business opportunities in many arenas. Interactive TV services create new profit centers for network operators, as well as for their suppliers of programming, hardware, and software.

Indeed, next-generation set-top boxes, which hit the market in 2001, will resemble personal computers. The new machines will have a hard disk drive and powerful processors for storing movies and product catalogs, handling e-mail, transmitting digital photographs, and playing games.

Unlike earlier devices, which were often given away by cable and satellite providers, the advanced machines will sport hefty price tags.

Major manufacturers of the boxes, such as Philips Electronics NV of the Netherlands, Matsushita Electric Industrial Co. of Japan, and Motorola Inc. of the U.S., were expected to price the machines high, seeing that the advanced boxes would cost between $349 and $436 to make. Analysts say that consumer prices will come down eventually to attract a mass audience.

PC makers were also hoping to capitalize on the digital TV market by offering software on their machines that can decode digital TV signals.

Fujitsu Siemens Computers, a joint venture between Germany's Siemens AG and Japan's Fujitsu Ltd., is offering a Windows-powered machine that combines a DVD player, CD player, MP3 music player, Internet access, games console, and telephone functionality. It was initially launched in Germany, but similar devices are expected to appear in the U.S. by 2002.

CBS had entered into a partnership with Microsoft to bring its traditional television programming into the interactive Internet and television worlds. David Katz, CBS vice president of strategic planning and interactive ventures, expected that with Web TV and Microsoft TV, Microsoft will kick-start CBS's interactive projects.

Stephen Baker, vice president of technology research for new media research firm PC Data, said, however, that comedy and drama will be more difficult to make interactive than news and sports, which inherently are more "participatory."

By 2003, some industry observers say, the television and the personal computer will converge to become the "one-device screen." By then, it is expected the infrastructure will exist to bring full PC functionality to television.

Currently, Europe is a bit ahead of the United States in the development of the digital television market. About 7 million European viewers now have access to interactive television, principally in Britain, France, and Spain, according to

Therese Torris, a media analyst for Forrester Research BV in Amsterdam.

The United States is still largely in the analog age. Up until recently, cable and satellite companies balked at the expense of installing set-top boxes that provide two-way communication. According to Jupiter Communications, fewer than 400,000 homes in the United States now have interactive television, but, Jupiter projects, the number of U.S. users will rise to 30 million by 2004.

Forrester Research predicts that by 2003, 71 percent of all businesses and 33 percent of all households will have broadband access. By 2004, program guides, enhanced broadcasts, and TV-based browsing will generate $11 billion in ads and $7 million in commerce.

Even Microsoft has secured a toehold. In March 1999, it signed a deal with China's top computer maker, Legend Holdings, to make inexpensive set-top boxes, nicknamed "Venus," using Windows CE, the consumer electronics version of Windows. Venus was targeted at turning Chinese TVs into Internet devices. But by the spring of 2001, sales of the device in China were virtually nonexistent. Analysts believed that was because PCs were already very cheap in China, and the popularity of the free Linux operating system was hurting Microsoft.

Meanwhile, rival AOL Time Warner had itself entered into a partnership with Legend to create a Chinese Internet portal.

While rivals were duking it out, in the works was a Microsoft alliance with News Corp. on a worldwide basis that would help the company keep up with AOL's moves and make headway in the interactive television market at the same time.

The two companies' separate scrambles for a viable presence in this market would unexpectedly come together by the spring of 2001 in a successful partnership through Sky Global Networks.

12

BUBBLE

In the spring of 2001, Rupert Murdoch was still pushing the plans for Sky Global and getting his hands on DirecTV. The Internet bubble had burst, and News Corp. was in the process of shutting down or scaling back numerous of its Internet-based ventures launched the previous year, and refocusing on the company's strengths.

The crowd is packed, body to body, and the room is full of pulsating music—the kind you can feel in the pit of your stomach. Four sinewy young men are jumping about in a spotlight in a Manhattan nightclub.

The mob heaves with each beat, and Rupert Murdoch nestles closer to his wife Wendi and son Lachlan, who leans over a balcony railing, loving every second of it. Actress Gwyneth Paltrow is mingling somewhere, and Lachlan's wife Sarah is by him, rocking to the sounds of the young shirtless men on the stage.

"It's too loud, but it has a good beat," says Murdoch, grinning ear to ear. "Half an hour's enough for me. I'm too old. I'm not used to this stuff." He'd arrived in time to hear his son's speech; the Red Hot Chili Peppers are playing a benefit for the philanthropic Robinhood Foundation, of which Lachlan is a board member and host for this event.

Murdoch protests, "It's very hard to catch a lot of the lyrics, it's like listening to those black rappers. I got a few words though." Murdoch had been intrigued by much of the music son James's hip-hop label Rawkus had published; there were markets to be served that he barely understood, but which fascinated him, like a big old lion out of his habitat, awkwardly sniffing about a new terrain.

Lachlan is a bit surprised that his father has shown up. "It would be something if he did," he'd said a few days earlier to a friend.

Murdoch, who, since his marriage and cancer treatment, has been on a good-health campaign—eating well and working out at the gym—is impressed by the strength of the scrawny lads entertaining the crowd. "Those guys, they gotta work out three hours a day! They're thin, but they have a lot of muscle! I reckon they're at the gym!"

Murdoch's mouth is moving and he is saying something, but the words can't be heard. He's being drowned out by the young crowd.

I t is a Wednesday night, March 14, 2001. The first generation of Internet businesses had landed with a thud, for the most part. Rupert is still waiting to hear if he can wrap his arms around GM's Hughes and DirecTV; Jack Smith needed to get that brother of his, Mike, with the program.

No one knew what the next round in new media would bring; broadband networks and not-so-far-off things to which not many had given much thought—like full-motion HTML—could change television and entertainment in untold ways. The dot-com bubble had burst—temporarily. If it had a chance of reviving, it might be through a more targeted and higher-profit-potential implementation of broadband services via interactive television. Murdoch had been betting on broadband and the television set all along.

The DirecTV acquisition would make things that much easier. So far, the deal was still alive. Not only had Microsoft's Ballmer said "no" to Mike Smith, Murdoch was pleased that "they're not only with us, they're with us for a set amount of money on a set of terms and we have a 99 percent completed deal with Microsoft that's waiting for these lawyers to write up."

The writhing musicians are still going at it under flashing lights, and the crowd is showing no signs of thinning. Above on the balcony, Lachlan Murdoch's head rocks like a piston.

Now Gerald Levin, the Time Warner honcho, is approaching Rupert with a lot of "record people" around him. (New York investor Henry Kravitz has made an appearance, but "didn't have much to say," Murdoch wryly observes.)

Prior to his hookup with AOL, Levin had missed the Internet boat big-time. He'd passed up the opportunity to buy portals like Lycos and Excite, and Time Warner's own Internet hub, Pathfinder, was a flop. Getting division heads at the media giant to focus on an Internet strategy had been extremely difficult. It remained to be seen if his new partner, Steve Case, and he would figure out the synergies that would make the century "the Internet century," as Case predicted.

Murdoch stops on the way out and shouts so Levin can hear him, "Jerry!" Levin looks up at his rival who is headed for the door. "Jerry, I'm getting a bit old for this, would you send me a copy of the lyrics tomorrow morning?" Murdoch asks, grinning.

Levin tells him he's sold 10 million copies of the stuff, the Chili Peppers' previous CD. "Yeah, they're good, the music is fine, they're physical, they get naked . . . they throw themselves around the stage, a lot of jumping like jumping jacks. . . ." Murdoch trails off. "I think by the end of it they get down to their tights."

Murdoch is being facetious; the Chili Peppers are infamous for often performing with nothing but socks covering their genitals.

Rupert Murdoch was not afraid of being vulnerable.

He was certain his original pact with GM would finally come through. "I'd say you'll see this completed within a month," Murdoch said.

But his optimism hasn't always paid off. The deal would take much longer than that. By late summer, it was still in limbo. Indeed, the press had dismissed the deal as dead, but Murdoch pressed on. His intuitions were often—but not always—right on the money.

Murdoch had been the opposite of optimistic about the prospect of Internet businesses. He'd doubted their viability until mid-1999, when pressure that he was "missing the Internet boat" began to mount. In nine months' time, he allocated more than $2 billion in resources to online projects. He told a group of executives at the company's annual meeting in November 1999, "You really see two companies here. One developing and extending its established and profitable businesses, the other investing energetically in the new technology-driven media, with opportunities that are just opening every day to us."

His enthusiasm for Internet-based business, however, lasted only a few months—despite the urgings of his sons. In early 1999, James, Lachlan, his son-in-law Alasdair MacLeod, eldest child Prudence, and wife Wendi all had been trying to persuade Rupert to get with the program.

Murdoch had never been confident in the business model for Internet startups, but the market was going wild, there was money to be made, and he decided to jump on the bandwagon. Yet he always believed it was folly to stray from his core business—and even James had said for years that the Internet was not a "business," but a "part" of doing business. More than anything, it was just another distribution vehicle for News Corporation.

Murdoch finally decided to go along for the Internet ride, and at the height of his optimism, while he was on his honeymoon in Tuscany with Wendi, he and a handful of his executives formed the plan for the new U.K. Internet division known as News Network. News Network, formerly News International Digital Publishing, had been created as the Internet arm of News International. (News International was comprised of News Corp.'s U.K. newspaper and magazine businesses, and had a 40 percent stake in BSkyB. It also had stakes in two German television broadcasters and a European radio music station.) News Network's stated mission was to "identify and build a network of on-line products and services for U.K. consumers building on the strengths of News International's advertising relationships and consumer reach."

A week after the formation of the division, Murdoch flew to London to announce a $300 million investment in the creation of e-partners, whose sole purpose was to invest in Internet businesses.

News Digital Media, which had been headed up by James since 1997 and which had launched Fox.com, Foxmarketwire .com, Foxsports.com, and Foxnews.com, stepped up its own minority investments. In the United States, it put some $7.5 million into Sixdegrees.com, a community web site; $20 million into Juno.com; $15 million in PlanetRX, the healthcare site; and $7.5 million into financial web site The Street.com. (By the end of 2000, all were failing or defunct.)

What's more, in the United Kingdom, BSkyB chief Tony Ball committed to pouring 250 million pounds into online ventures and putting millions more into such ventures as gaming site Gameplay.com and consumer site Letsbuyit.com. At the height of the spending, BSkyB purchased Sports Internet Group for 301 million pounds; by late 2000 SIG was worth only $3 to $5 million. However, News executives were still confident that venture would pay off—particularly with the increasing popularity of online betting.

News Network in December 1999 launched FiredUp.com as an events and entertainment-driven auction site. Its premiere event was the auction of "one-of-a-kind Spice Girls memorabilia including Posh's platform boots signed by her."

The web site also would cosponsor the broadcast of the Spice Girls concert on Murdoch's Sky One channel that month. Hopes were that FiredUp.com would be unique in offering real-time online auctions and entertainment-related events and merchandise.

Other auction events slated included "The Superbowl," which was billed as a once-in-a-lifetime opportunity to see America's number one sporting event with 50-yard-line tickets to the 2000 Superbowl in Atlanta, Georgia; and "Extra, Extra," the auction of a walk-on part to appear as an extra in such News Corp.–owned TV hits as *Friends, NYPD Blue, ER, Caroline in the City,* and *Veronica's Closet.* The auction would include "a seven-night stay in the homes of the stars," in Los Angeles.

News Network had also recently launched Bun.com, a free Internet service provider, and Page3.com, an offshoot of the *Sun* newspaper.

In July of 1999, Murdoch appointed son-in-law Alasdair MacLeod to be managing director of News Network. MacLeod had formerly served as general manager of Murdoch's Times Newspapers Ltd in the United Kingdom. In his position he would also oversee the company's new Internet service provider CurrantBun.Com, which would be rebranded as Bun.com, and the company's existing digital publishing operation that included the Internet editions of the *Times* and *Sunday Times*.

A separate unit that worked closely with News Digital Media, News Digital Ventures had worked closely with James Murdoch to identify investment opportunities in Asia and Europe. Ventures worked closely with News Corp. Europe, covering western and eastern Europe, consulting on potential Internet opportunities. The goal of the Ventures group had been to stay on top of the strategic goals of each division within News Corp., and help them fill in any gaps in an effort to bolster their strategies and build out their companies.

When Internet stocks took a dive in 2000, executives in Europe insist they did not panic, having been conservative about their endeavors all along. The group's edict, like Murdoch's own, was to take a longer-term view of the market. "We used a different risk profile than most companies," said Kathryn Fink, News Digital Ventures' president. "When we invested, we often invested in cash as well as in kind."

Even in rough times, the News Corp. investment strategy hadn't changed much. The valuations and the timing both changed, but the company's focus was on looking at platform development and securing distribution.

One of the new platforms the company was eager to develop was wireless, which inspired its investment in OmniSky, the wireless Internet service provider. In the spring of 2001, News boosted its stake to 20 percent in the U.S. operations of the company, as well as created a 50-50 joint venture internationally.

Broadband distribution was also of strategic importance.

It had fueled Star's partnership with Gigamedia in Taiwan. The area of content, of course, was also a hot spot for investments for News. It was searching for content complementary to what it already had, to build out its portfolio. In the area of sports in the United States, Fox Sports was very strong with national, regional, and local content, but really didn't have a lot of community-based content.

In response, News Digital Ventures made an investment in rivals.com, a network of some 900 small publishing affiliates focused on college team sites and communities. News also acquired a company, StatsInc, which did real-time sports statistics—content critical not only for the Internet business and entertainment, such as fantasy games, but also for use with interactive television and wireless broadcasts. The content fit across all of the News Corp. platforms, and could be sold to the companies' competitors, giving the company leverage in the market.

Murdoch still believed in these businesses. His goal was to create a network of the most compelling content available, draw it together, and distribute it in an absolutely ubiquitous way, across multiple platforms in ways that would optimize the strengths of each platform.

The adoption of broadband, however, had proven to be slower than expected. Ironically, it was rolling out more quickly in other countries' markets, particularly in certain markets in Asia.

Australian-born Fink says, "I think a lot of Americans are very surprised to hear how very far behind they are in terms of wireless development and wireless penetration. At the same time, it's an important stepping stone to enhanced television and interactive television, it's part of a spectrum of development in digital content."

News Digital Ventures had actually catalyzed the investment in Asia in January 2000 in Sinobit, a meeting place for venture capitalists and entrepreneurs. Sinobit was screening a lot of deals for News Corp. based out of Beijing, and operated similarly to garage.com.

In some cases, Murdoch got out just in time. While the market was still riding high, in March 2000, News International had a deal to sell Bun.com to Pan-European Internet service provider World Online for 64 million pounds, yet stated that News Network would continue to develop and build content and e-commerce businesses.

At the time of the Bun.com sale, managing director MacLeod stated, "Through News Network, News International will focus all of its Internet efforts on the areas where the company has the best opportunities for creating long-term value, and we are therefore concentrating on developing e-commerce businesses built around the massive reach and brand strength of our newspapers."

Indeed, at the time, with MacLeod and other top executives at his side, Murdoch was still pushing digital media hard. During the company's "new media" workshop in the spring of 2000, Murdoch had said, "We've pursued a three-part new media strategy: First, we're integrating interactivity into all of our key content assets, including entertainment, sports, news, and health, to name just a few."

He'd gone on, "Second, we're aggressively developing our existing platforms and building new platforms, establishing dominant positions in interactive television and direct-to-home broadcasting. . . . Third, we're making aggressive investments in targeted high-growth, dynamic new media assets."

Central to this strategy, Murdoch said, was "integration."

"Our goal is to extend our content as far as possible in our traditional media assets, and then across platforms into the new media world." Things would be drastically scaled back from Rupert's plan, however, in an alarmingly short time.

News Network was still in the process of developing online businesses as subbrands to the newspapers; Page3.com was an offshoot of the *Sun*. It had boasted almost 100,000 registered members during its first six weeks, and over one million page impressions per day. News Network still had plans to launch a range of consumer-driven e-commerce ventures over the coming 12 months exploiting the strengths of the relationships that the parent company had with its readers, customers, and business partners.

By the summer of 2000, however, the party was over. Internet spending was eroding the bottom line, and proving no return on the investment.

Less than a year later, after he'd "got it," having made no money on Internet ventures, Murdoch, Chernin, and CFO Dave Devoe ordered a retreat—in part pressured by a cash shortage and the U.S. economic slowdown.

In a Los Angeles bar in July 2000, Murdoch's top new media gurus were told that there was to be no more spending on Internet businesses. Months later News Corp. formally announced that it was folding all its online businesses that had been operated under News Digital Media back into their respective company divisions. What's more, the company was doing some hasty backpedaling from its partnership with WebMD and other online ventures.

Jon Richmond, who had taken over James's job earlier in the year as head of News Digital Media; his colleague MacLeod; Patrice McAree, director of new media for News Corp. in Australia; and others heading up new media projects all had been told in no uncertain terms: Your budgets are gone for anything Internet.

News International had begun layoffs. FiredUp.com was a dud, and a desperate attempt to relaunch the site was under way. The previous month, recruitment site Revolver.com had been launched and the reorganization was to affect that as well. MacLeod at the time insisted that the sites would continue operations as usual.

News Network, however, was being broken up. Control of newspaper-related sites were being returned to the individual newspapers. FiredUp.com had failed to find its niche in the fiercely competitive online auction market, and the company was having a hard time translating the success of its newspapers, such as the *Sun* and the *Times,* into Internet businesses.

All over the company, the axe came down on Internet activities. Even BSkyB had some 200 employees working on its online endeavors. Their numbers were severely slashed. In Britain, web sites Revolver.com and FiredUp.com were virtually abandoned.

I n the end, however, by the time Murdoch decided to bail out, only a fraction of the $2 billion he'd committed was ever invested in actual online businesses—his losses were not nearly as gargantuan as those of rivals like Disney, for example, which lost billions on its Go network.

What's more, existing pacts were readjusted without huge losses being incurred. By the end of 2000, News Corp. reduced its original $1 billion alliance with WebMD, the online health network, by $750 million, leaving intact only about $250 million in reciprocal content and services.

t the high point, Murdoch had hoped to launch a health site—most likely to be dubbed Sky WebMD— across digital cable, satellite, Internet, and print media. Strategic meetings had been under way to leverage a $1 billion, 10-year marketing and promotion partnership through a 50-50 international joint venture with Healtheon/WebMD. Murdoch had taken a 10.8 percent stake in the company, valued at $450 million.

The plan was to modify the WebMD Internet site and News Corp.'s Health Channel to include extensive data on the sale of health-related products and services, news on medical trends and developments, and electronic communication among consumers, doctors, suppliers, and insurance companies.

Former ABC Television president Pat Fili-Krushel had been lured onboard to head up the Healtheon/WebMD consumer division as CEO. Efforts to create and integrate TV, Internet, and print content and services were going full-steam ahead. One of Murdoch's shining stars, Anthea Disney, executive vice president at News Corp., had masterminded this "one-stop shopping" approach to content for consumers and business.

Son James liked to describe it as the "Martha Stewart model" for making money. The vision was that News Corp. would create advertising-supported revenue from cable, print, Internet, and digital and analog television, while simultaneously collecting money from marketers, consumers, and strategic partners.

Before the bubble burst, Murdoch hoped the Healtheon venture alone would result in a return on investment for News Corp. of several billion dollars within five years. What's more, WebMD and other new interactive content would be launched through a universal portal that News Corp. was secretly developing and testing.

An interactive interface, dubbed My Sky, was being developed that would offer several hundred video and audio channels; interactive navigation through Gemstar TV Guide;

e-mail and chat room functions; electronic commerce capabilities; and special-interest content, from movies to children's programming to health, business, and sports. In the
grand scheme, the portal could be accessed from any device—
digital TV, PC, or wireless Internet appliance. It was anticipated that its rollout would occur more quickly outside the
United States, where News Corp. had its British Sky Broadcasting and Star TV satellite platforms. The U.S. piece, with
any luck, would come with Hughes' DirecTV or some sort of
pact with Echostar.

Now it was all put on hold and narrowed to focus primarily
on interactive television offering very selective content—sans
the Internet piece.

When the *New York Times* in part blamed James for News
Corp.'s miscalculations about the WebMD venture, James dismissed that notion and said, "The *New York Times*, they don't
like us over there." The move to scale back was due to unexpected market changes that also led WebMD to refocus its
own business away from consumers and onto the business-to-
business market.

James said, "It's disappointing that WebMD had to realign
itself into their business-to-business operations—there is less
space for us in that. So that partnership really didn't make
sense looking at the new management of that company and
where they wanted to grow the businesses. At the time the
deal was negotiated, however, it looked like a pretty good solution to me, and I think the analysts would bear that out."

James continued, "The market has changed and [WebMD]
in particular has had a shift in management and a shift in
focus—earlier they were really building both the business-to-
business as well as the consumer health brand, and that latter
part is where our partnership fit in. Now they've really focused
on the former part, the business-to-business piece. We both

looked each other in the eye and said, let's be reasonable about this, let's figure out a way to accomplish some of our mutual commitments anyway."

Said brother Lachlan, evaluating his brother's initial role and optimism about that joint venture, "It was really unfair [for the press] to blame [the cutbacks] on James. It was a big deal for the whole company—it had to do with the cable health channel we had, and there were a lot of people involved. The truth is if you look back to when that deal was done, it was a pretty good deal in the mood of the day."

What everyone in the industry had their eye on, he said, was "how do media companies like News Corp. leverage our strategy internationally, how do we get into integrating cable plus print plus the Internet, with this content base? So it was structured in a way that was pretty clever, in the health category. You both have media outlets whether it's cable or whatever, plus we have this deal with all our newspapers which share content with WebMD back and forth. We leverage our international strength by showing them that we deserve to share rights to over half of their international business. And the question is, where is media going in terms of one-to-one relationships with consumers? How do you take a piece of the transactional revenue along the way? If you put yourself in the mindset everyone was in 18 months ago, it was a clever deal that you'd probably do again."

Of the deal's eventual demise, Lachlan said, "I think no one could foresee the change in the environment today, so it was the right thing to unwind it."

In fact, News Corp. was the first in a long line of media companies to see the writing on the wall. Its layoffs and shutdown of Internet ventures were followed by similar moves on the parts of GE's NBC, Viacom's MTV, Disney,

The *New York Times,* and Time Warner's CNN in the winter of 2001.

Murdoch through the mid- and late 90s had predicted that the Internet would "destroy more businesses than it creates." He was criticized for not "getting it," but by mid-1999 he'd gotten with the program—though in a much more careful and conservative way than his rivals.

In a number of cases, to be conservative, Murdoch made deals based on swaps for advertising via News Corp.'s properties versus cash. This was true of the WebMD arrangement.

Murdoch still believed that broadband networks would change everything, eventually. In the United States, News Corp. already had agreements for domestic distribution of broadband versions of its Fox News and Fox Sports to be carried on Excite@Home, Road Runner, Palm 7, and various cellular phone companies. Both DirecTV and Echostar had agreements to broadcast Fox channels.

Fox was reaching about 350 million cable subscribers worldwide and an average 30 million nightly broadcast TV viewers in the United States. Outside the United States, it had the capacity to reach 400 million homes, mostly through satellite and cable TV.

In Asia, however, where the Internet was still growing rapidly, James and his father were still optimistic about the long-term benefits of their earlier investments in such businesses as Netease.com and Indya.com and the $10 million investment in the Chinese-language community web site renren.com.

When sticking closely to its core businesses, while using the Internet to push content to broader audiences, News Corp. still had a winning formula.

In the United States, staffed by a tiny group—compared to other newspaper Web operations—the NYPost.com was turning a profit.

Epilogue

LEGACIES

Rupert Murdoch stands at the divide between the old world and the new. While his father, Sir Keith Murdoch, created Australia's first national newspaper chain, Murdoch created the first truly global media company. His expansion across world cultures rivals that of any other media company on the planet. Where does that leave the future of this vast and growing empire?

The economies of scale enabled by Sky Global will essentially fund Murdoch's future forays into underdeveloped regions of the world—such as China and India. In China, for example, while other media companies have taken a more conservative approach, doing little more than distributing their existing channels through platforms like Star TV, Murdoch is creating programming and distribution platforms where none existed.

In China, "CNN has its channels there, Viacom has its channels there, NBC, Disney have channels there. Most have taken a channel approach of their individual brands," says Tom Rogers, CEO of Primedia. Rogers, as head of NBC Cable in the mid-90s, worked with Murdoch to distribute NBC channels through Star. "Murdoch is the only one who has gone after a giant platform play, of being a major distributor. That is a bigger risk. Murdoch clearly has a vision that satellite television around the world is going to be a critical force."

While leveraging digital platforms for further reach around the globe, at heart Murdoch still possesses the aesthetics of his roots: the newspaper business. That tradition of print is in his blood.

In the newspaper world, his philosophy—like his father's—had always been that while other papers abandoned the working class, his media properties would be egalitarian and cater to popular tastes. No matter how high-tech the medium, for better or worse, that remained true. Whether through interactive betting on sports channels via digital TV, or via services of the future that would deliver personalized headlines to cell phones, Murdoch planned to get closer to individual consumers than he had ever dreamed possible. We can expect similar principles to govern the future of the conglomerate News Corporation.

His father's mentor, Lord Northcliffe, proprietor of the London *Times,* believed a newspaper should "deal with what interests the mass of people," that it should "give the public what it wants."

Indeed, Sir Keith had started a "women's page" when he took over Australia's Melbourne *Herald,* spotlighting the big news stories as well as the trivial. He even launched a beauty contest sponsored by the paper, as well as numerous reader contests. He, like his son, was accused by some of "yellow journalism."

Rupert, like his father—who went from a single newspaper to launching magazines, taking over other papers, and spreading out to radio broadcasting—would expand in many ways. Like his own children, as a schoolboy he was bullied because of his father's reputation and power.

Rupert was "anti-Establishment" for the most part, though he cozied up to the "establishment"—as in China—if it meant breaking into a huge, lucrative new market. Murdoch had almost a Dickensian love for common tastes, while he himself, a sophisticated man of the world with the best of everything, had risen above such things long ago.

His first preference, with his first child, Prudence, was to send her to a public school. In London, Murdoch had her initially attending a lowly comprehensive school, where she had a hard time of it.

"He didn't like all the kind of Establishment in England, so he wanted to probably just be a bit different," Prudence said. "I was his guinea pig, thank you very much."

Following that experiment, Murdoch dispatched her to a refined girls' school, Frances Holland. When he bought a country mansion outside London, she attended boarding school.

N ow Murdoch, with his sons' assistance, at every turn was confronting a changing new world, while still nurturing the old. He would not consider canceling his subscriptions to his favorite papers just because he could read them electronically, he says. He also only intermittently uses electronic mail and the Internet. "I get a lot of email. I have it in spasms."

Sitting in his Manhattan office, he ruminates on his habits and preferences, and the development of his empire. "I guess I've been too used to paper over the years," he muses. His favorite paper, he says, is the London *Sunday Times*. "I like the Sunday paper because you've got time to read. It's not like a sweat in the morning, 'God I should really read all these papers!' It would take at least an hour to do it proper, and I have to leave in about 10 minutes."

Murdoch pauses between thoughts with long "aaaahs," and "mmmms," and sometimes becomes so private in his thoughts that his words are barely audible. Talking about newspapers always gets Murdoch most animated, and opinionated.

"Some of them you get tired of reading. The *New York Times* on Sunday is very much the worst issue they put out for the week. All the news is what didn't get printed on Sunday," he says. "Not much gets printed on Sunday. The fact is they write for Monday, Tuesday, Wednesday, Thursday. Come Friday all those people are out at the Hamptons—their best reporters and editors. And it's leftovers on Sunday. They don't have their best people on."

Murdoch, still considering his newspaper rivals' Sunday habits, says, "Their business section, it's got a lot of life and they try very hard during the week, but it's unreadable on Sunday." Other than classified advertising, "I defy anyone to find anything of interest on Sunday," he says, noting that citizens all over the country "read the Sunday papers to see what's out there, what people are selling things for, mortgage rate listings—it's well done. But it's not what you'd call a normal newspaper giving you great insight into what went on during the week. 'The Week in Review' is really . . . I can't read it!"

Needless to say, Murdoch's favorite U.S. newspaper is the New York *Post*, "most days of the week." He says, "Other days, ahhh, I'd say we're flat today. The *Post* has always been a struggle. We never really put enough resources into it." He notes, however, that with a tiny staff, NYPost.com is quite profitable, and very much in demand with its classified section and other online features.

Contentwise, despite a lack of resources, says Murdoch, "It's very very good, it's the best in sports. It's the most unpredictable paper—you get a kick out of reading it. All the main news is there. You don't have to buy another paper—we cover all the big stories as well as anyone."

As for the prudishness and snobbishness with which some of his papers have been regarded, for example, the outrage over the years in some U.K. quarters regarding his Page Three Girls, bare-breasted beauties adorning one of his tabloids, the *Sun,* Murdoch says, "The feminists get pissed off, but they've even quieted down now. They're so harmless, those pictures. They really are. There's nothing pornographic. Bare top. That's all it is. . . ."

Page Three Girls came into existence, he explains, "in the early days." He says, "It happened when I was away, and I came back and was *stunned,*" with a huge smile on his face, clearly unbothered by controversy. "And even women like looking at it anyway. And it gradually became a total fixture. Then a few years ago there was a huge debate to move it off, on some days back to page 5 or 7."

The *Sun* had introduced Page Three Girls, wearing bras, in 1970. The pinups were known as Sunbirds. By November of that year, they were appearing completely bare-breasted. A caption told readers, "From time to time some self-appointed critic stamps his tiny foot and declares the *Sun* is obsessed with sex. It is not the *Sun* but the critics who are obsessed. The *Sun,* like most of its readers, likes pretty girls."

Editor Larry Lamb was originally responsible for the infamous page. Rupert had picked Lamb, the son of a Yorkshire colliery worker, as editor when he acquired the paper in 1969, after a bidding war with archrival Robert Maxwell. Lamb was left-wing and working class in his sensibilities. (The *Sun* had been a left-wing paper since its creation in 1964.)

"He's dead now. I think he certainly got the credit for it," Murdoch says, attributing some of the venom directed at himself in Britain to the fact that he turned the media business upside-down and unraveled the unions, knocking the competition off its feet.

Murdoch's deal-making skills were as acrobatic thirty years

ago as they are today, as demonstrated by his GM wrangling. Back then, he won the *Sun* with an arrangement to pay 50,000 pounds down, and installments of 2,500 pounds a week, up to a minimum of 250,000 pounds, which could be increased up to 500,000 pounds only if the paper continued to be profitable.

Murdoch quickly increased the *Sun's* circulation from a low of 1.5 million to 4 million. Murdoch, whom one of his colleagues involved in the GM wrangling describes as "understanding consumer behavior better than anyone I know," thought readers wanted more "fun" and hated being preached at; he thought investigative pieces on politics and socials issues—something rival papers were trying to push, going upmarket—were pretentious. His goal was to be brash, youthful, and uninhibited. By early 1971, the *Sun* was named Newspaper of the Year by the industry.

"We were a huge catalyst for change there, first on the newspaper scene—with the best popular paper in the world," Murdoch says. He got the paper after Maxwell had made the first offer and was rejected by the print unions.

The "Dirty Digger," as Murdoch was dubbed by critic Richard Ingrams, editor of the satirical paper *Private Eye,* did not believe he was vandalizing the British press, as his critics said, but merely delighting his readers.

At the end of the 1980s and into the early 1990s, the *Sun* was the biggest-selling English-language daily in the world. This was despite the fact that The Press Council, which monitored the British press till the late 80s, found it to be "racist," "sexist," and "manipulative." Indeed, over the years, Queen Elizabeth II sued the paper, and Elton John broke all British records by winning 1 million pounds in libel damages.

Says Murdoch, "The *Sun* is very very good now. I think they disliked us because we didn't show respect for the royal family. That's their Establishment. Ahhhh."

In 2001, Murdoch was once again shaking up the establishment. While thirty years ago Murdoch had made the U.K. newspaper world go all googly-eyed—sometimes with outrage, sometimes with awe and admiration—by the new millennium he had his competitors on the edge of their seats in the arena of digital television.

The prospect of Murdoch owning DirecTV, coupled with his increasing ownership of Gemstar and impending partnership with Microsoft, had many shaking in their boots.

Some competitors protested that Murdoch would be creating a "dangerous monopoly," once Gemstar's patent-rich electronic program guide was leveraged across the Sky Global platform. Said Tribune Media Services CEO David Williams, "Gemstar has used its patents as an offensive weapon to threaten to put small companies out of business. Murdoch's not going to back off. He'll probably take it even further."

By late April, just when his rivals were heaving a sigh of relief, believing the bid was dead, Murdoch relinquished his vow to not change the original terms and sweetened his play for the company. For the same amount of money, he agreed to a smaller stake in the proposed new company, scaling back News Corp.'s ownership share to 30 percent from the 35 percent previously proposed.

He'd also taken some assets off the table. The bid still would include more than $3 billion in cash from Microsoft Corp. and others. On Tuesday, May 1, the GM board debated the revised offer. The day before, the Hughes board reviewed its options.

Jack Smith, Harry Pearce, and others were urging their colleagues to go ahead. Mike Smith had been unsuccessful in securing a better deal. Still, difficult issues remained to be worked out with Murdoch.

In the new scenario, News Corp. would also consider giving up day-to-day management control. Heck, Murdoch was even open to allowing Mike Smith to remain in control—if it meant getting himself a piece of the DirecTV pie. In effect, by agreeing to a smaller ownership share without proportionately reducing the assets News Corp. intended to contribute, Murdoch had upped the premium he was willing to pay for Hughes, satisfying shareholders' concerns without giving up too much. As had often been his strategy, he was certain he could increase his share and control the company over time.

He'd taken off the table a stake in Stream, a small Italian broadcaster that had been losing money. It remained to be seen if he would structure the deal to still include Star. Murdoch and Rick Wagoner had explored the preliminary terms of the new deal during a personal meeting the previous week. Murdoch's gestures would help Hughes save face; shareholders and Mike Smith had been adamant about not selling out to Murdoch.

If something happens to finally derail the deal, Murdoch says his preference is to hold off on a Sky Global IPO, though the public offering still makes sense. Does it make sense to go public even without a U.S. piece to News Corp.'s satellite holdings?

"Oh yeah, absolutely," Murdoch says. "But we don't *have* to go public. It was an idea when the markets were flying high. A way to raise some money to put them [satellite assets] all together. But we don't have to do that at all."

Protean Murdoch is ready to mold himself into an alternative scenario at the drop of a dime.

Rupert Murdoch is fluid; he adapts to the moment and the market at the turn of a dime, say his colleagues. "Frankly, I'd rather not do it [an IPO] at the moment," says Murdoch. "There's quite a lot of pieces in there; they have a huge amount of development to do. I'd like to see that be a bit further along the way, a bit stronger, and then make an offering. But in this market you're going to need money very, very badly before you do an IPO. We don't need money badly, we're in sound shape. We have plenty of cash in the bank and we want to keep it there." He adds, "When we get it together it will be transforming for the company."

Musing over the evolution of Sky Global, Rupert Murdoch says, "As the success of cable shows, people want more choice than what they can get over free broadcast. And there's a big business creating distribution, and a big business creating programs for that distribution. I mean your ideas evolve of course, and technology opens up possibilities too."

After an IPO, "then the work starts," says Murdoch. "You've got to put the technology in, you've got to start putting in what programming you can do across continents."

Then there are questions of branding. "I think there'll be different brands in different markets. The brands are so well established, Sky is the name of pay television in Britain, even if you're on the cable, you're watching Sky channels. And it's the same in Asia—in China, Star is a bigger name than McDonald's, it's quite ridiculous, I don't know whether to believe it, but it's the biggest Western brand there," Murdoch says.

His strategies are "long distance," he says, "but I think we're making huge breakthroughs in India. Things are opening up much faster. And we've picked up a lot of business in places like Taiwan, which is 40 percent the size of Britain, it's not tiny. But the two big things really are India and China."

These days, in the spring of 2001, the Big Six meeting is "often a conference call," as it is difficult to have all six executives in the same location at the same time. The GM-Hughes deal "tends to take the first 90 percent of the meeting time," Murdoch says.

"We try and do it every Monday," he says. "We try to go through what we're all doing, and have done. So we know what's in the works. More or less it's just a contact meeting so we set the agenda—where do we stand on legal proceedings, what's the status on negotiations on Fox Family, for example. There's a checklist of things so we all know where we are."

Murdoch is unfazed about the market doldrums and the Internet adjustment that has taken place. He is 100 percent confident of his Sky Global plan, with or without Hughes.

On the Internet crash, Murdoch says, "We finally got beaten over the head by the investment community to get into it. But nearly all our investments, at least 50 percent were paid for in exchange for advertising. We've not lost much cash in it at all." Indeed, many of the companies he's invested in but has scaled back on "are still functional with a lot of money in them. . . . Are they going to succeed? How long before the stock prices go right up again? Who knows?"

An advertising-based model for making money on the Internet just doesn't work, Murdoch believes. "Well, I don't believe it ever will," he says. "As you can see at the moment, the idea of banner headline—advertising on a PC . . . I don't know, whenever I go to Yahoo!, I don't pay attention to banner ads. They annoy me. I'm going in, and I'm a very light user of the Internet I guess, but I'm told heavy users are all the same now. They want to go to a site, they want to go to etrade, or they mainly want to go do their e-mail. Or they want something special to be part of.

"Our attitude is very much broadband. The television is going to play a bigger part in people's lives than the PC," Murdoch says. "The fact is, particularly with the satellite, you can build a very intelligent set-top box with a TiVo recorder or whatever; you can do a lot of things. With the interactive television it will be whatever you [employ], whether its t-commerce, or enhancing the whole experience of watching

television, we do it now in Britain. You can stop news programs, and you can see the words on the screen, you can do
things like that. With football matches you can view different
players and different camera angles—and that will lend itself
to commercial applications too."

What's more, when Henry Yuen's technology is fully imple-
mented, Murdoch expects interactive TV to explode. "You'll
be able to get anything with one click. When you're watching
QVC, why should you pick up a telephone and say I want this,
here's my credit card number and everything else. You can just
click and the television set will know your credit card number.
Which makes it a lot easier to buy. That's an area of interactive
TV that I think is going to be very interesting."

As for the potential treachery of doing business with
Microsoft, Murdoch says he's comfortable that the company
is taking an approach with World Box that will ensure
Microsoft will not run away with its business and customers. "I
think we have that fairly worked out," he says. "It would be *our*
walled garden. There are still minor things to work out, but it
will be easy to get to MSN or anyone else," he says, and have
that be separate and walled off from Sky Global's business
transactions.

Murdoch expressed surprise at a U.K. newspaper
article in the spring of 2001, which, in a rare
acknowledgment, credited him as being a catalyst
for change in the media business.

"I try to be," Murdoch said. "We've been a catalyst with Fox
news. I can't say we were a catalyst with the *Post* but at least we
were an antidote to general, monolithic thinking in the city."

The most enormous change agent could be Sky Global. "It
has *enormous* potential for that," Murdoch said, letting out one
of his little roars on the word "enormous." It promises to

impact the entire media world, "without being political in the sense that it will certainly carry CNN, Fox News, or whatever— we'll have all sides. And we'll have to be very careful country by country."

Murdoch continued on about what he hopes Sky Global will be. "You want to cover all the major areas of the world, and I think you really want to make it a very key part of people's lives in terms of supplying everything from remote education to entertainment and information. . . . The key to its success would have to be the recognition that most countries want local programming. There are only certain things that are really going to become very, very high points of support. The biggest and the best American films are certainly international. It would be amazing, say, in a country like India— there will be an opportunity to have 100 channels and an opportunity for people to form a channel, get an audience, and express themselves artistically."

Murdoch became animated talking about it, sitting forward, his volume rising. "We can't own all the channels or even a significant proportion of them."

What's more, in the spring of 2001, Murdoch was still in talks lining up additional investors for Sky Global. Among those he courted, months earlier, was Prince Alwaleed, the renowned Saudi global investor and one of the richest men in the world. At a Manhattan dinner at the Plaza Hotel held in honor of the Prince, Murdoch and wife Wendi dined and talked with the billionaire investor all night long. "I sat next to him," Murdoch said. "He owns a very big piece of the Plaza, I think. He's a very, very intelligent investor, though he has no visions that I'm aware of that will change the world. He bets on good businesses."

Alwaleed had come on other occasions to visit Murdoch at his office. "I've not been to Saudi Arabia, we're not that close," Murdoch said.

Alwaleed, however, turned out to be an unlikely investor for Sky Global. According to News Corp. insiders, he had a large interest in an Arab satellite operation, along with his cousin, who hated the venture because both men and dozens of other Saudi investors lost billions of dollars on it. Alwaleed told Murdoch he was interested in putting his interest into Sky Global, and added some "real money"—a billion dollars or so.

"But it doesn't amount to much and we don't want to take a minority interest in a losing operation," said a News Corp. source. "We're watching what will happen in the Arab world. Something will happen between those people and there'll be an opportunity."

Said Murdoch, "I would hope that he would join us, but it will come in time after they sort out their problems between the competing platforms in those countries."

How does Murdoch draw the line when it comes to doing business in countries where human rights and freedom of speech are at issue? "I don't know. It's the popular thing to say that China abuses human rights. Their answer is there are plenty of human rights abuses in this country. And in every country."

Murdoch reflects on how the world will remember him for posterity. He hopes, he says, it will be as "someone who has hopefully had an impact on the world and an impact for good."

Says Murdoch, speaking in hushed tones now, "By creating competition and choice in the media, helping develop the media, the media has clearly for some time played a central role in the development of our society starting with the printing press." He says he hopes his good will come "by being someone who has done some important things in that huge field. I'll be very happy," he says, trailing off sadly. "Is that all right?"

"We've done a few important things." Starting in Australia, "we took broken-down newspapers," he says, and moved them to greatness. In the television arena, in the United States and Britain, News Corp., he says, has been "a huge guarantor for continued competition for generations."

In the United Kingdom, "we introduced a very important fundamental challenge to the whole television system. Which I think the public gained from a lot in terms of attitudes and competitiveness." In the United States, the Fox network and Fox News channel likewise brought more competition to the market, says Murdoch.

Murdoch says he has no idea why Ted Turner hates him so much. "We were good friends, I stayed on his ranch, we used to chat for stories and everything else. Then he came out about a week after I said I was going to start a news channel, which was only a throwaway remark at a chamber of commerce luncheon in Boston. And he made such a fuss about it. We never said we'd get on with it. We said we'd look at it, we cared to do it, but we didn't actually put a time on it. And I said to mutual friends, it's play acting, we're really good friends. And they said no no no, you don't understand, he really does hate you."

Of course, Murdoch *did* get on with it, and created Fox News which eclipsed CNN on many occasions over the years.

Murdoch was entertained when CNN's *Moneyline* host, Stuart Varney, quit because of an off-the-wall comment Turner had made. (Of course, Murdoch had for years been wildly entertained by Turner's mouthing off. He had the New York *Post* run the headline, "Ted Turner's Mouth Runs Amok at

U.N.," after Turner took the opportunity during a November 1996 forum at the United Nations to denounce Murdoch as wanting to "control the world," and "a no-good bastard.")

Murdoch is amazed by the latest. "He was getting a million dollars a year, he walked out. Then and there. Won't go back to work. Ted said some remark during a farewell for Bernie Shaw. It was Ash Wednesday and a few people turned up with ashes on their foreheads, and he said what are they doing with ashes, we got some Jesus freaks here, they ought to be over at Fox." Murdoch laughs. "Then he sent out an e-mail saying any religious-minded people are working at Fox."

Murdoch is sanguine about his own controversial comments over the years. He was viewed to be insensitive about Chinese censorship of Tibet and the Dalai Lama. "It was just a throwaway of mine," Murdoch says cheerfully. "He reminded me of a very political old monk shuffling around in Gucci shoes. There are quite a lot of people who quietly said to me you were dead right."

By early May, Hughes and GM boards had indeed approved reconsidering Murdoch's offer. Murdoch was quite happy. He'd compared the DirecTV business to *Mona Lisa*'s place at the Louvre.

Before a satellite industry conference a few weeks earlier, he'd emphasized that Sky Global would be a success, even without DirecTV and a U.S. presence.

"That's a bit like asking whether the Louvre could exist without the *Mona Lisa*," he said. "A U.S. presence is nice to have but it's not necessary to the overall success of the operation. We, like the Louvre, have plenty of other treasures to show off."

The companies were now working on establishing a definitive agreement to create what they hoped would be the world's premier satellite broadcasting enterprise.

Still being debated were whether News Corp.'s partly-owned Italian pay-TV business Stream and China's Star would be included as assets available to Hughes. Even Mike Smith was publicly acknowledging that Hughes was once again talking to News Corp.

Meantime, James Murdoch was busy lining up other opportunities in Asia. Around the same time his father was meeting with Hughes in early May, Star announced it had entered into a joint venture with Taiwan's Koos Group to set up a holding company that would help upgrade Taiwan's cable system and also invest in the country's cable companies. Star was preparing to put $240 million into the joint venture. Koos would also invest.

Once again, Murdoch's goal was to act as a catalyst, jump-starting the upgrade and digitization of cable systems in Taiwan, which of course would enable consumers in that country to partake of Sky Global's offerings in the future. Star's investment would also enable it to obtain equity interest in the cable systems concerned. It was expected that the first digital cable systems in Taiwan would be launched in early 2002.

Back in New York, the acquisition of an additional 17 percent interest in Gemstar-TV Guide had been completed, raising News Corp.'s stake to 38.5 percent.

John Malone had turned over 80 percent of Liberty Media's shares in Gemstar-TV Guide during the public announcement in September. Liberty officially was now the largest nonvoting shareholder of News Corp., with an 18 percent interest in the company, second only to Murdoch himself. Another 20 percent of Liberty's Gemstar interest was transferred to Sky Global Networks, so that Liberty owned 4.76 percent of Sky Global's outstanding equity prior to its IPO. Liberty also planned to invest $500 million in Sky Global shares at the time of the public offering. News Corporation, for its part, was now the largest Gemstar shareholder.

Unlikely was not a word that tempered Murdoch's ambitions in any arena, it seemed. Murdoch and sons were apparently empiricists, in the tradition of Keith Murdoch, who, in the early years as a journalist, pounded the pavement to see for himself what was going on in the world.

The Murdochs were driven by a need to "see" for themselves. It was personal experience that informed their actions, as well as their philosophies.

In college, as a philosophy major, Lachlan had a professor who was visiting from Cambridge, who indulged the young Murdoch for a year in the different aspects of Aristotle. "For a hard-core philosophy major it's sort of wimpy to say one of the ancient philosophers was your favorite because the concepts are simpler," Lachlan said. Nevertheless, he took a year on the *Nicomachean Ethics*, Aristotle's work on the meaning of life. "It was a good way to waste a year," Lachlan said.

One of the many things that Aristotle states, in the *Ethics*, is that practical wisdom is less a capacity to apply rules than an ability to see situations correctly. Human action is complex and variable; hence, practical wisdom involves issues that are not exact. Acquiring wisdom requires experience, one's being able to see what matters in certain circumstances, and why.

Experience in the world was a shifting terrain, and one had to adapt based on one's own observations.

Keith Murdoch's old guru, Northcliffe, had a mantra: "Explain, simplify, clarify!" Keith Rupert Murdoch was of like mind.

A signed editorial written by Murdoch in the *Sun* back in 1969 seems an apropos synopsis of his philosophy of life itself.

His goal was to be "truly independent, but politically mightily aware . . . ," to "never, ever sit on fences," and "never, ever be boring."

Source Notes

CHAPTER 1, pages 3 to 12

Rupert Murdoch in his office, on GM wrangling: author's interview.

General Motors/Hughes Electronics negotiations: author interviews with company executives, including Rupert Murdoch, Lachlan Murdoch, and numerous published reports.

The war between Mike Smith and Jack Smith: author interviews with News Corp. and GM sources and published reports. (Mike Smith would eventually resign from Hughes.)

Murdoch's view of his life as a series of wars: William Shawcross, *Murdoch: The Making of a Media Empire* (Touchstone, Simon & Schuster, New York, 1992).

Overview of GM relationships, Echostar, News Corp. strategies: author interviews, Rupert Murdoch, Lachlan Murdoch, James Murdoch, and other News Corp. executives.

Background on financial aspects of the deal: numerous newspaper reports, including March 19, 2001, New York *Times,* "G.M. May Be Running into Problems in Sale of Hughes Electronics"; and March 2, 2001, *Wall Street Journal,* "News Corp.'s Bid for Hughes Appears to Be at a Stalemate."

On the Smith brothers' relationship: published reports, including "How the Smith Boys Grew Up to Be CEOs," 10/23/1997, The *Wall Street Journal.*

On Mike Smith being out of a job if the News Corp. deal went through: interviews with News Corp. execs and numerous published reports, including "Hughes Electronics seeks to raise debt for spinoff," 3/10/2001, Reuters English News Service.

On shareholders, including Jeffrey Bronchick, chief investment officer for Reed Conner, objecting to News Corp.'s bid for Hughes: numerous published reports, including February 8, 2001, "Hughes Stock Falls 11% as Investors Question Terms of News Corp.'s Bid," *Wall Street Journal.*

Murdoch's 70th birthday party: author interview with Lachlan Murdoch.

Murdoch's opinion that no better deal was to be had, and that "they're with us for a set amount of money on a set of terms and we have a 99

percent completed deal with Microsoft that's waiting for these lawyers
to write it up": author interview with Murdoch in his office.

Account of due-diligence meeting in which Mike Smith walked out:
author interviews with Rupert Murdoch and several others who were
present at the meeting; author article in the *Financial Times*, March 22,
2001, "Murdoch Forced to Wait for His Biggest Piece of Pie in the Sky."

Who spilled the beans about Mike Smith's shopping the company to
Echostar and others? "I better not tell you who told me," Rupert said to
me in March 2001, and laughed about not wanting to blow his inside
source. Murdoch also told me, "I was pissed off because . . . I shouldn't
say this, but there was a very, very senior representative of GM, but
unknown to all the others at GM who had been negotiating with me."

Harry Pearce on ideas being "cheap": CNNfn: Market Coverage,
2/2/2000, "GM Names New CEO."

BSkyB business and impact on broadcast world: author interviews with
Rupert Murdoch, Lachlan Murdoch, James Murdoch, Merrill Lynch
analyst Jessica Reif Cohen, McKinsey & Co. partner George Wolf, Star
president Bruce Churchill, News Corp.'s Jon Richmond, NDS president Abe Peled, and others.

History of Hughes: Donald L. Barlett and James B. Steele, *Empire: The
Life, Legend and Madness of Howard Hughes,* January 1981, W.W. Norton
& Co.; Fortune, "Hughes Hasn't Been This Sexy Since . . . ," *Fortune,*
2/5/2001.

Rupert Murdoch's first dealings with GE, Hughes, and Cablevision for
Sky Cable venture: author interview with Rupert Murdoch; many pub-
lished reports, including 2/22/1990, *Wall Street Journal,* "Four Media
Giants Enter Venture for Direct-Broadcast TV Service," and 6/5/1991
Wall Street Journal, "Partners Pull the Plug on Sky Cable Project."

BSkyB and the interactive TV market in Europe versus the U.S.: *Business
Week* International Editions, "Europe's I-TV Advantage: Next-
generation broadcasting combines the best of a computer and a television," William Echikson, 2/19/2001.

Background on Tony Ball's career at News Corp.: author interviews and
published reports, including 7/26/2000, *Business Times,* "CEOs Having a Ball at BSkyB."

Background on Tony Ball and former CEO Mark Booth as well as Booth's
alleged difficulty with Elisabeth Murdoch: several published reports,
including 7/26/2000, *Business Times,* "CEOs Having a Ball at BSkyB."

Background on Hartenstein: author interviews and published reports
including 8/14/2000, *USA Today,* "DirecTV stays step ahead of cable."

Rupert Murdoch on Sky Cable: author interview with Murdoch.

History of Sky Cable, numerous published reports, including 2/22/1990, *Wall Street Journal,* "Four Media Giants Enter Venture for Direct-Broadcast TV Service," and author interviews with the Murdochs.

Robert Wright on the Sky Cable plan: news conference in New York, February 1990.

Murdoch on demise of Sky Cable and GE losing its nerve: author interview. DirecTV's other suitors: many published reports, including *Fortune,* 2/5/2001, "Hughes Hasn't Been This Sexy Since . . ."

Rupert Murdoch on GM's motivations to sell Hughes: author interview.

Background on FCC's Fowler, personal habits, and his relationship with Murdoch: Shawcross, *Murdoch;* other published reports, including *Broadcasting,* February 18, 1985, and *Business Week,* August 5, 1985.

Murdoch on being a catalyst for competition: author interview.

Murdoch on cultural imperialism, regulation, and doing business in different political environments: transcript of his speech in January 1999 at the Singapore Broadcasting Authority.

Lachlan Murdoch on Ergen: author interviews.

Lachlan on differences in taste re: *The Fight Club:* author interview.

History of American Sky Broadcasting (ASkyB): William Shawcross, *Murdoch: The Making of a Media Empire* (Touchstone, Simon & Schuster, New York, 1992); numerous published reports, including 5/22/1997, *Australian Financial Review,* "Murdoch's Satellite Plans Come Crashing to Earth."

Rupert Murdoch on cable threats: author interview.

Rupert Murdoch on Charlie Ergen: author interview.

Murdoch's plan for "World Box": author interviews with Rupert Murdoch, Lachlan Murdoch, James Murdoch, and other News Corp. executives; published reports, including author articles, *Talk* magazine, May 2001, "The Son Also Rises"; *Financial Times,* March 23, 2001, "Murdoch forced to wait for his biggest piece of pie in the sky."

On the deal being 99 percent complete, and set up in two parts, in case Hughes bailed out: author interview with Rupert Murdoch.

CHAPTER 2

Account of James Murdoch's wedding: author interviews with James Murdoch, Lachlan Murdoch, and numerous wedding guests.

Rupert Murdoch's introduction to James's wife: author interviews with Kathryn Hufschmid, James Murdoch, Lachlan Murdoch, and others.

Kathryn Hufschmid's background: author interviews with Kathryn Hufschmid, James Murdoch, and others.

Murdoch's long-term approach to investments: author interviews with Merrill Lynch analyst Jessica Reif Cohen and Booz Allen's Michael Wolf.

Murdoch's meeting with Bill Gates: author interviews with Lachlan Murdoch and others present.

Murdoch and sons' view of John Malone: author interviews with Lachlan, James, and other News executives.

Murdoch's partnership with Malone for Fox News: Shawcross, *Murdoch.*

Murdoch's vow that his Fox News would be better than CNN: *New York Times,* July 1996.

Murdoch on Turner's disparagement of him as schlockmeister: Murdoch speech at the National Press Club, February 1996.

Turner's loathing of Murdoch: scores of media appearances on Turner's part; publications documenting his legendary hate of Murdoch, including 5/17/1999, *The Guardian,* "The mouth of the south: CNN owner Ted Turner may be the anti-Murdoch"; and Shawcross, *Murdoch.*

Account of Sun Valley Lodge meetings: author interviews with those present.

James Murdoch's view of Sky Global and World Box: author interviews.

Microsoft's ambitions in the interactive television world: author interviews with company executives and analysts, including Booz Allen's Michael Wolf, Merrill Lynch's Jessica Reif Cohen, NDS's Jas Saini, NDS's Abe Peled, James Murdoch, Lachlan Murdoch, and many published reports.

Rupert Murdoch on World Box: author interview.

Murdoch's plans to "take out GM": author interview.

CHAPTER 3

Murdoch on assembling a world-class management team: his speech in January 1999 at the Singapore Broadcasting Authority.

Chernin history at company: 7/12/1999, *Newsweek.* "The Man Behind Rupert's Roll."

Chernin at company retreat: *The Age,* 7/10/1999, "New Successor Emerges from Rupert Love-in."

Chernin on global strategy: 8/14/2000, CNNfn: Market Coverage interview.

Rupert Murdoch's analyst briefing: 4/17/2000, "Murdoch loses $2.5 bln as News Corp. Shares Dive on ASX," AAP News; author interviews.

Jessica Reif Cohen on Murdoch diagnosis: author interview.

Lachlan and James Murdoch on rivalry wars: author interviews with both.

Lachlan on learning the ropes in remote parts of the world: author interview.

On Murdoch brothers' childhood and relationship personal details and high school and college days: author interviews with Lachlan Murdoch, James Murdoch, Rupert Murdoch, and long-time friends and colleagues who asked to remain unnamed.

Rupert Murdoch's preference for the real world: Shawcross, *Murdoch*.

James Murdoch's view of the English language versus world languages: author interviews and James's speech at an Edinburgh broadcasting conference, summer 2000.

Account of bachelor party: author interviews with those present, including James Murdoch, Lachlan Murdoch, and Robert Carlock.

Background on Rupert Murdoch's generosity toward his first wife, Patricia, and Prudence's comments on this: published reports, including "The Day I Screamed at My Dad Rupert," 3/21/1999, *Sun Herald*, London.

Rupert's continued support of his first wife after her second marriage ended: published reports, including 3/21/99, *Sun Herald*, and Shawcross, *Murdoch*.

Account of what went on in News Corp.'s corporate offices one day in the fall of 2000 when the stock took a dive: author observations at News Corp.

James's activities in India: author interviews with News Corp. and Star executives.

Chernin's activities in Washington: author interview with Rupert Murdoch and Lachlan Murdoch, and numerous news reports, including *Daily Variety*, 2/9/2001, "Chernin Enlists Publishers in C'right Fight."

CHAPTER 4

History of cryptography: For an in-depth and brilliant account, see Simon Singh's *The Code Book: The Science of Secrecy from Ancient Egypt to Quantum Cryptography*, September 1999, Doubleday & Co., New York.

Account of Murdoch's search for encryption technology, meeting with Peled, and the Michael Clinger affair: author interviews with Rupert Murdoch, Abe Peled, and numerous News Corp. and NDS executives.

Account of Hundertmark and Uzi Sharon: author interviews with NDS executives Abe Peled and Dov Rubin.

Account of News Corp.'s suit against Clinger and others, tax raid in Israel, and the investigation that ensued: author interviews with Rupert Mur-

doch, Abe Peled, Gary Ginsberg, and others, as well as published reports, including 2/24/1998, *The Jerusalem Post,* "NDS: Investigation to End Soon"; 11/10/1996, *Australian Financial Review,* "Secret Empire"; and *The Independent,* London, "The Man Who Got Smart with Murdoch."
Murdoch on Clinger being a "crook": author interview.

CHAPTER 5

Henry Yuen background and history: author interviews with Lachlan Murdoch, James Murdoch, Rupert Murdoch, Joe Kiener, and others, as well as numerous published reports, including 8/7/2000, *US News & World Report,* "Meet the Bill Gates of TV."
Murdoch on Yuen, and on James's pushing for a takeover: author interview.
Malone on Yuen: 9/29/2000, *Wall Street Journal Europe,* "Gemstar Is Key Player in Entertainment's Future."
Lachlan on James's early recognition of the value of Gemstar: author interviews.
On TV Guide's decline: author interviews and numerous published reports, including 9/4/2000, *Advertising Age,* "*TV Guide* magazine is fading, and that's fine with Joe Kiener."
Murdoch on Yuen's outrage at his takeover bid: author interview.
Murdoch on competitors' resentment of Yuen patents: author interview.
TV Guide and Gemstar background: author interviews with Joe Kiener, president, TV Guide; Lachlan Murdoch; James Murdoch; and Rupert Murdoch.
Murdoch's views on interactive television: author interview.
On competitors' suits against Gemstar, and Time Warner's blocking its guides: numerous reports, including 6/5/2000, *BusinessWeek,* "Gemstar Holds the Remote Control."

CHAPTER 6

Account of Beijing streets: author observations, early 2001.
Account of Rupert Murdoch's meeting with Jiang Zemin: author interviews with Rupert Murdoch and others present.
Rupert Murdoch on the Jiang meeting: author interview.
Rupert Murdoch comments on the impact of satellite TV on totalitarian governments: speech in January 1999 at the Singapore Broadcasting Authority.
James Murdoch on doing business in China and childhood memories in China: author interviews.

Patrick Murdoch on freedom of the press: Shawcross, *Murdoch*.

Michael Wolf's evaluation of Murdoch in China: author interview.

Lachlan Murdoch on his father and brother in China: author interview.

Murdoch on being "minnows," 2/10/2000, interview on Fox News: Your World.

Growth of technology in China: figures from China's State Administration of Radio, Film and Television, and other forecasts.

James's comments on the Falun Gong: his speech at the Millken conference in Beverly Hills, California, March 2001.

James's *Lampoon* cartoon: author interviews.

Rupert Murdoch on human rights and freedom of speech in China: author interview.

Mao posters in James's office: author interview with former News Corp. VP Matt Jacobson.

History of technology in China: Diamond, Jared, *Guns, Germs and Steel*, W. W. Norton, March 1997, which James was also reading during the winter of 2001.

James Murdoch on the sensitivities of doing business in China: author interview.

CHAPTER 7

Description of James's office and view of Victoria harbor: author observations in Hong Kong, December 2000.

Murdoch's mantra "Be global, think local": author interviews with James Murdoch, Star president Bruce Churchill, Star senior VP Gary Walrath, Star VP Jannie Poon, and others.

History of Star TV: author interviews with James Murdoch, Lachlan Murdoch, Star president Bruce Churchill, Star senior VP Gary Walrath, Star VP Jannie Poon, and others.

Bruce Churchill on changing the rules in China: author interview.

History of Star in India: author interviews with James Murdoch, Rupert Murdoch, Lachlan Murdoch, Star president Bruce Churchill, Star senior VP Gary Walrath, Star VP Jannie Poon, and others.

Background on Phoenix: author interviews with James Murdoch, Lachlan Murdoch, Rupert Murdoch, Star's Jannie Poon, and others, as well as published reports.

Background on CCTV: author interviews with Star president Bruce Churchill, Gary Walrath, and others; speeches by Zhang Hai Tao and many published reports.

Richard Li history: author interviews with Star and News Corp. executives and many published reports.

Murdoch and Jiang Mianheng: author interviews with Murdoch, and many published reports.

Secrecy of China Netcom deal: author interviews with those involved.

CHAPTER 8

Account of Zhang Hai Tao speech and Beijing conference: author interviews with NDS president Abe Peled, NDS VP Sue Taylor, James Murdoch, News Corp. China president Laurie Smith, Star president Bruce Churchill, and others.

Murdoch in L.A. with Tian Congming: author interviews with those present, and number of published reports.

Murdoch on China: his speech in Singapore, January 1999.

Murdoch during Jiang Zemin visit to London: numerous newspaper reports in the United Kingdom.

Jiang thanking Murdoch for his objectivity: numerous published reports.

Internet restrictions in China: numerous published reports.

Murdoch giving up his Australian citizenship: Shawcross, *Murdoch*.

Murdoch on the Dalai Lama: author interview.

The role of satellite versus cable in China: author interviews with NDS president Abe Peled, NDS VP Sue Taylor, James Murdoch, News Corp. China president Laurie Smith, Star president Bruce Churchill, and others.

Zemin's search for Huang Qi and "Shumin": numerous reports, including "China Detains Site Operator for 'Subversive' Postings," June 8, 2000, ABCNews.com, and report of the Digital Freedom Network at www.dfn.org.

CHAPTER 9

Account of James Murdoch's house, dog Sydney, and wife Kathryn, on The Peak in Hong Kong: author observations, December 2000.

James downplaying his house: author interview.

Kathryn on her courtship with James: author interview.

James's early years in new media: author interviews with James Murdoch, former News Corp. VP Matt Jacobson, senior VP Anthea Disney, Lachlan Murdoch, VP Kathryn Fink, and former News Digital Media programming executive Vladimir Edelman.

James Murdoch's profanities during Los Angeles speech and in general:

author interview, Matt Jacobson, former News Corp. VP, and published reports.

James Murdoch's comments on PCCW: text of speech he gave at Edinburgh broadcasting conference, summer 2000.

Richard Li's response via Alex Arena speech: several published reports.

James Murdoch's bafflement on his reputation of speaking in profanities: author interview.

Kathryn Hufschmid on the Murdoch clan: author interview and e-mail from Hufschmid to the author.

James Murdoch on his relationship with Wendi Deng: author interview.

James Murdoch on family versus business life: author interview.

Account of Shanghai and opening party thrown by Star there: author observations of the event, early December 2000 at Shanghai's Grand Hyatt.

Madame Jaio on James Murdoch: author interview, translated by a colleague of hers who was present.

Laurie Smith on James's reception in China: author interview.

James's "state visits": author interview with Gregory Tse, a Shanghai businessman present at the Star event.

Gary Walrath on James: author interview.

Bruce Churchill on rationale behind rejection of Hong Kong broadcasting license: author interview.

CHAPTER 10

Background on India market: author interviews with James Murdoch, Star India head Peter Mukerjea, Star VP Gary Walrath, and Star president Bruce Churchill.

Accounts of Indian arrest warrants for Rupert Murdoch: author interview with Rupert Murdoch, Peter Mukerjea, and several published reports.

Turner on Murdoch's trouble in India: numerous reports, including *The Guardian*, 5/17/1999, "The Mouth of the South: CNN owner Ted Turner may be the anti-Murdoch."

Account of Murdoch party in Delhi, at the Ashioki Hotel: author interviews with Star India head Peter Mukerjea, Star VP Gary Walrath, James Murdoch, and others.

Account of Murdoch's launch of the India version of *Who Wants to Be a Millionaire?:* author interviews with Star India head Peter Mukerjea, Star VP Gary Walrath, James Murdoch, Lachlan Murdoch, Star president Bruce Churchill, Star VP Jannie Poon, and others.

Figures on size of Indian television market: author interviews with Star executives, and published reports.

Mukerjea on Indian market: author interview.

Churchill on launch of ISkyB: author interview.

Account of James and Kathryn's trip to India, November 2000: author interviews with Star chief Peter Mukerjea, James Murdoch, and Kathryn Hufschmid.

Account of guard with shotgun protecting Rupert Murdoch during his earlier visit: author interviews with Star executives, and Rupert Murdoch.

Murdoch on his alleged "enemies" in India and his arrest warrants: author interview.

Chapter 11

Gates on Asian market: his speech at Korean summit.

Rejection of Gates and Microsoft in China: numerous published reports, including 4/26/2000, *Wall Street Journal Europe,* "Beijing Wants to Counter Entrenchment by Microsoft."

Microsoft interactive television problems: numerous published reports; author interviews with NDS executives, including Abe Peled and Jas Saini.

Accounts of NDS meetings with Microsoft: author interviews with NDS executives including Jas Saini, who was responsible for the deal.

Microsoft's statements about its television plans: white papers and documents posted on Microsoft's web site, spring 2000, and given to customers and clients.

Microsoft's Goldman on its television platform: documents posted on Microsoft web site, and other promotional materials.

Peled and Saini on Microsoft partnership: author interviews.

Microsoft's problems with UPC and AT&T: numerous published reports.

Jon DeVaan on AT&T relationship: published reports, including "Microsoft Delays Could Slow AT&T's Interactive Service," 8/27/2000, *Wall Street Journal.*

Microsoft's investments in cable companies: numerous reports, including 6/6/1999, "Gates Throws Cash at Next Thing," *Sunday Star-Times;* and 5/12/1999, "Microsoft May Buy Interest in UK Firm," *Wall Street Journal.*

Chapter 12

Account of Rupert Murdoch and Lachlan Murdoch at Red Hot Chili Peppers benefit concert, March 14, 2001: author observations at the event.

Murdoch on the Red Hot Chili Peppers: author interview.

Murdoch's sweetened bid for DirecTV: author interviews and published reports, including "News Corp. Sweetens Bid for Hughes, Agrees to a Reduced Ownership Share," *Wall Street Journal,* April 30, 2001.

On Murdoch's creation of e-partners, and numerous other new media ventures in 1999 and 2000: author interviews and published reports, including 7/12/1999, *BusinessWeek,* "Rupert Does the Cyberhustle."

Kathryn Fink on Internet investments: author interview.

On poor performance of new Internet ventures, and Murdoch's scaling back: author interviews and many reports including 7/28/2000, *The Guardian,* "Murdoch's New Media Venture Is Dismembered."

On publication of early Murdoch letters: 4/28/2001, ABIX—Australasian Business Intelligence: The West Australian.

James on demise of WebMD and other Internet ventures, & *NY Times* dislike of "us": author interview.

Lachlan on the Internet cutbacks: author interview.

EPILOGUE

Tom Rogers on Murdoch in China: author interview.

Background on Lord Northcliffe and Sir Keith Murdoch, and Rupert Murdoch's love of print media: author interviews, and Shawcross, *Murdoch.*

On Murdoch's daughter Prudence and her first experiences at an "egalitarian" school and being her father's "guinea pig": 03/21/1999, "The Day I Screamed at My Dad Rupert," *Sun Herald,* London.

Rupert Murdoch on his e-mail and newspaper preferences and habits: author interview.

Rupert Murdoch on the Page Three Girls: author interview.

Caption regarding the *Sun*'s "obsession" with sex: November 1970, *The Sun.*

Murdoch on Lamb: author interview.

Murdoch's deal when he purchased *The Sun:* Shawcross, *Murdoch.*

David Williams on impact of Murdoch alliance with Gemstar: author interview.

Negotiations of new terms with DirecTV and GM: author interviews and published reports.

Murdoch musing over going public *without* DirecTV; the evolution of Sky Global; branding; and Asia markets: author interview.

Murdoch on the Internet crash; interactive TV; doing business with Microsoft; on being a catalyst; Sky Global prospects; Prince Alwaleed; human rights; Ted Turner; and other issues: author interview.

Lachlan Murdoch on his studies of Aristotle: author interview.

Acknowledgments

There are many people whose support and assistance made this book possible. First are those who were there virtually every day to embrace me when I emerged from the trance induced by waltzing with thousands of words: my miraculous daughter Madeline; Amy and Christopher Dale; Liz Erkenswick; and Ric Murphy, who understands more than anyone the inscrutable process of creation.

Thanks also to Liz Sipes Liebeskind, Hank Liebeskind, and their beautiful daughters Charlie and Sam, for their warmth and Manhattan hospitality; Jim Donovan, for his wit, undying friendship, and numerous buoyant coffee breaks; and to Gene, Rick, and Marge, whose admiration and support helped me more than they can know.

I am indebted in ways they cannot imagine to the vivid imagination, liveliness, and endless friendship of Robert Auletta and Josip Pasic; the unflagging support of my parents; as well as the most precious comradery of Cindy, Gary, Jeff, and Adrienne.

I wish to thank my patient, talented, and supportive editor on this book, Airié Dekidjiev, and Andrew Stuart for his great work with foreign publishers. I am grateful also to Wiley's Jessie Noyes for saint-like patience and diligence in fielding phone calls, faxes, and many messages. Much gratitude to my original agent, Bill Gladstone, who got the ball rolling and kept it rolling with admirable skill.

Acknowledgments

A tip of the hat goes to Tina Brown and *Talk* magazine, whose support and publication of an early portion of my research kept me afloat at the right time.

At News Corp., Gary Ginsberg did a spectacular job providing background information and prying some doors open for me, as did Jannie Poon in Hong Kong. And, perhaps most importantly, I wish to thank the Murdoch family—particularly Rupert, James, Kathryn, and Lachlan—for their time, openness, honesty, joie de vivre, and willingness to confront any issue head-on.

Finally, I wish to thank Sterling Lord, whose rare and precious wisdom and gentle spirit are now leading me into surprising new worlds.

Index

Index